Early Modern Shipping and Trade

Brill's Studies in Maritime History

VOLUME 5

The titles published in this series are listed at *brill.com/bsmh*

Early Modern Shipping and Trade

Novel Approaches Using Sound Toll Registers Online

Edited by

Jan Willem Veluwenkamp
Werner Scheltjens

BRILL

LEIDEN | BOSTON

Cover illustration: A koff. Tile picture painted by Evert Hansen Koetsier (Harlingen 1769–1816), Delft painter at the Delft factory "Buiten de Kerkpoort" in Harlingen owned by Jacob Tjallingii (1789–1794) and Jan van der Veen (1794–1815). The picture has not been dated precisely. Collection Fries Scheepvaart Museum, Sneek.

The Library of Congress Cataloging-in-Publication Data is available online at http://catalog.loc.gov

Typeface for the Latin, Greek, and Cyrillic scripts: "Brill". See and download: brill.com/brill-typeface.

ISSN 2405-4917
ISBN 978-90-04-37177-4 (hardback)
ISBN 978-90-04-37178-1 (e-book)

This book is printed on acid-free paper and produced in a sustainable manner.

Contents

PART 3
Source Critical Arguments

PART 4
Name Data Analyses

Illustrations, Maps, Graphs and Tables

Illustrations

Maps

Graphs

Tables

Notes on Contributors

Loïc Charles
is full professor at University of Paris 8 (Vincennes Saint-Denis) and associate researcher at INED. His research focuses on French economic history and economic thought in the eighteenth century.

Ana Crespo Solana
is tenured scientist at Consejo Superior de Investigaciones Científicas (CSIC, Spain). She specializes in global maritime history with a focus on historical GIS, Flemish and Dutch merchant communities. She authored eight books and over 60 papers.

Guillaume Daudin
is full professor in economics at the University of Paris-Dauphine (LeDA-DIAL). He works on the early modern economic history of France and trade globalization. From 2014 to 2017, he co-directed an extensive project on eighteenth-century French trade statistics.

Maarten Draper
is a PhD student at the European University Institute in Florence. He wrote his MA-thesis at the University of Groningen in the framework of the STRO project. His current research focuses on Italian merchants in seventeenth-century Amsterdam.

Jerem van Duijl
obtained his MA at the University of Groningen with a thesis based on STRO. His current PhD research at Leiden University deals with the medieval possessions of the Teutonic Order in the bailiwick of Utrecht.

Jari Eloranta
is Professor of Economic History at the University of Helsinki and Docent at the University of Jyväskylä. He has published widely on the history of public spending, conflicts, and Nordic economic history.

Katerina Galani
Ph.D. (2011) Oxford University, is Post-Doctoral Fellow in Economic History at the Institute of Mediterranean Research/FORTH, Greece. She has specialised

in Mediterranean maritime history and banking in the eighteenth and nineteenth centuries.

Lauri Karvonen
is a master's student in history at the University of Jyväskylä. His research interests are on early modern trade and trade statistics. He has published on these topics in jointly written articles.

Yuta Kikuchi
is associate professor at the College of Economics of the Rikkyo University (Tokyo). His research focuses on Hamburg's trade in the seventeenth and eighteenth centuries with special consideration of its hinterland markets and networks.

Sven Lilja
is Professor emeritus of history at the University of Stockholm. His main fields of research are Swedish and Baltic urban and environmental history in the early modern period.

Maria Cristina Moreira
is an assistant professor at the Department of Economics, School of Economics and Management of the University of Minho, Braga, Portugal. She has published several articles on 18th and 19th century development of states and foreign trade.

Jari Ojala
is professor of comparative business history at the University of Jyväskylä, Finland. He has published widely on topics related to maritime history. Currently he coordinates a major research project to study Finnish early modern growth (c. 1500–1860).

Pierrick Pourchasse
is Professor at the University of Western Brittany in Brest, France. He researches eighteenth-century economic relations between France and Northern Europe. He authored *Le commerce du Nord. Les échanges entre la France et l'Europe septentrionale au XVIIIe siècle.*

Magnus Ressel
is assistant professor at the Chair of Early Modern History, University of Frankfurt/Main. He has published mostly on maritime history, German-Italian

trade relations, migration, the history of slavery and intercultural relations in the premodern era.

Klas Rönnbäck
is associate professor in economic history at the University of Gothenburg, Sweden. He studies issues related to development and early modern globalization. Previous research focused on the impact of technological improvements on the speed of transatlantic shipping.

Werner Scheltjens
Ph.D. (2009), is assistant professor at the University of Leipzig. He has published on preindustrial maritime history, including *Dutch Deltas. Emergence, functions and structure of the Low Countries maritime transport system ca. 1300–1850* (Leiden / Boston, 2015).

Siem van der Woude
studied history at the University of Groningen. He works at the Frisian historical archives (Ryksargyf, since 2002 Tresoar) and is one of the initiators of Sound Toll Registers Online.

Jan Willem Veluwenkamp
Ph.D. (1981), was associate professor of early modern history at the University of Groningen until he retired in 2017. He has published on commercial history, including *Archangel. Nederlandse ondernemers in Rusland, 1550–1785* (Amsterdam, 2000).

A Closer Look: STRO as an Instrument for the Study of Early Modern Maritime History[1]

Werner Scheltjens, Jan Willem Veluwenkamp and Siem van der Woude

1 The Aim of This Book

Early modern trade and shipping through the Danish Sound has attracted the interest of many historians since a long time. A prominent reason for this is that the route via the Sound connected Europe's main economies with the economically important Baltic Sea region. It can be maintained that one of the pillars supporting the Dutch Republic's Golden Age in the seventeenth century was the import of Baltic grain to feed the country's population. The Baltic Sea region was Europe's main source for raw materials and one of the main markets for its exports. Indeed, Baltic grain, especially wheat and rye, fed large parts of the European population not only in times of famine. Baltic iron, copper, timber, tar, pitch, hemp, flax were indispensable for the production of the merchantmen and warships of virtually all major European countries. Potash was vital for the production of soap and the bleaching of linen. Linen, hides and skins (mainly furs and Russia leather) were processed in the making of clothes and home furnishings.[2] Reversely, the Baltic Sea countries soaked up the consumer goods of the west – first and foremost textiles of all sorts and qualities and both basic and exotic foodstuffs like salt, wine, herring, spices, sugar, coffee and tea, but also a wide variety of skins and hides, from sheep to rabbit.[3] As most of these cargoes were less heavy and voluminous than the west bound cargoes, many ships sailed east in ballast, carrying cheap and heavy building materials like bricks, roof tiles and floor tiles which found, as an additional benefit, ready markets in their ports of destination.[4]

The other reason why trade and shipping through the Sound attracted the attention of so many scholars is the fact that they are so very well documented

1 Earlier versions of parts of this paper have been published as parts of Veluwenkamp, "Die Sound Toll Registers Online," and Scheltjens and Veluwenkamp, "Sound Toll Registers online".
2 Compare Faber, "De Sontvaart," 92; Unger, "Trade," 213, 218.
3 Compare Faber, "De Sontvaart," 92; Unger, "Trade," 207, 218.
4 Veluwenkamp, "Lading," 44–46.

 | DOI:10.1163/9789004371781_002

by the Sound Toll Registers (STR) – or *Øresundstoldbøgerne*, as they are known in the original Danish. The STR are the records of the toll levied by the king of Denmark on the passage of ships through the Sound, the main strait between Denmark and Sweden, connecting the North and Baltic Seas. They are stored by the Danish National Archives, where their more than 700 volumes occupy about sixty meters of shelf space and cover about 300 of the 360 years between 1497 and 1857, including a practically uninterrupted series from 1574 to 1857 and scattered records for the period between 1497 and 1574. The STR hold information on about 1.8 million ship passages. This information includes the date of passage, the name of the shipmaster, his place of residence, his port of departure and – from the mid-1660s – his port of destination, the composition of the cargo and the toll paid.[5] For that reason, the STR are well-known as one of the great serial sources of early modern history and the only one with rich and detailed information on European shipping and trade that spans a period of four centuries. They are considered to be the main measuring point of commodity transport in Europe and contain vital information on trade, transport, production and consumption. Moreover, the STR are cherished as a vital source of information on the origins, lives and economic activities of a host of shipmasters from many countries. They are, in short, a central source for social, economic and maritime history on all levels: global, European, national, regional and local.[6]

Although the Sound Toll Registers have always been widely known as crucial, their sheer volume and detail make them virtually impossible to handle. Consequently, and this is quite a paradox, they have been used only scarcely for historical research. Instead, historians have preferred to use the Sound Toll Tables (STT), or, in the original Danish, *Tabeller over skibsfart og varetransport gennem Øresund*. This monumental seven-volume publication, produced by the Danish historians Nina Ellinger Bang and Knud Korst in the first half of the twentieth century, provides an ample summary of the STR and make them digestible for the researcher.[7] Ever since the publication of the first volume of the STT in 1906 these tables, and not the STR themselves, have been used in almost every major study of early modern European transport and trade.[8] What is more, many scholars have even cut across and reached for the

5 Gøbel, "The Sound Toll Registers Online project," 305–308.

6 Veluwenkamp, "Sound Toll Registers," 3.

7 Bang and Korst, *Tabeller over skibsfart*.

8 See also: Van Tielhof, *The 'Mother of all Trades'*, 42. There are, of course, exceptions. Christensen, *Dutch trade*, uses both the STT and the STR. The same applies to Boon, 'West Friesland'. Scheltjens uses the STR in: Scheltjens, *De invloed van ruimtelijke verandering*; Scheltjens, "The Influence of Spatial Change"; Scheltjens, "The changing geography".

review articles published by the Dutch historian Willem Sybrand Unger upon the publication of new volumes of the STT.[9] To mention a few examples from Dutch historiography, Van Bochove, Van Tielhof, De Vries and Van der Woude, Israel, Faber, Harder-Gersdorff, Snapper, Bruijn, Knoppers discuss various aspects of shipping and trade between the Baltic Sea area and the Dutch Republic and other parts of Europe, referring not to the STR but mainly to the STT and Unger's review articles.[10]

However carefully the STT – not to mention Unger's review articles – are used as a source, almost any analysis based on them lacks the depth, detail and nuance that could be achieved if the STR themselves would be used. This is caused by the fact that, despite all due admiration for Ellinger Bang and Korst and their team, and the enormous significance their work has had for the writing of early modern economic and maritime history, the STT have major flaws – which have been amply discussed in the historiography.[11] The first shortcoming to be mentioned is that the STT only cover the years 1497–1783 and do not include the period 1784–1857 which the STR cover, too. Second, the STT only present data on a high level of aggregation. Individual passages, shipmasters, and cargoes have disappeared from sight.[12] Third, in the commodity transport tables for the period 1562–1657, the STT combine commodities in categories, which in major cases are of no or hardly any use. The most striking example involves the category that shifts from 'pepper, rice and sugar' in the early years to 'colonial commodities, subtropical fruit, dyestuffs, tanning stuffs, drugs etc.' by the middle of the seventeenth century.[13] It is true, the STT specifies the relevant individual commodities below each annual table, but here, the connection with the countries or ports of departure has been lost. The STT restores the connection between the commodity categories and the ports of

9 Unger, "De Sonttabellen"; Unger, "De publikatie"; Unger, "Trade".

10 Van Bochove, *The economic consequences*, 264–265; Van Tielhof, *The 'Mother of all Trades'*, 43, 49, 51, 53, 55, 59, 70, 73; Unger, "The Dutch trade in rye," 127; De Vries and Van der Woude, *Nederland 1500–1815*, 481, 485; Israel, *Dutch primacy*, 57, 93, 118, 129, 139, 144, 202, 214, 216–217, 301, 366, 381; Faber, "Friesland"; Faber, "The decline," 33–40; Faber, "Structural changes," 90; Faber, "Shipping"; Harder-Gersdorff, "Avoiding Sound traffic," 242–244; Snapper, "Commerce," 420–422; Bruijn, "De vaart in Europa," 217, 219 and references; Bruijn, "Scheepvaart in de Noordelijke Nederlanden 1580–1650," 146; Bruijn, "Scheepvaart in de Noordelijke Nederlanden 1650–1800," 223; Knoppers, "De vaart in Europa," 235, 241, 244, 248 and references.

11 See for example: Gøbel, "The Sound Toll Registers Online project"; Jeannin, "Les comptes du Sund"; Christensen, "Der handelsgeschichtliche Wert"; Heckscher, "Öresundsräkenskaperna".

12 Gøbel, "The Sound Toll Registers Online project," 321.

13 Compare Jeannin, "Les comptes du Sund," 9.

departure for every tenth year in this period (1562–1657), but here the specifications of the individual commodities are omitted.

The fourth shortcoming of the STT is that no tables combining ports of departure and destination are included, even though the STR provide this information for every passage from 1669 on.[14] True, starting in 1661, the STT list the annual number of ships per country or port of departure subdivided by country of destination. For each resulting connection, the list is grouped by the 'nationality' of the shipmasters and provides per 'nationality' an overview of the commodities shipped and their quantities.[15] Statistical analysis of these numerous and detailed data is only possible by entering them in tables – a task that may not be as time consuming as working with the STR themselves, but must be executed by the individual researcher. Moreover, these lists are incomplete and of limited detail. The unspecified term 'colonial commodities' (*Kolonialvarer*) features prominently where it hardly occurs in the STR. Moreover, a check of the STT against STRO revealed that a 'small' product like rhubarb appears not to have been included. All this means that the STT provide only laboriously accessible and incomplete information on transport routes and the composition of the relevant commodity flows.

A prominent example of the limitations of historical analysis based on the STT involves the study of commodity flows through the Sound. Our relevant insights into these flows result from the research of generations of historians who naturally accepted the many shortcomings of the STT.[16] Consequently, their studies are confined to the period up to 1783 and to exports and imports from individual countries and ports. The STT have not allowed them to study the commodity flows between ports and/or countries. For example, it is clear that in the sixteenth and seventeenth centuries most Rhine wine and about half of the French and, less prominent, Spanish and Italian wines were shipped to the Baltic Sea area from the Dutch Republic, whereas the rest was shipped directly from the countries of production. It is also clear that about half of all this wine went to Danzig and the rest to various other destinations.[17] However, inevitably, the literature remains silent about the individual routes this wine followed. We do not know, just to mention one tiny example, to which Baltic Sea ports the wine exported from Malaga went. Thus, generally speaking, the

14 Jeannin, "Les comptes du Sund," 9.

15 Manish Kumar has kindly drawn our attention to this.

16 For example: Bogucka, "The role"; Faber, "De Sontvaart"; Unger, "De publikatie"; Unger, "De Sonttabellen"; Unger, "Trade"; Van Tielhof, *The 'mother of all trades'*; Van Tielhof, "Ostseehandel". See further: Veluwenkamp, "Die Sound Toll Registers Online".

17 Unger, "Trade," 208–213.

STT has allowed contributing to the history of trade and transportation but fails to make STR's riches fully available.

To overcome the problems the STT pose and to make the STR fully and quickly accessible to researchers, the University of Groningen and Tresoar, the Frisian Historical and Literary Centre, Leeuwarden, The Netherlands, have engaged in entering the STR data into an online database: Sound Toll Registers Online (further: STRO). This endeavor is funded by the Netherlands Organisation for Scientific Research (NWO), several Frisian cultural foundations, *Fonds 21*, the *Samenwerkende Maritieme Fondsen* (Cooperating Maritime Funds), the University of Groningen and Tresoar. The Danish National Archives (Copenhagen), the Fryske Akademy (Leeuwarden) and the University of Leipzig provide scholarly advice and support.

Since 2010, STRO has been becoming gradually available. Already, it has been used by many researchers. The articles collected in this volume are prominent examples. Together they achieve the aim of this book: to demonstrate how STRO overcomes the drawbacks of the STT, how it boosts the writing of the history of European maritime transport and trade and how its use contributes to our knowledge of that history. Of course, both the STR and STRO bring their own source critical and methodological problems. For a better understanding of these problems, we first discuss the intricacies of the two sources at some length in the following two sections. Subsequently, we introduce the articles.

2 The Sound Toll Registers

The Sound Toll – Danish: *Øresundstold* – was introduced by the Danish king Erik VII about 1429.[18] It was abolished in 1857 after diplomatic pressure from the main maritime powers of the time, including the United Kingdom and the United States of America. The Sound Toll contributed considerably to the income of the Danish state. By the late seventeenth century, it amounted about 4.5 % of that income and this percentage subsequently increased to about 10 % during many years in the first half of the nineteenth century.[19] Today, we know the records of the Sound Toll kept by the Danish authorities as the Sound Toll Registers.

The king's bureaucrats levied the toll and kept its records at the small town of Elsinore, north of Copenhagen, where the Sound is at its narrowest. Initially,

18 Olesen, "Den rette, sædvanlige Strøm," 27. According to Hill, *The Danish Sound Dues*, the Sound Toll was introduced in 1426.

19 Gøbel, "The Sound Toll Registers Online project," 305–308.

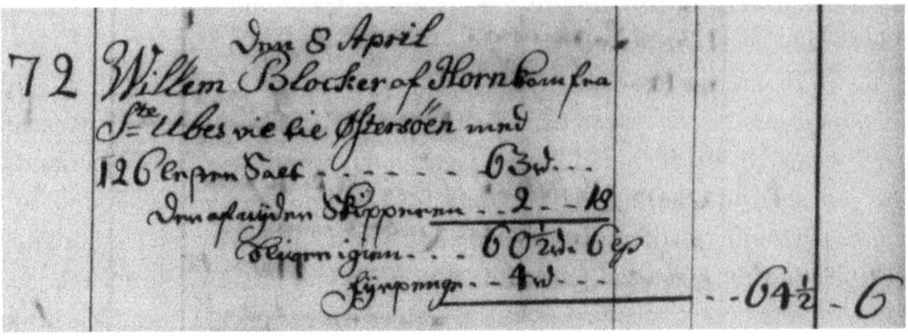

ILLUSTRATION 0.1 Entry from the Sound Toll Registers, 1734
SOURCE: DANISH NATIONAL ARCHIVES, COPENHAGEN

the information for each passage entered in the registers was limited to the year of passage, the name of the shipmaster, his place of residence, the toll amount paid for the passage and, when relevant, the toll amount paid for the wine cargo.[20] The information density increased with the gradual introduction of additional tolls in the course of the decades and centuries. The information of the individual passages had reached its more or less definitive extension by the eighteenth century when for each individual passage, both westward and eastward, the STR contain the date of passage, the name of the shipmaster, his place of residence, his port of departure and port of destination, the composition of the cargo and the toll paid. Illustration 0.1 reproduces a typical eighteenth-century entry in the STR.

Transcription:

Den 8 April

72	Willem Blocker af Horn kom		
	fra Ste Ubes vil til Østersøen, med		
	126 lester salt	63 rd.	
	Deraf nijder skipperen	2 18	
	Bliver igien	60 ½ rd. 6 s.	
	Fijrpenge	4 rd	64 ½ 6

20 For the year 1497, see for example www.soundtoll.nl > all scans > rolnrs 1 > scans 531 and 532.

Translation:

Willem Blocker of Hoorn, comes
from Setubal wants to sail to the Baltic Sea, with
126 lasts of salt 63 rigsdaler
Thereof enjoys the shipmaster 2 rigsdaler, 18 skilling
Remains 60.5 rigsdaler, 6 skilling
Beacon money 4 rigsdaler 64.5, 6

Explanation:

Shipmaster Willem Blocker, living in Hoorn,[21] departed from Setubal,
destined to the Baltic Sea with as cargo aboard his ship
126 lasts of salt, for which a toll of 63 rigsdaler is due
Subtracted as a contribution in favor of the shipmaster: 2 rigsdaler, 18 skilling
Remains: 60.5 rigsdaler, 6 skilling
Added: beacon money for the maintenance of the beacons in the Sound: 4 rigsdaler
Grand total to be paid: 64.5 rigsdaler, 6 skilling

It is clear that 1.8 million entries like this provide an immense quantity of information about the shipmasters passing the Sound, the routes they sailed, the cargo of their ships and the toll they paid. This, however, does not mean that the STR may be used without criticism. One has to keep in mind that they are a fiscal source. The Danish bureaucracy did not produce statistics for future researchers, but submitted accounts for the toll they levied to the king. Several reservations need to be made.

First, there were other routes to the Baltic, including the Little Belt, the Great Belt, the over-land route, the route to Russia via the North Cape and, from 1784 on, the Schleswig-Holstein Canal. Although each of these routes individually may not have offered a serious alternative for the Sound, taken together they should not be omitted. Hardly anything is known about the traffic through the Little Belt except that this strait was hardly navigable and meant a long detour

21 There is a protracted historiographical discussion concerning the implication of the Danish word 'af' in the STR. Of course, it means 'from'. Most likely, this implies that the shipmaster lives in the place that follows, in this case Hoorn. Some, however, have argued that rather the homeport of the ship is mentioned.

for ships sailing to and from the Baltic Sea.[22] Only for strictly local transport, it may have been of significance.[23] Only a minority of the shipmasters sailed the Great Belt, as this channel was much harder to navigate than the Sound while the same toll tariffs were applied in both straits.[24] The relevant traffic was mainly of a regional character, predominantly connecting Lübeck and Rostock with Danish and Norwegian ports.[25] The overland route to the Baltic area was clearly only relevant for the transport of low-weight, low-volume and expensive commodities.[26] The Schleswig-Holstein Canal between Tönning on the North Sea and Kiel on the Baltic was opened in 1784, but only small ships could pass through it and it never attracted a lot of traffic.[27] Lastly, the sea route to Russia via the White Sea port of Archangel was the main gateway to Russia during the long seventeenth century, when Russia did not have its own Baltic port. It was the main and preferred alternative for the routing of Russia's foreign trade via the Baltic Sea and the Swedish and other possessions lying between the sea and Russia. Vital as it was to Russia, Jeannin argues that this route involved usually much less than 10 % of the Sound traffic.[28]

The second qualification to be made concerning the reliability of the STR involves fraud. Fraud hardly included stealing through the Sound without paying the toll. The chance of success in this respect was very low as the strait was observed and guarded from Kronborg castle and the royal guard ship cruising it. It is widely accepted that all ships that passed the Sound in the years that are covered by the STR, are recorded in it. However, shipmasters certainly evaded payment of the total toll due by making false declarations of the commodities their ships carried. Clearance was based on the documents carried aboard the ship. The customs officers were entitled to search the ships, but this did not stop the shipmasters from trying their luck. Comparison with other sources, especially customs accounts of individual ports, the dependability of which is incidentally problematic, too, has shown that the information on cargoes in the STR is generally correct but not complete.[29] The size of the fraud differed per period and per commodities category. Expensive commodities of

22 Gøbel, "The Sound Toll Registers Online project," 319–320 – Gøbel mentions that toll registers of the Little Belt have been preserved for the years 1816–1857; Jeannin, "Les comptes du Sund," 12.

23 Jeannin, "Les comptes du Sund," 12.

24 Gøbel, "The Sound Toll Registers Online project," 319; Jeannin, "Les comptes du Sund," 12.

25 Jeannin, "Les comptes du Sund," 12.

26 Jeannin, "Les comptes du Sund," 4, 6. Compare Kikuchi's article in this volume.

27 Gøbel, "The Sound Toll Registers Online project," 319–320.

28 Jeannin, "Les comptes du Sund," 4–5.

29 Gøbel, "The Sound Toll Registers Online project," 319–321.

small volume were always subject to fraud.[30] For bulky commodities like grain, flax and hemp the picture is slightly different. Here, before 1618, especially in the period 1580–1618, fraud was enormous, oscillating perhaps between 25 and 50 %. This may be explained by the fact that the customs officers hardly seem to have checked the declarations. In 1618, this changed. From then on, the customs officers carried out more systematic checks so that in the case of the conspicuous bulk goods fraud was no longer a serious problem.[31]

A third reason why the STR must be handled with care is the fact that parties were sometimes exempted from the toll. This applies throughout to Danish ships and goods and it applies to Swedish vessels and commodities between 1650 and, practically, 1710.[32] Exempted passages were registered, but the relevant cargoes, and especially their volumes, are usually not known.

Alternative routes, fraud and exemptions cannot alter the fact that the STR are a great source for trade and transport. Even to the very critical historian they provide a rich starting point for the analysis of European trade and transport. As always, the researcher must be aware of the limitations of the source, in this case especially with regard to cargoes.[33]

3 The Sound Toll Registers Online

The shortcomings of the Sound Toll Tables and the drive to improve the accessibility of the Sound Toll Registers have induced several historians to continue, in a way, Ellinger Bang and Korst's work, especially when the possibilities of the use of computers increased. In the 1950s, Desfeuilles endeavored the methodical use of the STR for the years 1784–1793. He has preliminary presented his results in several articles but seems not to have published an addendum to the STT.[34] In the 1970s, Johansen created an electronic database with the detailed data of all Sound passages for the period 1784–1795. He presented his analysis of these data in a monograph in 1983.[35] The Danish Data Archive at Odense, Denmark, administers Johansen's database and puts it at the disposal

30 Jeannin, "Les comptes du Sund," 33, 38; Van Tielhof, *The 'Mother of all Trades'*, 42.

31 Jeannin, "Les comptes du Sund," 21, 37–39.

32 Jeannin, "Les comptes du Sund," 39–40.

33 Gøbel, "The Sound Toll Registers Online project," 319.

34 Desfeuilles, "La Navigation"; Desfeuilles, "La Navigation"; Jeannin, "Les comptes du Sund," 8.

35 Johansen, *Shipping*. Also: Johansen, "Ships" and Johansen, "Demand", where he combines his own database with STT. Other scholars have used Johansen's database, too. See for example Minchinton and Starkey, "Ships".

of researchers. In 2009 and 2010, Welling reconstructed and edited Johansen's database and made it accessible via the internet.[36] Not to be confused with the STR are the "Dutch Sound Registers", the lists of Sound passages which the Dutch representatives in Denmark made and sent to the Estates-General in the eighteenth century, kept by the National Archives of the Netherlands in The Hague. These 'Registers' only cover part of the eighteenth century and contain much less detailed information per passage than the STR. The website of The National Archives contains a database with the relevant data of thirteen sample years.[37]

As was mentioned above, since 2009, the University of Groningen and Tresoar, the Frisian Historical and Literary Centre, Leeuwarden, The Netherlands, are engaged in the realization of an electronic database of the complete Danish Sound Toll Registers. The resulting relational database, Sound Toll Registers Online, or STRO, is free of charge and instantly accessible for all via the internet: www.soundtoll.nl. STRO currently (September 2017) roughly covers the period 1600–1857 and contains about 1.6 million passages. Work is in progress to enter the data of the remaining 200 thousand passages and complete the database – containing the information of 1.8 million passages – in the years to come.

Sound Toll Registers Online is in many ways the delayed continuation of Johansen's pioneering effort. In 2000, after several years of preparation and data gathering, the Frisian National Archives (now Tresoar), supported by a number of private Frisian cultural foundations, acquired a complete set of the microfilms of the STR. The Frisian maritime transport industry flourished in the eighteenth century but left only few sources so that relatively little is known about its organization and extent. Compensating the lack of local sources, the STR may be considered as a major source for its history. The years following acquisition were devoted to finding a partner in the academic world, which would initiate research into Frisian merchant shipping in the period between 1600 and 1800. In 2007, contact was made with Jan Willem Veluwenkamp of the University of Groningen. During the discussions that followed about possible research, it was established that the digitization of the Sound Toll Registers and the subsequent creation of an electronic database containing the STR data was essential for the comprehensive study of Frisian merchant shipping. Furthermore, it was recognized that such an electronic database would have the potential to become a vital research tool for European social and economic history in general.

36 http://www.let.rug.nl/welling/sont/johansen.htm.

37 http://www.gahetna.nl/collectie/index/nt00338.

In 2008, the project, then dubbed REDS – Realization Electronic Database Sound Toll Registers – received funding from NWO, several Frisian cultural foundations, the University of Groningen and Tresoar. The initial project team of Sound Toll Registers Online included Jan Willem Veluwenkamp, lecturer of early modern history, and George Welling, lecturer of digital history, both at the University of Groningen, and Frank Bosmans, head of ICT, and Siem van der Woude, research team leader, both at Tresoar. This team had the STR microfilms digitized in order to facilitate data entry from digital images rather than directly from the microfilms and contracted, through a tender procedure, Breed, the sheltered workshop of the city of Nijmegen to enter the data.

Breed started its work in 2009. Breed entered the data as much as possible in the original spelling of the STR and delivered the data files to Tresoar. The University of Groningen (RUG) and Tresoar accepted or rejected the data after a quality check by random sample.[38] Initially it was agreed that they would accept an error rate of 2%, allowing two out of hundred passages Breed entered to contain serious faults. Gradually, it became evident that this quality level was set too ambitiously. By mutual agreement, it was increased to 5%. After acceptance, Tresoar and RUG corrected the data. Correction to the degree of a flawless reproduction of the original data was impossible, but the resulting quality allows all queries to produce accurate results. Moreover, as the image of the original is available in the database, researchers may always check results. In 2011, the first results were made accessible via the website: www.soundtoll.nl. About 1.5 million of the 1.6 million passages for which the data are now online have been entered by Breed's employees.

In 2013, the cooperation with Breed was terminated with mutual consent. One of the reasons was of a financial nature. From 1634 onwards, each individual passage was recorded in one entry in the original Sound Toll Registers and, consequently, has been entered in one record in database. It appeared that in the years before 1634, however, each individual passage was recorded in one or several entries in the STR. Consequently, they would have to be entered in one or several records in the database. In 2013, it was estimated that, in order to process the remaining 300 thousand passages and complete the database, some 700 thousand entries would have to be made. There was no budget for that and the data entry had to be organized in another way. It was decided to rely on skilled volunteers instead. Based on the experiences of the Meertens Institute at Amsterdam and Tresoar, among other parties, it was assumed that it should be possible to find many people in the Netherlands

38 Mark de Lannoy, Johan Steendam and Ubo Kooijinga (Tresoar) have carried out the checks.

and other countries willing to participate in the data entry and the checking procedures. To facilitate this, the Meertens Institute was contracted to adapt to our needs a data entry application, which it had developed for other purposes. This application allows participants with a laptop and internet connection at their disposal to work from home or any other place. In October 2013, a few volunteers began entering data and testing the system live.[39] When it was clear that everything worked properly, the recruitment of volunteers started on a larger scale. By the spring of 2016, there were 50 active participants entering data. One year later, this number had proved to be stable.

The database, Sound Toll Registers Online, includes for each passage[40] – in general – the following information:

the date of passage
the shipmaster's name
the shipmaster's domicile
the port of departure
the port of destination (from the mid-1660's)
the nature and quantity of the cargo
the toll paid

The database is designed to enable all conceivable search actions, to allow the making of all conceivable cross tabs and to facilitate statistical analysis.[41] For this purpose, the data are entered in four basic tables: *passages, cargoes, taxes* and *images*. The *passages* table contains one record per passage including fields for the date and the shipmaster's name and domicile. It does not contain fields for the cargo and the ports of departure and destination as many ships carried several commodities and the ports of departure and destination could differ per commodity. Accordingly, the *cargoes* table contains a record for each commodity of each passage including fields for the commodity's ports of departure and destination and the tax paid per commodity. The separate *taxes* table contains fields for the tax or, in many cases, the several taxes levied per passage. The *images* table contains fields making the connection with the scans of the relevant folio of the original source. The four tables are connected by a common identity field.

39 In particular, volunteers Siep Maat, Klaas Dantuma and Anneke Westerhuis have done excellent work.

40 Here and below strictly speaking: for each STR entry, as passages often were recorded in more than one entry in the STR before 1634 – see main text.

41 George Welling (University of Groningen) and Frank Bosmans (Tresoar) have designed the database.

The data are entered into the database in the language of the original source, i.e. in Danish. As there was no standard spelling in the centuries in which the STR were produced, the spelling variations of personal names, geographical names, commodity names, measures and weights are almost without limit. To facilitate the analysis of the data geographical names and commodity names, measures and weights will be standardized.[42] In addition, Werner Scheltjens carries out the conversion of measures and weights into the metric system as part of a separate research project.[43] All standardized terms are entered in additional tables so that the original input is preserved. The same procedure is followed for the categorization of terms. For the time being, the shipmasters' personal names are not standardized. As it is hard enough to standardize personal names occurring in one region, e.g. Friesland, it is anticipated that the results of a general standardization of personal names would yield unreliable results. In the case of the STR, which contain names of shipmasters from many places, regions and countries, names must be standardized differently depending on the place where the men lived. Perhaps this nut will be cracked at a later stage.

STRO is an interpretation of the STR and not a direct copy or a source edition. Therefore, it should be handled with care and with understanding of its power and limitations. Besides the limitations inherent to the original source (STR), the individual researcher must be aware of STRO's characteristics when he or she makes use of it.

First and foremost, only the STR toll collection entries proper have been entered into the database. The large quantity of additional information contained in the STR has been omitted. This information mainly involves the recurrent introductory, accounting and justifying texts of the toll officials. In addition, as the database has a strict format, the extra information the officials sometimes added in the passage entries could not be included. This information is diverse. It may involve the owner or addressee of part of the cargo, a ship having stranded, or a rotted part of the cargo. In order to preserve that information, as a rule, a reference was added to the electronic database in the field 'opmerking bron' – 'remark about the source'. Usually, this reference was worded as 'stuk Deense tekst' – 'piece of Danish text' – during data input.

42 George Welling (University of Groningen) and Frank Bosmans have standardized the geographical names.

43 The first results of this project as well as a detailed description of the methodology of the conversion can be found in: Scheltjens, "The volume of Dutch Baltic shipping"; Idem, "Het ontstaan"; Idem, "French imports"; Idem, "Die krisenhaften Auswirkungen"; Idem, "Maße und Gewichte"; Idem, *Dutch Deltas*.

Even after having dealt with – or having shed – extra information in this way, not all entry problems had been solved. The STR have organically developed during more than three and a half centuries and their form and precise content change and vary from one period to the next. This means that all kinds of peculiarities had to be dealt with to provide a proper fit of the content of the original STR into the electronic database. The three most conspicuous examples concern the recording of commodity values, the formulas 'giør' and 'er' and references in one STR entry to another.

Usually, commodities – the components of the cargo – are recorded including its unit of measurement and quantity: '60 læster rug.'[44] Sometimes the unit of measurement and the quantity involve an amount of money: 'for 800 rd. kramerie.'[45] But is also occurs that both the unit of measurement and the value of the commodity are recorded: '156 fad stads viin à 52 rd.'[46] In this case the value indications were entered into the database as part of the commodity name, treating 'stads viin à 52 rd.' as a separate commodity.

Sometimes commodities are recorded with a second measure: '42 læster rug etc. giør 50 2/5 læst.' or '36 læster hveede er 45 læst.'[47] The formulas 'giør' and 'er' were interpreted as 'that is to say' or 'i.e.' The second measure was entered in a separate field as an alternative measure.

In less than 0.6 % of the STR entries there is a reference to another entry, characterized with the formula 'Vide Fol.' followed by the relevant folio and passage number.[48] These references usually involve corrections of earlier entries by other shipmasters. These references are concisely indicated in the field 'opmerking bron' – 'remark about the source', mentioning the folio and passage numbers and the shipmasters name and domicile. At the present stage of the project, it is up to the researcher to process these references further.

Finally, despite all scrutiny that has been employed to maximize correct reproduction of the content of the STR entries, it has been unavoidable that the database contains many small errors and perhaps a few omissions. Errors in the original spelling of geographical and product names and measures and weights will largely be overcome by their standardization. In other cases, the user will have to rely on his critical mind and wit to avoid mistakes and errant interpretations.

---

44 www.soundtoll.nl, record 152363, 25 August 1783.

45 www.soundtoll.nl, record 81863, 11 November 1783.

46 www.soundtoll.nl, record 96205, 16 May 1783.

47 www.soundtoll.nl, record 75437, 23 March 1783; record 82520, 5 May 1783.

48 For example www.soundtoll.nl, record 119865, 21 August 1783.

4 STRO as Instrument of Historical Analysis

STRO is a powerful instrument for historical research. It opens up the STR in much more detail than the STT do. The user interface gives easy access to the database without the requirement of query writing skills.[49] STRO's builders have tried to fit an organic historical source into a much more sterile database, which allows the user to select records containing data of individual passages using search terms, including time periods, names and domiciles of shipmasters, ports of departure and destination, and commodities. The results of those selections, including basic time series and cross tables, can be downloaded easily and processed further using spreadsheet and relational database programs. Researchers wishing to write their own queries can download 'raw' tables from the database. The project team continuously works on enlarging the ease of use of its interface both in terms of technical stability and availability and, as mentioned above, standardization.[50]

STRO's significance has already been illustrated by the papers, which were presented in annual workshops and conferences to promote STRO. They were held in Groningen, the Netherlands in June 2010, in Leeuwarden, the Netherlands, in October 2010, again in Groningen in October 2012 and in Leeuwarden in October 2013, and then they went abroad, to Helsingør, Denmark, in October 2014, to Antwerp, Belgium, in October 2015, to Leipzig, Germany, in October 2016 and to Marennes-Oléron, France, in October 2017. Many of these exploratory studies, produced by scholars from many different countries, have been published as working papers at www.soundtoll.nl.[51] Some of the authors have rewritten their papers into the articles collected in this book. They have all used STRO as one of their research instruments. This enabled them to take their analyses to a level of detail and sharpness and a scope of conclusions, which were unattainable before. In that sense, the result is a collection of groundbreaking contributions to early modern European maritime and commercial history. Equally important, the articles show the methodical and technical challenges, which full use of STRO demands. They show that it takes ingenuity, expertise and skill to use the new 'reservoir' of data STRO offers for historical analyses.

The challenges associated with using STRO are formulated implicitly in the work of some authors while taking center stage in that of others, but all contributors to this volume have developed different ways of applying the data

49 Frank Bosmans (Tresoar) has produced the user interface.

50 Frank Bosmans is the key officer here.

51 www.soundtoll.nl>Research>Workshops and papers.

they extracted from the database. Consequently, alongside making a significant contribution to the history of early modern European shipping and trade, this volume explores the methods for exploiting the novel instrument upon which these contributions are based. This aspect of the various contributions is reflected in the structure of the book. The contributions are grouped according to the problem areas and methods prevailing in them rather than the subjects, places and times they discuss.

In the first part of the book, the articles of Sven Lilja, Pierrick Pourchasse and Magnus Ressel use STRO to analyze and explain the size, structure and development of trade flows between places east and west of the Sound. Ressel surveys the impact of the Partitions of Poland on maritime trade between Western Europe and the Baltic Sea's southern ports. He finds that the shifting of the state borders and the mercantilist policies of Prussia and Russia fundamentally rechanneled the trade flows. Essentially, Memel's commerce thrived and Danzig's trade suffered. Sven Lilja analyzes Stockholm's maritime trade with Western Europe and the Swedish west coast in the 1770s and 1780s. Stockholm mainly exchanged commodities with the Netherlands, Great Britain and Ireland, France, Portugal and Sweden's west coast. Generally, Stockholm supplied iron, copper, pitch, tar and timber and demanded mainly salt, wine, fish and a variety of other consumer goods, among which textiles stand out. Pourchasse tests if the British trade blockade of the ports of France of 1793–1795 was effective. It turns out that the blockade was rather porous and that merchants from neutral powers, especially Danes, supplied France quite easily with huge quantities of grain.

In the second part of the book, the chapters of Galani, Crespo Solana and Kikuchi employ STRO to compare and contextualize broader historical developments that occurred in areas that may seem to be only remotely related to the Baltic. These authors have turned to STRO to find quantitative and episodic data to support their arguments about the connections between distant European regions (Crespo Solana), to analyze complementarities between overland and maritime trade (Kikuchi) and to study similarities between Baltic and Mediterranean trade (Galani). Rather than commodity flows Crespo Solana analyzes the commercial network connecting Southern Spain and the Dutch Republic in the first three quarters of the eighteenth century making use of, among many other sources, STRO and a database on Hispanic Atlantic commerce, which is part of her – unpublished – DynCoopNet Data Collection. She argues that this network connected the economies of large parts of the Baltic Sea area, Scandinavia and Northern Europe with the south of the Iberian Peninsula. The numerous Dutch merchants living in Cadiz, which was an important commercial hub between the Americas and the Mediterranean, played a prominent role. They realized direct commercial connections between Cadiz and many foreign ports, frequently featuring Baltic Sea ports. Kikuchi explores the factors, which decided the choice between the two alternative transport routes in Hamburg's Baltic trade in the seventeenth and eighteenth centuries – the one over land via Lübeck and the other over sea via the Danish Sound. He argues that, in the course of the seventeenth and eighteenth centuries, the commodity transport from Hamburg to the Baltic Sea shifted from land to sea as larger ships became essential for the transport of large quantities of colonial products. The overland route stayed in use mainly as a substitute when war, ice and lack of shipping capacity frustrated maritime transport and formed a subsystem of trade between Western Europe and the Baltic. Galani examines British shipping to the Mediterranean and the Baltic and the repercussions war had on it in the period 1765–1820. Both areas were integral parts of Great Britain's commercial network, each providing specific markets for British supply and demand. Galani makes use of two electronic databases, STRO for the Baltic and her own, unpublished database of *Lloyd's List* for the Mediterranean. The figures show that war seems to have hit British shipping to the Baltic harder than that to the Mediterranean.

A different approach to STRO is pursued in the third part of the volume. Charles and Daudin and Ojala c.s. mainly contribute to the source criticism of the STR and STRO and explore methods of using them for historical research. They use STRO to compare the STR with other primary sources to assess the value of the STR as a source for trade and shipping. They also suggest methods to study the STR via STRO and to give meaning to the data they contain. Charles and Daudin compare STRO with the French bureau of balance of trade statistics for the period 1750–1789 to find common trends and structures and to present suggestions for further research. They apply a comparative methodology to both datasets in order to improve our understanding of the nature of the information they contain, to assess how economic historians could use them meaningfully and to provide new tools and methodologies for the further development of comparative analyses of early modern trade databases. The basic problem of this comparison is that STRO records commodity flows in physical quantities and the French source presents commodity flows measured in values. The two series, the authors conclude, do not match and their comparison does not produce any valuable economic information. However, the Sound Toll Registers tax indicator is a reasonable proxy for the flow values and tally quite nicely with the values measured by the French bureau. Ojala c.s. compare time series from STRO with those of the Swedish Board of Trade Statistics and the Portuguese General Balance of Trade focusing on the bulk commerce between Sweden and Portugal carried by Swedish ships in the period 1738–1800. They argue that the data the Sound Toll Registers and the Swedish and Portuguese sources provide on trade volumes match quite well and that the three sources, therefore, may be considered to be fairly accurate. They stress that the STR are an effective barometer of transactions in Northern European East-West trade but call for caution when the source is used to study the cargoes of individual ships or less traded commodities. They recommend the use of complementary shipping documents in those cases. They support Erik Gøbel's observation that the STR are correct but not complete.

Finally, the two chapters of the fourth part of the volume move away from commodity flows fully acknowledging and exploiting STRO's rich alphanumeric data. Rönnbäck explores the speed of transport as an aspect of the productivity of shipping. He uses the names of the shipmasters, the names of their Baltic ports of call and the dates they were recorded at Elsinore in the STR to make sound quantitative statements about the speed of shipping in the Baltic. The tentative results seem to indicate that the speed of shipping in the Baltic might have increased to a quite substantial degree in the course of the eighteenth century, i.e. prior to the nineteenth century transport revolution. Draper and Van Duijl focus on the people who sailed the ships, and analyze and explain the decline of Baltic maritime transport by shipmasters from the Dutch West Frisian Islands in the eighteenth century. They employ the names of shipmasters as registered in STRO as a means to identify and study their communities and patterns of group behavior in their activities. They argue that these shipmasters specialized in sailing trade routes, which were prominent in the early eighteenth century but were largely abandoned in the course of the second half of the century. The shipmasters were dependent on this traffic and were unable to switch to emerging new routes.

The essays collected in this volume cover a wide range of historical case studies with STRO as a common element. The volume makes a double contribution to the history of European shipping and trade in the early modern period: on the one hand, it provides selected examples of case studies substantiating the power of STRO as an instrument for novel historical research; on the other, the different contributions serve to distinguish between different methods and techniques for using STRO. In the concluding remarks to this volume, the latter are briefly reviewed and some recommendations are made to enhance STRO's potential for future research.

PART 1

Commodity Flows

CHAPTER 1

The Impact of the Partitions of Poland on the Structure of Baltic Trade

Magnus Ressel

1 Introduction

This paper analyzes the commercial ramifications of the Partitions of Poland on the Baltic and beyond.[1] Poland was not only large; it was also a state of substantial economic importance. Although it was not home to a large manufacturing sector or an entrepreneurial middle-class, the state encompassed vast areas of arable land that traditionally furnished Western Europe with cereals, timber and raw materials. Their importance generally increased in the second half of the eighteenth century, a time marked by the intensification of naval warfare, a secular trend of early industrialization, continuous population growth and the increasing integration of the European economy. The overall frequency of passages through the Sound is a testament to this (see graph 1.1).

Interestingly, the number of passages grew substantially after 1763. A significant factor influencing this development has hitherto not been properly recognized: Prussian mercantilism. Under Frederick's II reign, a fundamental goal of Prussian trade policy was to strengthen its Baltic harbors. In order to achieve this, the flow of Eastern European goods to Hamburg was diverted to the Prussian Baltic harbors.[2]

Prussia was well-situated to expand its Baltic ports. With Cleves, Magdeburg and after 1772 also the town of Fordon in West Prussia, the Kingdom controlled three crucial nodes of Rhine, Elbe and Vistula. Along the Rhine, the Prussians hardly hampered trade,[3] yet, they did much more so on the Elbe. Magdeburg was used as lever against Hamburg by means of the reintroduction of its staple rights in 1747.[4] Prussian policy found a temporary relaxation during the Seven Years' War. When its Baltic harbors were blocked, Prussia opted for opening

1 On the topic in general: Müller, *Die Teilungen Polens*; von Aretin, "Teilung und Länderschacher".
2 More extensively on Hamburg's hinterland, see Yuta Kikuchi's contribution to this volume.
3 De Vries, *De Economische achteruitgang*, 38–39, 99–103; Van Dillen, *Van rijkdom en regenten*, 399, 484, 515, 627–629; De Vries and Van der Woude, *The First Modern Economy*, 191–192, 489–490.
4 Henderson, *Studies*, 118.

 | DOI:10.1163/9789004371781_003

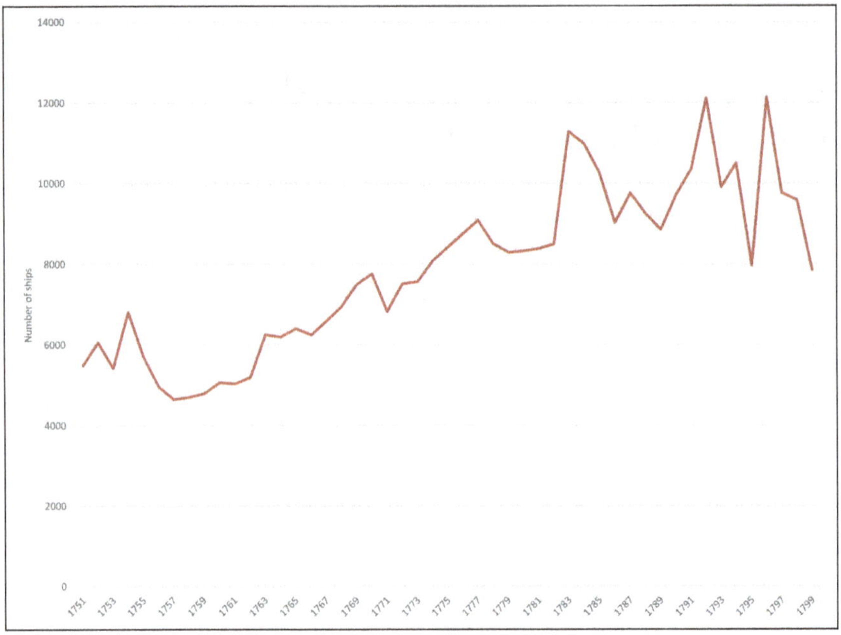

GRAPH 1.1 Number of passages through the Sound, 1750–1799
SOURCE: STRO

the Elbe-route.[5] Thanks to the accompanying increased demand for cereals by the Prussian army,[6] this proved to be a good time for Hamburg's trade[7] to which, not by chance, a short-term depression in shipping through the Sound corresponds.[8]

From the mid-1760s onwards, Prussia's goal of weakening Hamburg's entrepôt position was pursued yet again.[9] The results of this policy are reflected in the income of Hamburg's *Admiralitätszoll*.[10] From 1770 to 1782, this toll yielded less than half of its peaks of 1768 and 1783. The Prussians were able

5 Kikuchi, *Hamburgs Handel*, 221–225.

6 Bömelburg, *Zwischen polnischer Ständegesellschaft*, 193–194; Pantel, *Die hamburgische Neutralität*, 73, 174.

7 Büsch, *Versuch einer Geschichte*, 109–113; Beutin, "Die Wirkung des Siebenjährigen Krieges," 219.

8 North, *Geschichte der Ostsee*, 180.

9 Wohlwill, *Aus drei Jahrhunderten*, 66–88; Rachel, "Der Merkantilismus," 972.

10 This toll was levied on the incoming and outgoing goods from and to Hamburg west of the Scheldt, with some exemptions for short distance trade and specific goods, cf.: Krawehl et al., eds., *Statistik des seewärtigen Hamburger Einfuhrhandels*, 10–13.

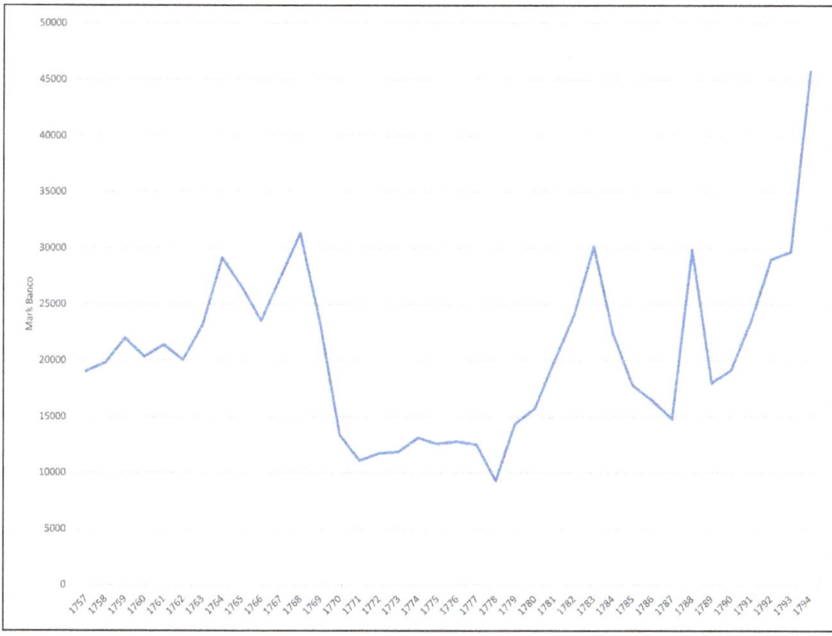

GRAPH 1.2 Admiralitätszoll Income of Hamburg, 1757–1794, measured in Mark
SOURCE: STAATSARCHIV HAMBURG, CL. VIII, I, 174

to ruin Hamburg's shipbuilding industry, marginalize its timber trade and reduce the city's beer brewing and luxury industries.[11] Only the combination of intense warfare of the western powers between 1776 and 1783, and some relaxation on the part of Prussia after 1786 led again to the strengthening of Hamburg's hinterland-trade.[12] The death of Frederick II in 1786 had resulted in a shift of Prussian commercial policy. Hugo Rachel has put forward a fascination of Prussian elites with the ideas of Adam Smith as the principal reason for this change after 1786.[13]

It seems that not only did the reduced attractiveness of Hamburg result in a general push of European vessels into the Baltic for the better part of the second half of the eighteenth century. Frequent wars in Western Europe increased the demand of Baltic products while the costs for seaborne transport fell in

11 Büsch, *Versuch*, 104–106, 132–142; Baasch, *Quellen*, 224; Rachel, *Die Handels, Zoll- und Akzisepolitik Preußens*, 285; Weber, *Deutsche Kaufleute*, 227.

12 Wiskemann, *Hamburg und die Welthandelspolitik*, 132–135.

13 Rachel, "Der Merkantilismus," 990–992; Kraus, "Der „nervus rerum“ in Publizistik und Wissenschaft," 42–44.

these decades due to nautical and logistical innovations.[14] The fact, that the Partitions of Poland took place in the years when the Baltic attained the greatest importance it ever had may be a historical coincidence, yet, this overall background only increases the significance of these events.[15]

From the side of historical research, interest in the economic consequences of the Partitions of Poland has been rather small.[16] Even historians who explicitly wrote about the economic history of Prussia tended to shy away from this topic.[17] This picture differs strongly in the case of Danzig and the province of West Prussia, which have been the focus of interest of many German and Polish historians. The underlying aim of many resulting studies was to confirm a "respective" national standpoint. This could oscillate between the extremes of seeing an economically decaying city and province, saved after 1772/1793 by the enlightened and modern Prussian Kingdom, or an economic strangulation of a hitherto flourishing city and province, which was brought to its knees after 1772 and annexed in 1793 against resistance of the (mostly German) burghers.[18] Often, adherents of the second standpoint conclude that this was not to the great economic benefit of the city or the province.[19] Regardless of any bias, the research undertaken has been of great use and furthered our understanding of the economic aspects of the Partitions of Poland for Danzig and West Prussia.

---

14 North, "Sources of Productivity Change," 953–970; Lucassen and Unger, "Labour Productivity," 127–141; Lucassen and Unger, "Shipping, Productivity and Economic Growth," 3–46.

15 On the inner-Baltic trade: Rasch, "Kopenhagen," 55–68; Cieślak, "Aspects of Baltic Seaborne Trade," 239–270.

16 Even a standard title hardly mentions the Partitions: Johansen, *Shipping and Trade*. This is reflected in this citation from a modern anthology on the Partitions: "Eine wirtschaftshistorische Analyse der Teilungen findet lediglich in der älteren geopolitisch beeinflussten polnischen Forschung statt, wenn etwa der Verlust des Zugangs zum Meer und die preußische und russische Zollpolitik in ihren ökonomischen Konsequenzen nachgezeichnet werden." in: Gestrich et al., "Die Teilungen Polen-Litauens," 32. The topic is mostly avoided in other recent publications: Lukowski, *The Partitions of Poland*; Lawaty et al., *Deutsch-polnische Beziehungen*, 277–280.

17 Treue, *Wirtschafts- und Technikgeschichte Preussens*, 196–199.

18 The resistance of the citizenry against the Prussian occupation has always been highlighted by Polish historians, see e.g.: Cieślak and Biernat, *History*, 293–294; it has been, albeit somewhat uneasily, downplayed by the German historians of the period from 1871–1945, e.g.: Keyser, *Danzigs Geschichte*, 151–154. A more balanced account of the relations between Danzig and Prussia from 1772 to 1793 can be found in: Bömelburg, *Zwischen polnischer Ständegesellschaft*, 376–393.

19 The relevant chapter-subtitle in a standard account bears the title: "The years of decline (1814–1850)", a time during which the population nearly doubled and many indicators point towards an overall growth, c.f.: Cieślak and Biernat, *History*, 331–364.

The most eminent Polish historians who specialized on Danzig and its hinterland (which extends down to Southern Poland and deep into Ukraine) are Maria Bogucka,[20] Czesław Biernat,[21] Barbara Grochulska[22] and Edmund Cieślak.[23] More recently, Szymon Kazusek has published detailed statistical material on the exports and imports of the Crown of the Kingdom of Poland (*Corona Regni Poloniae*) from 1786–1790.[24] In Germany, research concentrated on Prussia's trade and toll policies (Hugo Rachel), the German trade balance between 1789 and 1833 (Andreas Kutz) and the economic policies applied to "South Prussia" between 1793 and 1806 (Adelheid Simsch).[25] Additionally, Hans-Jürgen Bömelburg's analysis of West Prussia focuses on the multiple facets of its society and its transformation via the Prussian acquisition.[26]

Of interest here are the effectiveness and repercussions of political upheavals and mercantilist measures in the late eighteenth century in the Baltic. Since any acquisition of territory by absolutist rulers in the late eighteenth century meant first and foremost a different taxation and customs regime in specific territories, we can gauge herewith the effects and/or limits of the fiscal-state on the economy at large. In the following, a general survey of the repercussions of the Partitions of Poland on western European maritime trade with the Baltic is presented. These observations shall serve to formulate hypotheses on the impact and efficacy of political factors (warfare/mercantilism) in channeling trade flows from and to the Baltic.

1.1 *Methodology*

Shipping and trade of five southern Baltic cities or towns during the years from 1751 to 1799 are compared: Lübeck, Barth, Stettin, Danzig and Memel, which are deemed to reflect the politico-geographical diversity on the shore of the southern Baltic Sea area. More ports could have been included, especially Rostock (belonging to the Duchy of Mecklenburg, to gauge the potential of a small state

20 Bogucka has always shown a predilection for the sixteenth and especially the seventeenth centuries. For some of her most important publications c.f. the literature in one of her own recent articles: Bogucka, "Danzig als Metropole," 89–98.

21 Biernat, *Statystika*.

22 Grochulska, *Handel*, 174–193.

23 Cieślak, has concentrated his research on Danzig and the partitions: Cieślak, "Bilan et structure," 105–118.

24 Very useful is the introduction with its overview of the existing literature on early modern Polish trade: Kazusek, *Handel zagraniczny Korony*.

25 Rachel, *Die Handels-, Zoll- und Akzisepolitik*, 382–549; Kutz, *Deutschlands Außenhandel*; Simsch, *Die Wirtschaftspolitik*, 148–154.

26 He concluded with an overall rather negative assessment of the Partitions, especially in economical respects: Bömelburg, *Zwischen polnischer Ständegesellschaft*, 470–474.

to develop its trade after the end of the Warnemünde toll in 1748[27]) or Riga (the foremost competitor for the Prussian ports with regard to Russian goods). The sample suffices to show how different political entities, serving diverse but not too dissimilar hinterlands, dealt with the changing circumstances. The overall legitimization for the choice of these five specific ports is the fact that they were intensely affected by the Partitions. Other ports in the area seem to have been affected less by the shrinking and disappearance of Poland-Lithuania.[28]

The numbers of ships from a specific homeport and their nationalities as they were registered at Helsingør are compared. The parameters are as follows:

- *Sound passages* represents the number of passages through the Sound, in both directions, of ships domiciled at the chosen port. This will provide a general overview of the standing and the performance of the respective port's fleet.
- *Atlantic shipping*, a subsample of *Sound passages*, represents the number of passages through the Sound in any direction with a destination at or departure from the Atlantic coast of France, Spain and Portugal, i.e. between Brest and Gibraltar, of shipmasters domiciled at the chosen port. This shows the capability of shippers from the chosen port to engage in long-distance transport activities.
- *Trade* represents the number of passages westwards through the Sound of ships of any nationality whose last port of call within the Baltic was the analyzed port. This will show us how important the chosen port was for the delivery of products to Western Europe. The last harbor within the Baltic that a ship had visited was usually the place where the goods to be sold in Western Europe were fetched, thus only westward passages are counted.

1.2 *Analysis I – Overview*

In order to illuminate the impact of the Partitions of Poland, the analysis of five Baltic ports is conducted. Memel, Danzig and, with some distance, Stettin, are obviously ports with a large trade. Barth and Lübeck are nearly only centers of a shipping sector. This reflects the most basic principles of Baltic trade. At the beginning of the seventeenth century, the ports at the mouths of the great rivers had lost most of their shipping to the Dutch and from then onwards had contented themselves mostly with the hinterland trade. Ports with a weak connection to the hinterland by a small river either had to seek an active role in shipping or were left to a marginal and anemic existence in the shadows of

27 On this toll and its abolition cf.: Barnewitz, *Geschichte*, 137–154.

28 On Königsberg: Straubel, *Die Handelsstädte*, 664–665; on Riga: Handrack, *Der Handel*, 58–86; Harder-Gersdorff, "Riga als Handelsmetropole," 276–277, 294; on Stralsund: Müller, *Die Entwicklung*, 75–99.

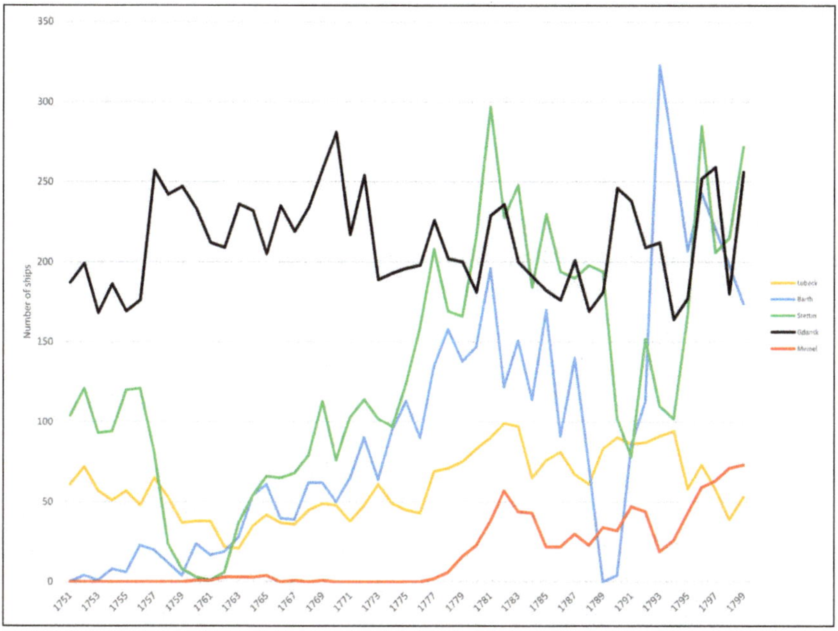

GRAPH 1.3 Number of Sound passages of shipmasters domiciled at one of the five selected ports
SOURCE: STRO

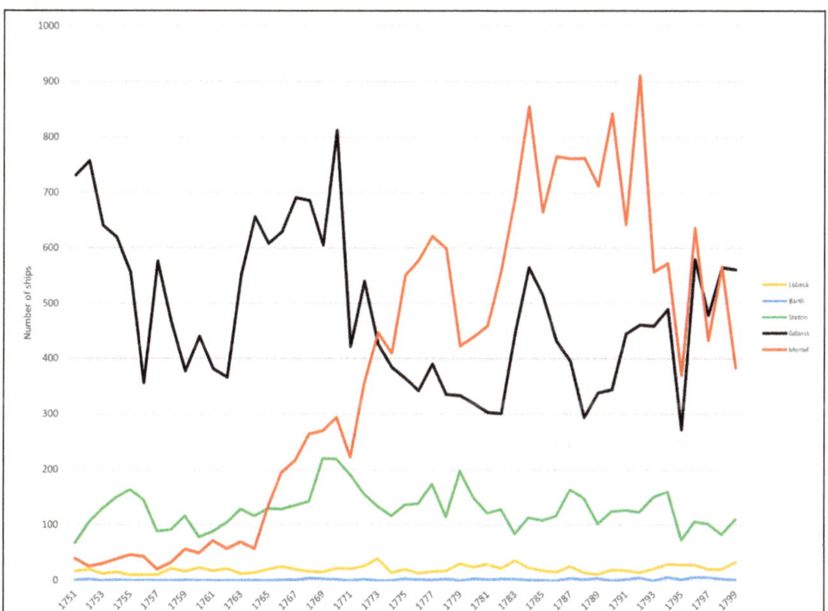

GRAPH 1.4 Number of westward passages through the Sound from selected ports
SOURCE: STRO

the large centers, a destiny not uncommon for many Baltic coastal towns and villages.[29]

1.3 *Analysis II – Lübeck*

In the two decades from 1750 until 1770 Lübeck's shipping underwent a time of recession. Having started strongly in 1751, most likely a late effect of the neutrality in the war of Austrian succession,[30] its shipping nearly vanished after the end of the Seven Years' War. The year of the First Partition of Poland, 1772, was the starting-point for a modest upswing in shipping. From 1780 until 1795 Lübeck's shipping had its best time, yet, in the Atlantic, it lost strongly after 1785.[31] The Second and Third Partitions of Poland had, if any, only a negative effect. Striking is the inability to profit from the dropout of the Dutch after 1795, although they had always been traditionally the strongest competitors of Lübeck.[32] Impressive is the degree of Lübeck's shipping towards the European Atlantic coast. This reflects a disproportionally strong standing in the French wine trade.[33] Only Lübeck's trade remained stable at a low level. However, compared to the preceding century, Lübeck's position seems to have been severely weakened.[34] Its loss of performance in the eighteenth century and especially in the 1790s indicate a general breakdown of Lübeck's traditional position as a carrier of Baltic goods to the West.

The weakness of Lübeck's shipping during the Seven Years' War might be due to the relaxation of Prussian mercantilism on the Elbe. This gave Hamburg a strong impetus to the detriment of the shipping of its Hanseatic partner.[35] The question as to why Lübeck fared better in the 1770s and early 1780s than in the late 1790s, also in regard to its long distance shipping towards France

29 Beutin, *Der deutsche Seehandel*, 90–91; North, *Geschichte*, 163.

30 Vogel, "Beiträge zur Statistik," 137–138.

31 Vogel, "Beiträge zur Statistik," 138–139.

32 Lübeck's shipping had mostly and for centuries followed a triangular structure, i.e. the Lübeckers sailed to a Baltic port to fetch goods and transport them to the West. This structure was most vulnerable to Dutch competition: Vogel, "Beiträge zur Statistik," 127–133; Olechnowitz, *Handel und Seeschiffahrt*, 45–48; Jeannin, "Die Rolle Lübecks," 13–14; Pelus-Kaplan, "Eine Hansestadt," 127–128.

33 Beutin, *Der deutsche Seehandel*, 69–71; Unger, "Trade," 216.

34 Decisive for the decline of Lübeck were the English Navigation Acts: Jörn, "Dietrich von Brömbsen," 205–213. Illustrative for the subsequent waning of Lübeck's fortunes is a glance at the tax-income of the "Schoß", which was at its apex in the 1650s and 1660s and fell to its absolute low in 1742: Hammel-Kiesow, "Schoßeinnahmen," 301–312.

35 Not only did the connections of Hamburg with Eastern Europe via the Elbe increase, in times of war the land route between Hamburg and Lübeck was intensely used for trade and, thus, the need for Lübeckers to use the sea route declined, cf. Yuta Kikuchi's contribution in the volume.

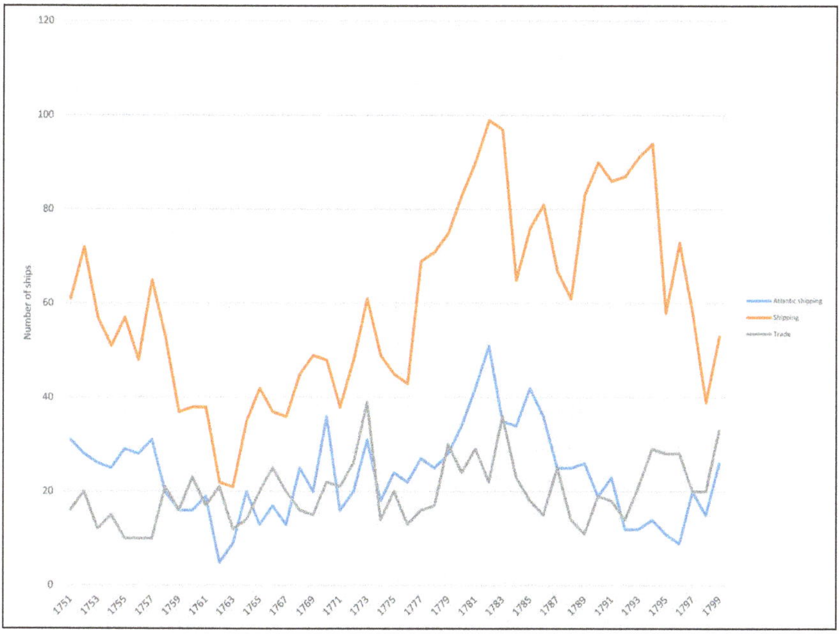

GRAPH 1.5 Lübeck's trade and shipping, 1751–1799, measured in numbers of passages through the Sound
SOURCE: STRO

and Iberia, is most pertinent. One could point towards the League of Armed Neutrality that had forced the British to abstain for some time from privateering in the early 1780s. Yet, if one looks at the strong growth of Hamburg's and Bremen's shipping towards Iberia in the 1790s and the absence of growth for Lübeck's shipping in the same years, the 'corsair' factor seems to be overestimated.[36] An important reason for Lübeck's weakness can only be found in Lübeck's immediate neighborhood. The strong growth of Hamburg in the years after 1795 may have been disadvantageous to Lübeck's trading position.[37] Yet, Lübeck's crisis began in the mid-1780s. Furthermore, even with a strong growth of the Hamburg market, the Trave city, due to the different range of products offered here in contrast to the Elbe, should still have been able to increase its shipping to furnish goods to and from Baltic ports. The question as to why this did not happen can only be answered by looking at Lübeck's eastern neighbors.

36 On Hamburg: Kresse, *Materialien*, 58. On Bremen: Beutin, *Bremen und Nordeuropa*.

37 This is hinted at by: Beutin, *Der deutsche Seehandel*, 83.

1.4 *Analysis III – Barth*

Until 1755, Barth hardly appeared as a place of maritime transport services. After the First Partition of Poland, however, the shipmasters of the town substantially increased the intensity and range of their activities and after 1778, they developed substantial shipping towards France and Iberia. Once having acquired expertise in southwestern waters, Barth became an important regional hub of Baltic shipping for some years, although it never developed any importance as a trade-emporium.[38] The shipping of this small port, however, dwarfed that of its competitors in the area.[39] A short crisis from 1788–1791 can be explained by the Russian-Swedish war and some uncertainty regarding Sweden's stance in the upcoming wars in the west in its immediate aftermath. The Second and Third Partitions of Poland had beneficial effects on the community of shipmasters of Barth, the members of which now often stated Danzig as the last port of call when passing the Sound westwards.

One potential explanation for Barth's rise might be that it was not hampered by traditions. In the elder literature, we find the Baltic ports of the old Hansa (of which Barth was never a part) described as backward-looking in the eighteenth century. Clinging narrow-mindedly to guild constitutions and entrenched in a strong conservative outlook, they allegedly hindered innovations in shipping.[40] If this really had been the case remains to be proven, but it is true that Stralsund's shipping did not grow impressively in the second half of the eighteenth century when ships under the Swedish flag drastically extended their range.[41] Furthermore, cheap prices for land and houses reduced the costs of living substantially and extended the possibilities for mercantile

38 Lindblad has strangely identified a boom of Swedish Pomeranian shipping from 1745–1760, which was then allegedly halted by Swedish competition: Lindblad, *Sweden's trade*, 32–33. This may hold true for shipping towards Amsterdam, but the truly international engagement of Swedish Pomeranian shipping began only in the 1770s: Ressel, "Swedish Pomeranian Shipping," 76–77; Müller, "The Forgotten Age," 15–16. The fact that ships from Barth and Swedish Pomerania operated mostly as carriers for other nations was already remarked with some amazement by the contemporaries: Oddy, *European Commerce*, 31–34.

39 The potential competitors, i.e. ports in the southeastern Baltic which had difficult access to a rich hinterland, consisted mainly of Lübeck, Wismar, Rostock and Stralsund. On the latter: Techen, *Geschichte*, 257–268; Müller, *Die Entwicklung*, 71; Gadebusch, *Schwedisch-Pommersche Staatskunde*, 189–191; Müller, *Rostocks Seeschiffahrt*, 17.

40 Müller, *Die Entwicklung*, 95–96; Olechnowitz, *Handel*, 105.

41 Stralsund's underperforming shipping and trade was noted by contemporaries and explained by the high costs of living in the town (due to garrison and fortress), the poor quality of Pomeranian products (cereals and wool), the bad condition of the harbor, as well as 'the lack of experienced and well-connected enterpreneurial merchants': Von Reichenbach, *Patriotische Beyträge*, 52–95.

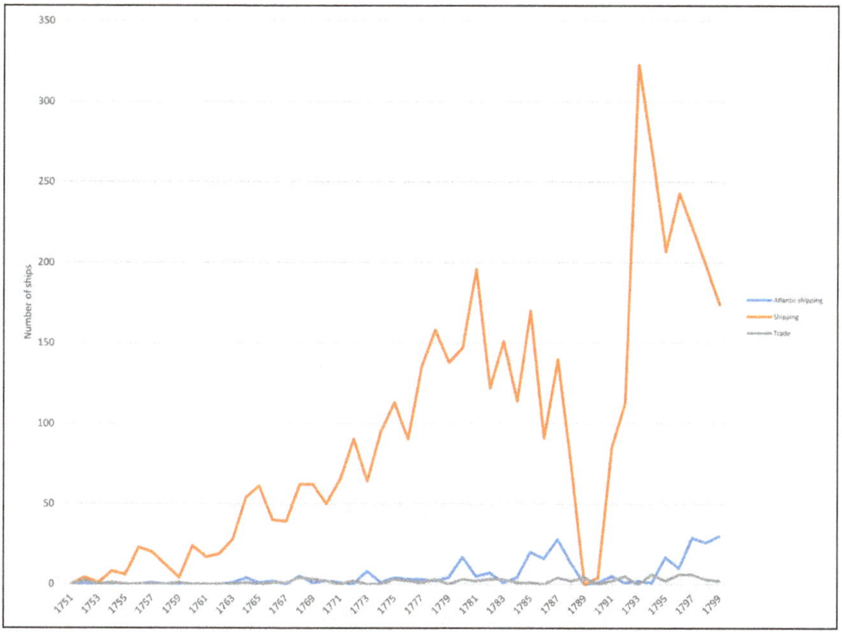

GRAPH 1.6 Barth's trade and shipping, 1751–1799, measured in numbers of passages through the Sound
SOURCE: STRO

activities (e.g. land cultivation, retail trade) at a spot that turned out to be in many aspects an ideal harbor.[42] The missing river connection to the hinterland did not hinder the ships from Barth to engage in providing maritime transport services between the major ports in the Baltic and western and southern Europe.[43] An important factor that cannot be discussed here in detail is the beginning liberalization of Swedish mercantilism in its German province after 1766.[44] Protected by the Swedish flag, which enjoyed the highest possible respect of all European flags in the revolutionary years, Barth benefited from the turbulences of the age.

42 Reichenbach, *Patriotische Beyträge*, 55, 132–138.

43 The reason was a very good connection to the foreland, i.e. a favorable location for shipbuilding and a natural protection of the harbor by the peninsula of Zingst. Disadvantageous was the low depth of the water, which forced all Barth ships to dock in either Wismar or Rostock, cf.: Reichenbach, *Patriotische Beyträge*, 123–146.

44 Initially these reductions of the Licenten were considered a failure: Töpffer, "Unvorgreifliches Bedenken," 203–226; Findeisen, "Progressive Kameralisten," 111–112. With a time lag of a few years, however, the results were even greater than expected: Ressel "Swedish," 76.

1.5 *Analysis IV – Stettin*

Stettin had undergone a time of stagnation between 1678 and 1720, caused by the Brandenburg-Swedish rivalry at the mouth of the Oder.[45] In contrast, the eighteenth century became a period of relative prosperity. Enjoying strong mercantilist protection from the Prussian kings, the port became a regional commercial hub.[46] Stettin's shipping and trade had reached a solid level until both were reduced by the outbreak of the Seven Years' War in 1757. The peace of Hubertusburg in 1763 was the starting point of a vigorous comeback of the port, which then became, at a time when an economic crisis and Prussian mercantilism were haunting Hamburg,[47] an import harbor for many western and southern European products.[48] Interesting is the lasting contraction of trade between 1771 and the end of the eighteenth century, which immediately begs the question whether this is connected to the First Partition of Poland. Did it not weaken a principal competitor, Danzig, and should it therefore not have had a beneficial effect to the attractiveness of Stettin as an entrepôt in the Baltic?

Stettin's lack of growth as staple after the first partition of Poland seems to have been connected to the foundation of the "Preußische Seehandlung", which got the monopoly of trade towards Poland with salt and from Poland with wax; both principal products in the Polish-Prussian trade relations.[49] This mercantilist act, however, not only weakened Danzig and reduced the hinterland-connections between the Baltic ports and Galicia. It also caused a general loss of attractiveness for all Prussian ports in international shipping and diverted substantial trade flows of the Baltic hinterland to the ports of Swedish-Pomerania, Poland or Russia.[50] The loss of attraction as a port of call was not offset by the strong rise of shipping after 1770. This growth becomes less impressive when we take into account that the range of its ships remained mostly local; in long-distance shipping the Prussians were underachievers.[51] Furthermore, the absence of any profit from the Russo-Swedish War is surprising and proves structural weaknesses of the Prussian shipping sector.[52]

45 Schmidt, "Geschichte des Handels," 46–58; Naudé, *Deutsche städtische Getreidehandelspolitik*, 35–36.

46 Müller, *Die Entwicklung*, 91–93; Wachowiak, "Stettin," 83–96.

47 Büsch, *Versuch*, 128–130.

48 Beutin, *Der deutsche Seehandel*, 93.

49 Schrader, *Geschichte*, 1–7; Straubel, *Zwischen monarchischer Autokratie*, 48.

50 Zottmann, *Die Wirtschaftspolitik*, 71; Straubel, *Die Handelsstädte*, 136–146.

51 Stettin's shipping in the eighteenth century was done mostly by small ships with short life spans. Their range was mostly limited to the Baltic and North Seas: cf. Kozłowski, *Rekonstruktion*, 224–225; Baziński, *Handel morski Szczecina*, 181–201, 268–281; Knitter, "Verifizierung von Schifffahrtsstatistiken," 49.

52 This observation stands in contrast to: Johansen, "Østersjøhandelen," 47–50.

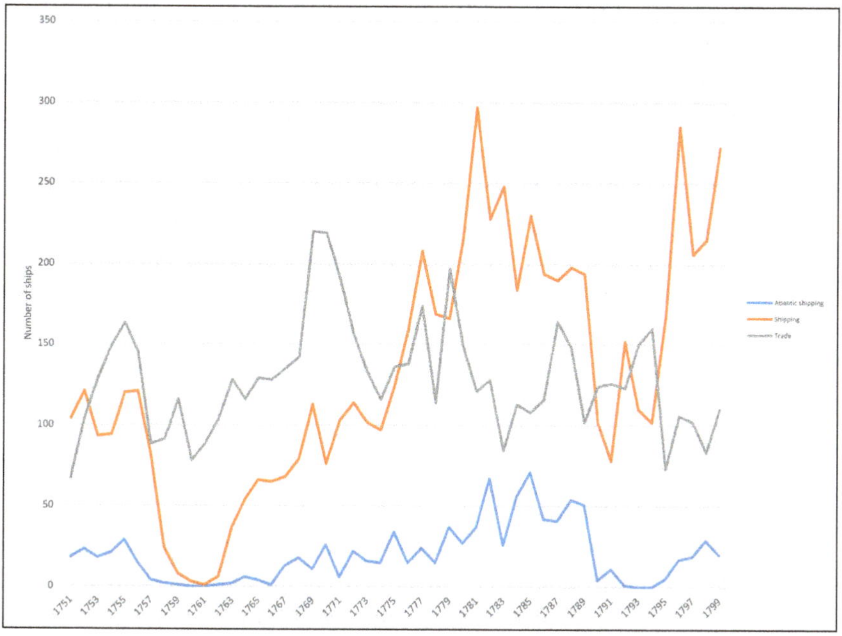

GRAPH 1.7 Stettin's trade and shipping, 1751–1799, measured in numbers of passages through the Sound
SOURCE: STRO

The war against France from 1791–1795 was disadvantageous for the town's shipping, yet, not so much to its trade. The strong surge in shipping after 1795 remained again limited to the short-distance lanes. The town's long-distance shipping was even weaker than in the decades before.[53]

In many regards, Stettin is exemplary for the successes and failures of Prussian mercantilism. A wide range of state measures had furthered the possibilities of Stettin's merchants, but also limited and hampered them.[54] The second half of the eighteenth century was a time when the town became a staple of colonial goods and acquired an important position as exporter of cereals and timber.[55] The densification of trade between Berlin and Stettin via the reduction of the staple rights of Frankfurt on the Oder in 1751 was perhaps the most important measure of the Prussian government to further the

53 Kozłowski, *Rekonstruktion*, 234–296.

54 This refers to the many limitations or prohibitions, but also to the subsidies on the salt-, grain- and timber-trades, cf. Schmidt, "Geschichte des Handels, III," 1–4; Braun, "Zur Stettiner Seehandelsgeschichte, Teil II," 65–98.

55 Johansen, *Shipping*, 70–72; Unger, "Trade," 212–214.

development of Stettin.[56] The construction of the Havel-Elbe Canal in 1745 and the Finow Canal in 1751 further strengthened the attractiveness of the Oder as a commercial lane.[57] The basis of Stettin's wealth was its role as distribution center for imports to Brandenburg, New Brandenburg and Silesia.[58] The result of the Prussian liberalization of trade with colonial goods on the Elbe after 1787 was therefore detrimental to Stettin.[59] Due to the following rise of Hamburg as primary supplier of colonial goods to the Prussian monarchy, Stettin's trade declined.[60] The sudden growth of Stettin's shipping after 1795 was mostly due to a neutrality-bonus and not connected with an internal strengthening of the commercial situation.[61] Stettin had achieved its potential maximum attractiveness under King Frederick II, but his reign had thus more or less proven that Stettin, for all the qualities it possessed, could never become a staple of international standing during the eighteenth century.[62]

1.6 *Analysis V – Danzig*

Danzig is the most important example to illustrate the effects of the Partitions of Poland. The Seven Years' War was a period of depression for Danzig's trade, though not of its shipping. The former could be attributed to Russian operations in East and West Prussia during the war,[63] yet in fact, it is much more likely due to the rise of Hamburg's trade, after Frederick II had opened up trade on the Elbe in 1757. Consequently, after 1763 Danzig's trade grew again. The First Partition of Poland, which put a toll-line between the city and its hinterland, was nearly as effective at reducing the trade flow as the short-term interruption of the Prussian anti-Hamburg mercantilist measures from 1756–1763 had been. Even though the loss for Danzig after 1772 was marked, strongly visible in the breakdown of long-distance shipping, the city retained trade of some substance.[64] Elbing was the great winner for the next 20 years.[65]

56 Matschoss, *Friedrich der Große*, 36. On the further Prussian attempts to stimulate the trade within the state: Straubel, *Die Handelsstädte*, 404–520.

57 Berner, *Geschichte*, 373–374; Treue, *Wirtschafts- und Technikgeschichte*, 75.

58 Naudé et al., *Die Getreidehandelspolitik*, 161–166; Beutin, *Der deutsche Seehandel*, 91–96.

59 Schmidt, "Geschichte des Handels III," 4; Rachel, "Der Merkantilismus," 990–992.

60 Kikuchi, *Hamburgs Handel*, 225–234.

61 The Prussians explicitly did not favor shipping, cf. Kozłowski, *Rekonstruktion*, 56: "in our state commerce is much more important than shipping."

62 Neugebauer, "Marktbeziehung und Desintegration," 183–184.

63 This is erroneously done by: Vogel, "Beiträge zur Statistik," 114–115; much more cautious is: Biernat, *Statystika*, 48.

64 Biernat, *Statystika*, 80–81, Cieślak, "Sea-borne Trade," 54–55.

65 Straubel, *Die Handelsstädte*, 218–234. On p. 219, n. 590 Straubel criticizes some conclusions of: Bömelburg, *Zwischen polnischer Ständegesellschaft*, 470–474.

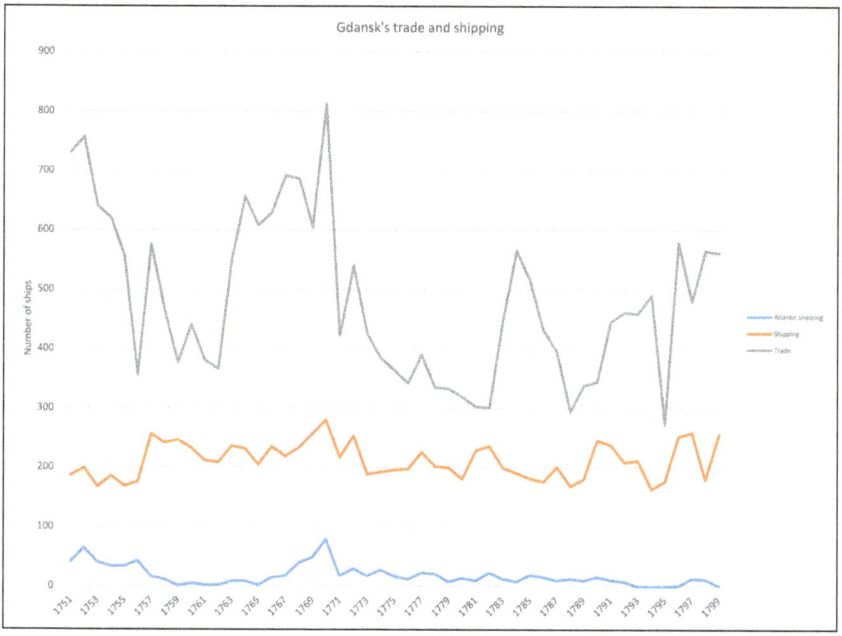

GRAPH 1.8 Danzig's trade and shipping, 1751–1799, measured in numbers of passages through the Sound
SOURCE: STRO

However, it is important to remember that within Prussia this was an exception; the entire provinces of East Prussia and Silesia, suffered from the loss of Polish hinterland to Austria and Russia.[66] Between 1782 and 1785, Danzig was able to hamper the Prussian competitor by curtailing the trade flow through its territory into the Prussian enclaves.[67] Danzig's shipping in general remained rather constant, not visibly affected by either war or peace, or the changing fortunes of Poland. Due to the Russo-Swedish war and its accompanying increase of demand for timber and cereals on the side of the belligerents the city grew again as a trade-hub after 1788. The takeover of Danzig by Prussia in 1793 is at first only visible in the shipping of the city. The peace of Basel in 1795 brought

66 In the case of East Prussia, part of its trade was diverted to Riga and Libau by the Russian toll policy until 1783: Von Baczko, *Versuch einer Geschichte*, 87; Armstedt, *Geschichte*, 250–251; Critical on this: Straubel, *Die Handelsstädte*, 41–55. On Silesia: Fechner, *Wirtschaftsgeschichte*, 185, 467, 527, 530; Wendt, *Schlesien*, 183–184; Kargol, "Wirtschaftliche Beziehungen," 34–35; Straubel, *Die Handelsstädte*, 518.

67 Damus, "Die Stadt Danzig," 102–136; Cieślak, "Bilan et Structure," 113–115; Cieślak, "Aspects," 240–244.

an overall increase in Danzig's performance in trade and shipping.[68] The next years were boom years; the visits of the city by ships sailing under a foreign flag nearly doubled from an already high level in 1799 up to 1803. The number of ships from Danzig registered in the Sound reached its peak in 1805 with 361 vessels, in 1794, the figure had been 164.[69] Thus, while the city lost attraction as a port of call already after 1803, it continued to grow as a center of shipping.[70] Danzig's prosperity around 1800 becomes even more extraordinary if we take into account that, in 1799, an economic crisis hit Northern Europe. Danzig's continuous rise shows us just to what degree the city had been restrained by the mercantilist measures of Prussia.

We may go back over 150 years to put this into perspective. In 1625, Danzig had lost the potential for long-distance trade to the Dutch and other shipping powers.[71] Since that time, its most important goods had been transported mostly by foreigners and the city's own long-distance shipping had remained underdeveloped. As a trade-emporium, it had stood in many regards in direct competition with Hamburg, both being connected to the Central and Eastern-European hinterland. Yet, while in the case of Hamburg, the importance of cereal exportation fell off from a peak that had been reached around 1650, Danzig's fortunes were mostly, at least until 1800, based on selling this commodity.[72]

Even if this is taken into regard, the mercantilist diversion of Prussian grain from Magdeburg to the Kurmark instead of Hamburg greatly affected the grain market of the city on the Elbe and helped Danzig to re-establish its former position as a cereal emporium after 1763.[73] When the First Partition of Poland cut the city off from its hinterland, the damage to Danzig's trade was profound, though not to its shipping. We know from the literature that the First Partition severely reduced the imports and exports of the city, a fact clearly reflected in the picture above.[74] With the Second Partition and the Prussian annexation of South Prussia in 1793, the city was reunited with its hinterland and became again an attractive trade emporium.[75] Probably helpful for Danzig in

68 Kozłowski, *Rekonstruktion*, 178–183.

69 It took the city until the 1840s to attain a trade as intense as in 1802 again: Grochulska, *Handel*, 184: "Aż do lat czterdziestych nie osiągnął poziomu z r. 1802."

70 Biernat, *Statystika*, 82–83, 100–101; Kozłowski, *Rekonstruktion*, 180–185.

71 Van Tielhof, *The 'Mother of all Trades'*, 43–50. Some exceptions in the next 150 years confirm the rule: Cieślak, "Sea-Borne Trade," 52–54.

72 Naudé, *Deutsche städtische Getreidehandelspolitik*, 54–60; Vogel, "Beiträge II"; Tielhof, *The 'Mother of all Trades'*, 50–62.

73 Naudé et al., *Die Getreidehandelspolitik*, 123–127; Biernat, *Statystika*, 96–97.

74 Cieślak, "Bilan et Structure," 109–112.

75 Biernat, *Statystika*, 20, see esp. the grain exports: 82–83; also: Kutz, *Deutschlands Außenhandel*, 286.

this regard was the decision of the Prussian authorities to integrate the newly acquired provinces of South and New Prussia into the administrative fabric of the Prussian state.[76] Grain production in the newly acquired territories was stimulated[77] and thus supported Danzig's recovery after years of stagnation and recession. No city had been as affected as Danzig from the Partitions of Poland. From 1772 to 1793 mostly negatively; afterwards it boomed stronger than it had ever before. Polish historiography does not fail to mention this.[78]

1.7 *Analysis VI – Memel*

Memel is in most regards the inverse of Barth. A port with practically no shipping but an intense trade, which only emerged in the late eighteenth century.[79] Memel's boom starts with the Russian takeover in 1757 and the following five years of occupation; this connected the local timber industry with lasting effects to the Russian forests.[80] Consequently, the visits of foreign ships increased markedly.[81] The pace in the growth of trade increased after 1763 and the First Partition of Poland was advantageous to Memel. The port now developed some importance as salt staple, and as an exporter of flax and cereals, presumably because some of the trade flows from and to Danzig now were diverted to Memel.[82] More important, however, was the growing demand for timber in Western Europe.[83] This brought a strong dependence on access to the Russian hinterland. When Russia raised its tolls at the Polish border in order to strengthen the Russian Baltic ports, especially Riga, this caused a short-term crisis between 1777 and 1781.[84] Only a Russian *ukaz* of 1782 to force its traders away from Polish-governed Libau resulted in a strong push of these not to Riga but to Eastern Prussia, namely Memel.[85] It was not by chance that the prime years of Memel's trade position were between 1784 and 1792, i.e. during

76 The alternative of a 'colonial' exploitation had been deliberated: Simsch, *Die Wirtschaftspolitik*, 54–59.

77 Simsch, *Die Wirtschaftspolitik*, 198–212, 255.

78 Cieślak/Biernat, *History*, 304: "the Prussian administration attempted to eliminate the most striking anachronisms and allowed far greater freedom than hitherto as regards production and marketing."

79 Johansen, *Shipping*, 78–81; Goldbeck, *Vollständige Topographie*, 31–32.

80 Straubel, *Die Handelsstädte*, 158–159.

81 Sembritzki, *Geschichte*, 260–263.

82 Straubel, *Die Handelsstädte*, 43, 148, 161–168.

83 Straubel, *Die Handelsstädte*, 170.

84 Rachel, *Die Handels-, Zoll- und Akzisepolitik*, 436, 496, 524–525, Straubel, *Die Handelsstädte*, 58–59.

85 Rachel, *Die Handels-, Zoll- und Akzisepolitik*, 563–565; Eckard, *Livland*, 467–475.

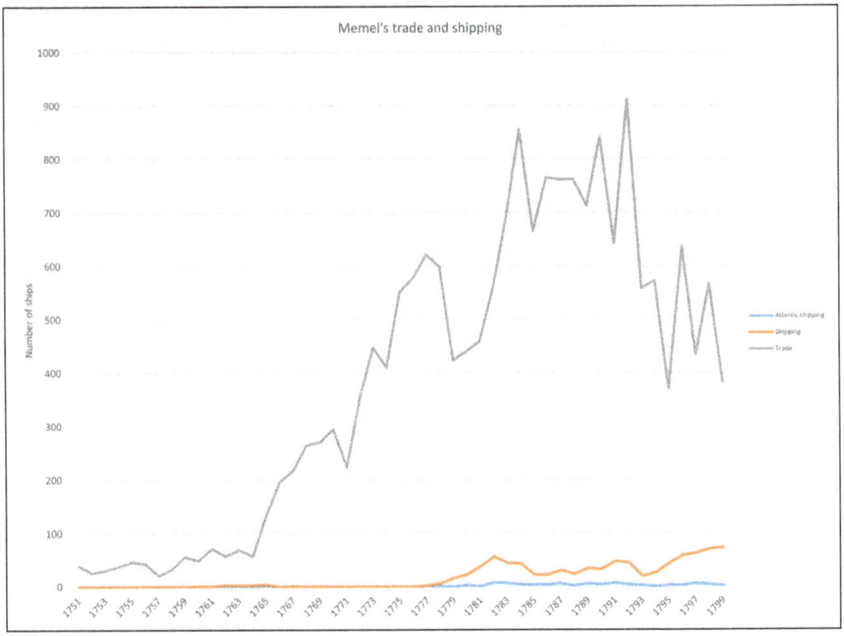

GRAPH 1.9 Memel's trade and shipping, 1751–1799, measured in numbers of passages through the Sound
SOURCE: STRO

peacetimes. The revolutionary wars and the Second and Third Partitions of Poland overlapped with a depression of trade to and from Memel.

In Memel's case, we see a combination of Prussian and Russian mercantilism and the growing demand of timber as the strongest factors influencing its fortunes. Contemporaries dated the beginning of Memel's flourishing in 1764.[86] This can be explained by the marginalization of Hamburg's timber-trade by the Prussians after the end of the Seven Years' War.[87] The First Partition of Poland had only limited effects on Memel, mostly by weakening the entrepôt position of Danzig. Since Danzig and Memel had different structures, the former being more a cereal staple, the latter more of a timber staple, this should not be overestimated. More important was the rising demand of timber and the continuing openness of a still vast Poland-Lithuania for the merchants of Memel. The relaxation of Prussian mercantilism after the death of Frederick II

86 Oddy, *European Commerce*, 221.

87 Büsch, *Versuch*, 129–130; Baasch, *Beiträge*, 29–30.

did not pose problems for Memel, since this did not affect the timber trade.[88] Problematic for the town was deforestation of its hinterland in the late 1780s, the simultaneous arrival of American timber on the European and especially British market and the surge of St. Petersburg and Narva, both heavily bolstered as timber-exporting places by Russia.[89] The port remained a passive staple-place frequented mostly by foreigners. Thus, Memel seems to have gone into stagnation with the prospect of a long-term decline in the last years of the eighteenth century.[90]

2 Conclusion

The impact of the Partitions of Poland on the structure of Baltic trade is remarkable. The changes of the borders played a primary role in channeling and diverting the trade flows. Thus, what is structurally much more important than warfare is mercantilism. Prussia had been able to weaken Hamburg's entrepôt-position in the years before and after the Seven Years' War via Magdeburg, to the advantage of many Baltic ports. Once the lower Vistula was in the hands of Prussia, i.e. after 1772, Danzig began to suffer, to the advantage of Elbing. The relaxation of Swedish mercantilism in 1772 was, with some time lag, advantageous to Swedish Pomerania. The flourishing of Danzig's trade and Stettin's shipping after 1795 are not only related to the situation of warfare, but perhaps even more to the annexation of large stretches of Poland, which increased the hinterland of the Prussian Baltic coastline. The simultaneous reduction of Memel's hinterland with the now very near Russian border was to detriment of the port. Barth, standing for Swedish Pomerania, profited probably most from the last two Partitions of Poland; its ships became principal carriers of the by-now Prussian products.

We know from the literature that the First Partition of Poland had been disadvantageous for Silesia and East Prussia, where the territorial expansion of Prussia, Austria and Russia led to an overall reduction of a hitherto vast free agricultural market zone.[91] This also holds true for other parts of Prussia. In times of strong Prussian mercantilism, it seems as if the winnings in the Baltic went mostly to the non-Prussian actors (Swedish Pomerania, Lübeck) and the

88 In fact, Prussia continued to hamper Hamburg's timber trade: Rachel, *Die Handels-, Zoll- und Akzisepolitik*, 697–700.

89 Straubel, *Die Handelsstädte*, 200–201.

90 Macgregor, *Commercial Statistics, I*, 675–681.

91 See n. 67. This partly explains the strong longing of the Prussians to get an alliance with Poland in 1791, cf.: Lord, *The second partition*, 124–127, 168–184, 488.

meagre benefits for a Prussian port like Stettin, Memel or Elbing could not make up for this. The overlap of the Second and Third Partition with the relaxation of Prussian mercantilism was to the benefit of most Prussian ports along the Baltic, even for Stettin, which had previously experienced mercantilist 'support'.

These observations allows us to conclusively formulate a hypothesis concerning the results of the Partitions of Poland. Whereas Poland had always been a non-mercantilist state,[92] Russia, Prussia and Austria certainly were. Prussian mercantilist policy between 1772 and 1786 was, as the statistics show, overall to the detriment of the standing of the state in world trade. Thus, the switch towards more liberal policies after the death of Frederick II does not only reflect the stronger fascination of Prussian elites with Adam Smith. The limits that Prussia found with its mercantilist measures after the First Partition of Poland could not but constantly sap away the vestiges of mercantilist thinking in Berlin.[93]

92 Hasse, *Geschichte der Leipziger Messen*, 4.

93 In this vein: Zimmermann, *Geschichte*, 1–13.

CHAPTER 2

The Sound Toll Registers as a Mirror of Stockholm's Foreign Trade c. 1770–1790

Sven Lilja

1 Introduction

In the early 1780s, Johan and Sven Westberg were actively engaged in maritime transport to and from Stockholm, the capital of Sweden. They were busy skippers with an extensive geographical range. In the Sound Toll Registers, their activities can be followed in some detail.[1] On 2 June 1782, Johan Westberg was registered for a passage from Stockholm to Port à Port (Oporto, Portugal). His ship carried 612 *skippund* and 7 *lispund* iron (probably bar iron) for which he had to pay a toll of 51 talers and 2 skillings. He also exported 10 *tylt* of boards and around 2.3 *last* of train oil. His total customs fee amounted to 54 talers.[2] Between 1782 and 1785, Johan Westberg was registered with eight passages through the Sound. He did not only call at Oporto, but also at Setubal (St. Ubes) and Aveiro in Portugal and at Rouen in France and St. Petersburg in Russia. He transported mainly iron, steel, boards and planks, as well as lesser amounts of brass wire, tar, train oil, alum, red paint and potash from Stockholm abroad and he conveyed salt, wine and small goods (*kramerie*) to Stockholm, and sugar from Oporto to St. Petersburg. He was registered for one to three Sound passages each year.[3] Sven Westberg had a similar sailing pattern. Between 1782 and 1785, he was registered in the Sound six times. He had connections with Portugal through Lisbon and Setubal, but also called at the Swedish west coast towns of Gothenburg, Kungälv and Marstrand and at Plymouth in England.

1 Unless otherwise indicated all quantitative data and other references to skippers, shipping and cargo traffic in this article are based on STR Online (http://www.soundtoll.nl). The core data for this article were extracted in 2010 from tables in a provisional version of the STR online database, roughly covering the period 1769–1792 http://www.let.rug.nl/~welling/sont/. This provisional version might have some errors and has been standardized only (and incompletely) for geographical names and cargo categories. However it seems to give a fairly correct picture of Stockholm's traffic through the Sound during the 1770s and 1780s.

2 www.soundtoll.nl, passage ID 136280, 02-06-1782.

3 www.soundtoll.nl, passage ID 136280, 02-06-1782; passage ID 137845, 29-09-1782; passage ID 95603, 13-05-1783; passage ID 120899, 26-07-1783; passage ID 120539, 16-09-1783; passage ID 130652, 14-07-1784; passage ID 96566, 20-05-1785; passage ID 77262, 16-09-1785.

 | DOI:10.1163/9789004371781_004

In the Baltic Sea, one of his ports of call was Riga. He mainly transported iron, but also tar, copper and herring. One of the loads he carried from Stockholm to Gothenburg included no less than 15 products; among them were iron, copper, nails, ropes, tobacco, textile, sheet metal, butter, brandy, refined salt and small goods. Both Johan and Sven Westerberg sailed mainly between Stockholm and foreign coast towns, but occasionally they also transported goods between foreign towns, for instance from Marstrand to Riga, from Riga to Lisbon and from Oporto to St. Petersburg.[4]

Johan and Sven Westberg were fairly representative of the Stockholm cargo traffic through the Sound in these years. Jacob Westerling, another Stockholm skipper, displays a similar pattern, with Dutch (Amsterdam), French, Russian, Portuguese and Irish ports of call. But there were shipmasters with geographically more specialized connections. Samuel Dixon, who was registered with 15 passages through the Sound in 1769, 1776–78, and 1780, had regular contacts with London. He seems to have been a somewhat larger actor in the Stockholm traffic, but the range of the export products he transported was much the same as that of other Stockholm shipmasters; he shipped iron, bar iron, tar, boards, beams, and heavy timber, and smaller amounts of butter, and sheet metal. The products carried from the London market to Stockholm were often more varied. He imported, among other things, cheese, tobacco, wild cat skins, coffee beans, oriental spices, and rice.[5]

It is clear from these examples that the STR contain a host of varied and valuable data for any researcher that is interested in the details of a port's foreign shipping. At the same time, it is possible to interpret the information in the registers as idiographic and to use it as a basis for studies into the economic biographies of individual skippers. The preceding examples may serve as a first illustration of the potential of STRO for the execution of such detailed studies, not at the least because its electronic form has greatly improved the possibilities to penetrate and search the wealth of information gathered by the toll officers at Elsinore.

4 www.soundtoll.nl, passage ID 142161, 11-11-1782; passage ID 100872, 05-06-1783; passage ID 140425, 10-05-1784; passage ID 103360, 19-10-1784; passage ID 90898, 02-12-1784; passage ID 69188, 25-07-1785.

5 www.soundtoll.nl, Jacob Westerling: passage ID 188156, 30-06-1777; passage ID 149622, 17-11-1780; passage ID 127385, 18-05-1782; passage ID 131117, 16-08-1782; passage ID 137866, 29-09-1782; passage ID 162619, 30-11-1782; passage ID128243, 11-08-1783. Samuel Dixon: passage ID 24207, 27-06-1769; passage ID 244769, 18-09-1769; passage ID 246604, 12-11-1769; passage ID 248998, 30-04-1769; passage ID 195072, 26-06-1776; 208672, 29-08-1776; passage ID 187923, 14-08-1777; passage ID 191651, 12-07-1777; passage ID 196556, 28-09-1777; passage ID 220042, 27-05-1777; passage ID 200102, 14-05-1778; passage ID 205967, 16-09-1778; passage ID 212197, 07-11-1778; passage ID 224349, 09-07-1778; passage ID 165177, 19-12-1780.

In this article, some quantitative compilations are used to illustrate how STRO reflects Stockholm's maritime trade with Western Europe and the Swedish west coast in the 1770s and 1780s. The study focuses on some basic data concerning skippers and cargoes and asks how they mirror the product variation and geographic range of shipments through the Sound. In this way, the tendency in maritime transport to specialize in certain destinations and products as well as – more generally – Stockholm's role in the eighteenth century trading system are addressed from the perspective of the *idiographic* information in STRO. Finally, some thoughts on various non-economic research possibilities offered by STRO are added.

2 Stockholm-Based Shipmasters in STRO

Research on Stockholm's pre-industrial foreign trade and shipping has been concerned mostly with the eighteenth century. The Swedish economic historian Eli Heckscher's description and analysis of this trade were based on his conviction that all state regulations are, and forever will be, harmful to economic development and welfare. Since the eighteenth century was a century of mercantilism, when the Swedish crown tried to regulate foreign trade in order to defend its national interests, foreign trade must have been hampered by all regulations.[6]

Staffan Högberg partly confirms Heckscher's view of the declining relative importance of Stockholm's shipping and trade, but also points to the reorientation of Sweden's maritime trade when Gothenburg and the other west coast towns drastically expanded their shipping fleet.[7]

Based on court protocols (*tänkeböcker*), the Swedish geographer Nils Friberg was able to map Stockholm's medieval trade connections, which ranged from the northern tip of the Bothnian Sea to the Swedish west coast.[8] A more recent study by Åke Sandström has confirmed the wide geographical range of the city's trade connections for the late sixteenth and early seventeenth centuries. Sandström argued that Stockholm played an intermediate role in the large international shipping and trading network that connected Sweden to the European world-system (as put forth by Immanuel Wallerstein). According to Sandström, the center-periphery relations of different economic regions within the world-system were as important as state relations and state competition

6 Heckscher, *Sveriges ekonomiska*, 2. Heckscher, *Svenskt arbete*.

7 Högberg, *Utrikeshandel*, 44–45, 239.

8 Friberg, *Stockholm*.

within the system.[9] More recently, the economic historian Klas Nyberg has initiated a project on Stockholm's manufacturing industry and export trade in the eighteenth century. So far, this project has resulted in the publication of several studies on Stockholm's textile production and export in the middle of the eighteenth century.[10] Thus, the earlier interpretations of Stockholm's role in maritime trade confirm that the city was part of an international trade system that was, if we follow Immanuel Wallerstein and other world-system proponents, one of Sweden's links to the larger European world-system. As a semi-peripheral state, Sweden was situated between the core areas of Western Europe and the periphery of Northern and Eastern Europe. Sweden's position was characterized by economic dependence to a certain degree, but also by a strong state protecting trade and shipping against foreign competition. In this context, Stockholm had a strategic position as Sweden's gateway to the larger European market.[11]

In spite of Stockholm's importance as a port city in the Baltic Sea the shipments to and from the city through the Sound were limited compared to Sound traffic as a whole. A comparison of Sound traffic in its totality with the Sound traffic of the Stockholm-based shipmasters[12] clearly reveals what a small part of the traffic was in the hands of the Stockholm shipmasters (graphs 2.1 and 2.2).[13] In straight numbers, there were normally between 8,000 and 11,000 registered passages going through the Sound on a yearly basis in the 1770s and 1780s. However, Stockholm skippers normally executed only between 290 and 340 passages per year; a share that seems to have been fairly stable. Thus, the Stockholm-based shipmasters' average annual share of passages through the Sound was just above 3 %.[14]

---

9 Sandström, *Mellan Torneå och Amsterdam*. Concerning Wallerstein's world-system model see, for instance: Walllerstein, *The Modern World-System*, especially 15–61 and 346–357, and Wallerstein, *The Modern World-System*, 2. Wallerstein has given several applications of his model. For a short presentation of the world-system as such, see his *World-Systems Analysis*.

10 Nyberg, *Köpes: ull*.

11 Wallerstein, *The Modern World-System*, 2, 203–221. Sandström, *Mellan Torneå och Amsterdam*, 385.

12 The expression "Stockholm-based skippers/shipmasters" or "Stockholm skippers/shipmasters" refers to skippers registered with Stockholm as their domicile in the STR.

13 For comparative purposes I have restricted this part of the study to fully registered years only. For general references see note 1 above.

14 Six of the seven normal years 1777–80 and 1783–85 (excluding the two extreme years of 1789–90) are registered for a minimum of 8,292 passages (1778) and maximum of 11,297 passages (1783). Of these seven years the Stockholm shipmasters had 292 (1779) to 343 shipments (1785), ranging between 3.1 % (1784) and 3.5 % (1778 & 1779); only 1780 deviated somewhat with 209 shipments (2.5 %). The Stockholm shipmasters' average share was 3.2 %, with median 3.3 %.

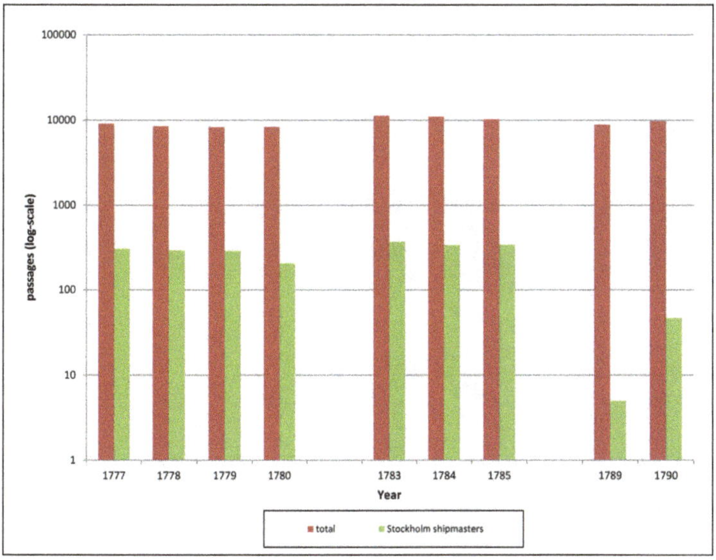

GRAPH 2.1 Number of passages from/to Stockholm through the Sound 1777–1780, 1783–1785 and 1789–1790
NOTE: The diagrams show only years that were fully available in the 2010 database.
SOURCE: TOTAL NUMBER OF SOUND PASSAGES FROM STR STATISTICS IN HTTP://DIETRICH.SOUNDTOLL.NL/PUBLIC/STATS.PHP?STAT=PY

During the seven normal years 1777/1780 and 1783/1785 there were approximately 670 Stockholm-based shipmasters active in traffic through the Sound with close to 2,200 passages, which gives an average of almost 3.2 passages per skipper for all seven years, and 0.7 passages per skipper and year. Many of the skippers were registered with only one or two passages; some were registered with a few more passages; and a small number of skippers was intensively engaged in traffic through the Sound.

Of course, in extreme situations the share of Stockholm's shipmasters in the Sound traffic could vary a lot. In the years 1789 and 1790, there was a drastic reduction of this group's registered passages through the Sound. From the normal average amount of around 310 passages, the numbers fell to 5 and 47, respectively. Apart from the possibility that data might be faulty, everyone educated in European history might have one or two guesses concerning the underlying causal factors. To explain this drastic drop of shipments by the revolutionary events that occurred in France in these years would be stretching things too far. If there were a connection to the French Revolution, why should it only affect Stockholm's traffic through the Sound and not all traffic? There appears to have been a slight reduction in the total number of passages

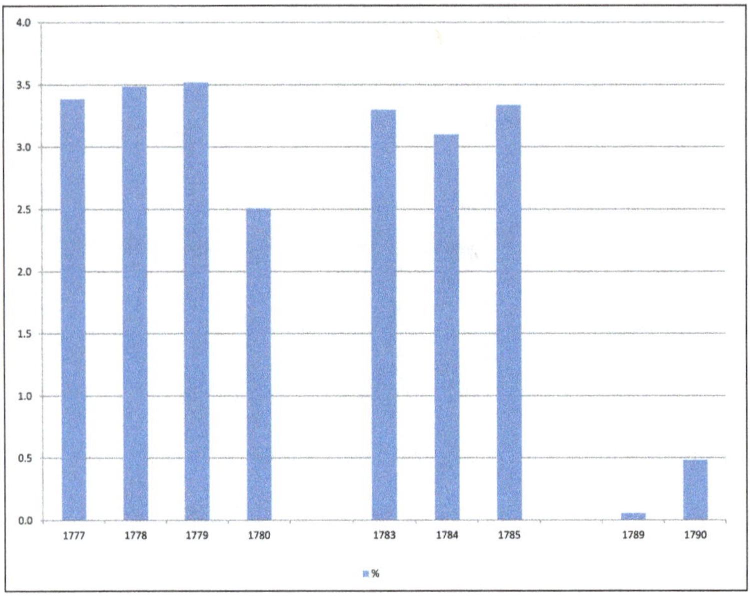

GRAPH 2.2 Stockholm-based shipmasters' share of Sound passages, 1777–1780, 1783–1785 and 1789–1790. Percentage share of total number of Sound passages.
NOTE: The diagrams show only years that were fully available in the 2010 database.
SOURCE: TOTAL NUMBER OF SOUND PASSAGES FROM STR STATISTICS IN HTTP://DIETRICH.SOUNDTOLL.NL/PUBLIC/STATS.PHP?STAT=PY

through the Sound in 1789 and 1790, but nothing like the near elimination of traffic that occurred for Stockholm. It is more likely that the Swedish-Russian war in 1788–90 had this catastrophic effect on the Stockholm skippers' traffic through the Sound.[15]

3 Patterns of Product Specialization

In table 2.1, the cargoes[16] exported from Stockholm have been counted and classified by the main product categories and a few dominant products. The table presents the number of registered cargoes distributed into major product

15 For the dip in Sweden's shipping trade in these years, see Högberg, *Utrikeshandel*, 18, 33.
16 I have used the cargo concept from the sources mentioned in note 1 above. There could be several loads of different products in a single shipment. For example: a shipment from

categories. Metal and forest products amounted for more than three quarters of the total number of cargoes exported through the Sound. Among the most important metal products, iron (most of it probably bar iron) constituted a 21 % share of the cargoes, but iron plates, steel and various products of copper and brass also had significant shares. Boards and planks of different kinds, tar and a smaller amount of pitch dominated the forest products. The forest product group had a 38 % share of the outgoing cargoes. No other category or individual product came close to the exports of iron, boards and planks, and tar.

Among the other product categories, a fair share was taken by the heterogeneous group of wares here labeled "urban market goods." This category was characterized by its variety and its many small loads; it included exotic products such as tobacco, saffron, porcelain stoves, anise, books and pepper, but its main sub-categories were various kinds of textiles and a noteworthy category of unspecified small goods (*kramerie*). The "urban market goods" constituted 9 % of the cargoes, thus substantiating that, besides exporting staple products from the Swedish mining and forest industries, Stockholm also played a role as a transit port of European and non-European consumer goods.

It is no surprise that there was a strong contrast between Stockholm's exports and imports (Table 2.1). "Urban market goods" constituted no less than 31 % of Stockholm's incoming cargoes, with small goods and various kinds of textiles amounting to 15 %. Three products dominated food and drink imports (47 %): fish (19 %), salt (7 %), and wine (6 %).

Together food, drinks and "urban market goods" accounted for almost 78 % of the cargo items registered as destined to Stockholm. The share of metal wares and forest products, on the other hand, amounted only to an insignificant 3 % of the import traffic, a figure that contrasts sharply with the product structure of exports from Stockholm, with its 76 % share of metal wares and forest products.

4 Patterns of Geographical Specialization

The cargoes registered in the STR as destined for Stockholm in the 1770s and 1780s were mainly coming from major port cities of the European west coast and the British Isles and Ireland, but there was also a substantial trade with the Swedish west coast (see Table 2.2). Amsterdam was the most important single port of departure for ships destined to Stockholm in these years. More

Amsterdam to Stockholm (passage ID 5406, 12-05-1789) carried no less than 15 cargoes of various products (*kaffee, quicksölv, couchenille, uld*, etc).

TABLE 2.1 Export and import products from Stockholm through the sound, 1769–1790

		Export cargoes		%		Import cargoes		%	
metals		**4,241**		**38**		**319**		**3**	
	iron, bar iron		2,340		21				
	iron plates		708		6				
	steel		508		5				
food and drink		**496**		**4**		**5,157**		**47**	
	fish						2,058		19
	salt						738		7
	wine						608		6
forest products		**4,234**		**38**		**61**		**1**	
	planks		2,141		19				
	tar, pitch		1,808		16				
urban market goods		**980**		**9**		**3,388**		**31**	
	small goods		647		6		865		8
	textiles		333		3		717		7
chemicals		**632**		**6**		**1,028**		**9**	
various and unknown		**490**		**4**		**929**		**9**	
	ballast						331		3
Total		**11,073**		**100**		**10,882**		**100**	

SOURCE: EXTRACTS FROM TABLES IN A PROVISIONAL VERSION OF THE STR ONLINE DATABASE, ROUGHLY COVERING THE PERIOD 1769–1792. (HTTP://WWW.LET.RUG.NL/~WELLING/SONT/).

than 2,600 of the registered cargoes going to Stockholm, or almost one-fourth (24 %) of its cargo traffic, came from Amsterdam. Thus, the Dutch Republic was a major country of departure, where Amsterdam was clearly predominant: almost all 'Dutch' cargoes destined to Stockholm came from Amsterdam (99 %). With its almost 2,000 cargoes, France was the second most important area of departure for imports to Stockholm via the Sound in the 1770s and 1780s. The French traffic to Stockholm constituted 18 % of the shipments destined for the Swedish capital. In France, the geographic range of the traffic was more widely spread than in the Dutch Republic. No less than 18 French ports were involved in this incoming traffic to Stockholm, and some of them had a significant share of the traffic. Bordeaux, for instance, had c. 1,040 cargoes destined for Stockholm, or almost 10 % of the traffic. Other important French port cities were Marseille, Cette and Rouen.[17] As in the French case, the traffic coming from the British Isles was spread out among many port cities. More than 1,400 cargoes (13 %) left the British Isles and Ireland for Stockholm from as many as 41 ports of departure. However, this traffic was, like the traffic departing from the Dutch Republic, heavily centralized. London took a 9 % share of the traffic through the Sound destined to Stockholm, and with its more than 1,000 registered cargoes, it accounted for 72 % of all British or Irish traffic destined to Stockholm. No other British or Irish port city came close to these shares.[18] Portugal and Germany were also significant import countries in Stockholm's traffic through the Sound during the latter part of the eighteenth century. The Portuguese traffic to Stockholm amounted to almost 5 % (506 cargoes). There were five Portuguese ports involved in this business. Most important was the traffic from St. Ubes (Setubal), with 423 cargoes.[19] In Germany, Hamburg dominated imports to Stockholm; with 394 cargoes it had a share of 85 % of Germany's total.

These figures clearly illustrate how unevenly the Sound traffic to Stockholm was distributed. Only three countries (the Dutch Republic, France, and Britain with Ireland) were registered with more than 1,000 cargoes, and only three foreign cities (Amsterdam, London, and Bordeaux) with more than five hundred cargoes destined for Stockholm. There was a sharp contrast between the dominant port cities of Amsterdam, London and Bordeaux and the many minor ports that sent shipments to Stockholm in these years. However, many of these minor ports carry interesting information about the geographic range of Stockholm's Sound traffic. Among the quantitatively less important ports we find distant places such as St. Bartholomey (12 cargoes), St. Domingo (7 cargoes) and Philadelphia (9 cargoes). Stockholm also had a significant traffic coming in from the Mediterranean, with Spain and Italy as the main areas of departure. Both countries were good for a full three hundred cargoes, which amounted to approximately 3 % each. A small number of cargoes originated further south and east in the Mediterranean; from Constantinople (38 cargoes), Smyrna (13 cargoes), and Algiers (4 cargoes).

---

17 With respectively 433, 257 and 151 cargoes.

18 Newcastle, with its eleventh ranking position among the ports of departure, reached only 1 % with its 102 cargo loads destined for Stockholm.

19 Lisbon had the next largest share of the Portuguese traffic to Stockholm, but only with a rather small number of 71 cargoes.

The geographical distribution of the traffic from Stockholm through the Sound was similar to the incoming traffic, but with some noteworthy differences. Approximately 25 % of outgoing traffic was directed to the British Isles and Ireland (see Table 2.3). As with the incoming cargo traffic, London was the main port of call (about 900 cargoes, 8 %). The geographic distribution of the traffic from Stockholm to Britain/Ireland was somewhat more evenly spread than in the opposite direction, though. Cities like Hull (405 cargoes, almost 4 %) and Dublin (364 cargoes, over 3 %) were significant ports of destination. This is explained by the British ports' unfavorable shipment balance with Stockholm, with almost 2,800 cargoes coming from Stockholm and only c. 1,400 going to Stockholm. Except London, the British and Irish port cities were heavily dependent on Swedish staple products, but did not have much to supply to Stockholm. It is symptomatic that these cities are registered with more than 160 cargoes of ballast. This finding seems to illustrate the importance of Swedish staple products for the British economy at the brink of the industrial revolution.

Ballast was a noticeable part of London's traffic to Stockholm too (101 ballast cargoes), but – at least in terms of the number of different cargo items registered in STRO – the balance between both capitals was more even with 893 cargoes coming from Stockholm and 1,024 cargoes going to Stockholm. In relative terms, however, there was a marked imbalance. London received only 32 % of the total British and Irish cargo traffic departing from Stockholm, whereas it supplied 72 % of all registered cargo items to the Swedish capital. On one hand, this imbalance reflects London's dominance as a deliverer of food and "urban market goods" to Stockholm, on the other, it highlights the need for the Swedish staple products from metal and forest production at the other British and Irish port towns. France was the second largest destination of Stockholm's outgoing shipments through the Sound. France's traffic with Stockholm was fairly balanced, with close to 2,000 cargoes in both directions. Marseille and Rouen, with more than 400 cargoes each, were important ports of destination, and even surpassed Bordeaux in this respect. Portugal's traffic with Stockholm was approximately at the same level as that of France. With more than 1,800 cargoes from Stockholm, it constituted over 16 % of all exports from Stockholm – again insofar as the number of different cargo items informs us. The cities of Lisbon and Porto stand out as the most important Portuguese destinations of exports from Stockholm. The Dutch Republic was significant as a destination for Stockholm's outgoing goods as well, but not nearly as much as this region's importance as deliverer of incoming goods to Stockholm. Amsterdam dominated heavily with its more than 900 cargoes, or 85 % of the total traffic to the Netherlands, but there were a few other ports with some traffic as well. Thus, the balance of the traffic with the Dutch Republic was an almost complete reversal of Stockholm's traffic with the British and Irish ports, where the number of outgoing cargoes was twice as large as that of incoming cargoes. Other West European countries were less important, but Italy (496 cargoes, almost 4 %) had a noticeable share of the outgoing traffic from Stockholm.

Although Stockholm had a wide range of geographical destinations and products in its traffic through the Sound, the traffic was, to a relatively high degree, specialized in only a few commodities obtained from or sent to a small number of destinations. Metal wares and forest products constituted no less than 76 % of the outgoing cargoes. Insofar as the British and Irish imports from Stockholm were concerned, the share of metal wares and forest products exceeded 93 %. The situation was much the same for the traffic with other countries: France 86 %, Portugal 94 %, Spain 86 % and Italy 78 %.

In the other direction, the leading ports delivered foodstuffs (mainly salt and wine) and "urban market goods" to Stockholm. In the exports from the Dutch Republic, France and Spain to Stockholm both of these product categories played an important role (77 %, 86 % and 92 %, respectively). London, on the other hand, had a more diversified export to Stockholm with noticeable shares not only of food and drink and "urban market goods" but also of chemicals and metal wares (food and drink 17 %, "urban market goods" 37 %, chemicals 12 %, metal wares 15 %) (see Table 2.3). The traffic from Portugal and Italy was dominated by food – almost exclusively salt.[20]

TABLE 2.2 Geographic distribution of import and export goods, 1769–1791 (number of cargoes and percentage share)

A) incoming from	food	%	urb	%	chem	%	metal	%	forest	%	varia	%	total	%	% of total
Netherlands	1,041	39	1,010	38	368	14	47	2	5	0	177	7	2,648	100	24
Britain & Ireland	216	15	404	28	124	9	190	13	9	1	488	34	1,431	100	13
France	716	36	1,001	50	200	10	10	1	6	0	58	3	1,991	100	18
Portugal	468	92	23	5		0	5	1	6	1	4	1	506	100	5
Spain	196	57	120	35	23	7		0		0	7	2	346	100	3
Italy	248	78	62	19	6	2		0		0	3	1	319	100	3
Mediterrania, remaining	11	41	12	44	2	7		0		0	2	7	27	100	0

20 Portugal 365 cargoes of salt (93 %), of which 306 came from St Ubes (Setubal); Italy 220 cargoes of salt (79 %).

TABLE 2.2 Geographic distribution of import and export goods, 1769–1791 (*cont.*)

A) incoming from	food	%	urb	%	chem	%	metal	%	forest	%	varia	%	total	%	% of total
America & West India	3	11	16	57	3	11		0	3	11	3	11	28	100	0
Germany	111	24	199	43	96	21	1	0	2	0	54	12	463	100	4
Denmark & Norway	169	74	17	7	3	1	2	1	2	1	35	15	228	100	2
Swed W coast	1,950	71	476	17	194	7	55	2	10	0	76	3	2,761	100	25
Baltic Sea & unknown	28	21	48	36	9	7	9	7	18	13	22	16	134	100	1
Sum cargoes to Sthl	5,157	47	3,388	31	1,028	9	319	3	61	1	929	9	10,882	100	100
B) outgoing to	food	%	urb	%	chem	%	metal	%	forest	%	varia	%	total	%	% of total
Netherlands	16	2	70	7	99	9	414	39	437	41	29	3	1,065	100	10
Britain & Ireland	5	0	77	3	21	1	1,107	40	1,472	53	111	4	2,793	100	25
France	12	1	85	4	137	7	901	46	775	40	49	3	1,959	100	18
Portugal	16	1	33	2	13	1	938	51	786	43	39	2	1,825	100	16
Spain	2	1	17	7	8	3	115	47	96	39	8	3	246	100	2
Italy	5	1	36	7	48	10	194	39	193	39	20	4	496	100	4
Mediterrania, remaining	2	1	4	3	8	6	63	43	64	44	4	3	145	100	1
America & West India	10	17	6	10	8	14	17	29	13	22	4	7	58	100	1
Germany	1	1	9	6	19	12	54	35	66	43	4	3	153	100	1
Denmark & Norway	1	1	3	3	5	5	39	41	46	48	2	2	96	100	1
Swed W coast	417	19	632	29	261	12	376	17	270	12	209	10	2,164	100	20
Baltic Sea & unknown	7	10	8	12	5	7	22	33	16	24	9	13	67	100	1
Sum cargoes from Sthl	496	4	980	9	632	6	4,241	38	4,234	38	490	4	11,073	96	100

NOTE: Percent shares greater than or equal to 35 % are marked with grey shades.

SOURCE: EXTRACTS FROM TABLES IN A PROVISIONAL VERSION OF THE STR ONLINE DATABASE, ROUGHLY COVERING THE PERIOD 1769–1792. (HTTP://WWW.LET.RUG.NL/~WELLING/SONT/).

Thus Stockholm's trade with foreign countries and ports was an exchange of semi-manufactured goods, such as bar iron, planks and tar, for a more varied and exclusive range of urban products with a large share of salt, wine, and small goods. This is a trade pattern that comes close to a semi-peripheral status, as it has been proposed by Immanuel Wallerstein and other world-system advocates.

Several important ports of departure of the traffic to Stockholm were located on the Swedish west coast. In fact, this area was the most important region for incoming shipments to Stockholm and the second most important region (after Britain and Ireland) of outgoing shipments. Approximately 25 % of Stockholm's incoming, and almost 20 % of its outgoing traffic through the Sound, came from or went to the Swedish west coast. This was domestic traffic, although it went around the southern tip off Scandinavia, and thus was registered in the STR. This domestic traffic was dominated by Gothenburg, the most important and largest port on the Swedish west coast, with almost 1,897 cargoes from Stockholm (17 % of Stockholm's outgoing cargo traffic), and almost 1,589 cargoes to Stockholm (15 % of Stockholm's incoming traffic) (see Table 2.3). Thus, the overseas traffic between Stockholm and Gothenburg was fairly balanced, however with a minor dominance of the outgoing cargo traffic. The products from mining and forestry were much less important in this domestic traffic than in the city's international traffic, but they still had some significance. These product categories amounted 19 % and 12 % respectively of Stockholm's outgoing traffic to Gothenburg, compared to the averages of foreign countries and ports close to 40 % (see Table 2.3). Thus, the share of Stockholm's staple products to Gothenburg differs fundamentally from the corresponding pattern of its cargo traffic with Western Europe. At least in part, this can be explained by the fact that Gothenburg had as easy an access to Sweden's staple products as the capital city. Gothenburg's hinterland stretched to the northeast along the Göta Älv and Klarälven river systems and included one of Sweden's most important forestry and metal production regions.

In both directions, food and "urban market goods" were more important. The exchange of "urban market goods" was rather balanced between Stockholm and Gothenburg, with c. 400 incoming and 550 outgoing cargoes, whereas food was mostly imported to Stockholm.[21]

The two cities' urban character might explain why the exchange of urban market goods between Stockholm and Gothenburg was fairly balanced. At this time, Stockholm was a relatively large city with approximately 70,000 inhabitants; Gothenburg was Sweden's second largest city, with a mere 12,000

21 Urban goods: in 395 (4 %) and out 545 (3 %); food: in 949 (9 %) and out 368 (5 %).

TABLE 2.3 Geographic distribution of import and export goods from/to major ports

port	% food	% urb	% chem	% metal	% forest	% varia	% sum	towns total	ports of total %	ports of country %	country
incoming cargoes											
Amsterdam	39	38	14	2	0	6	100	2,634	24	99	Netherlands
London	17	37	12	15	1	19	100	1,024	9	72	Britain & Ireland
Bordeaux	34	53	11	0	0	2	100	1,039	10	52	France
Marseille	29	53	13	2	0	3	100	433	4	22	France
St Ubes	95	4	0	0	0	1	100	423	4	84	Portugal
Hamburg	22	45	24	0	1	9	100	394	4	85	Germany
Gothenburg	60	25	9	3	1	3	100	1,589	15	58	Swed W coast
Marstrand	85	7	4	0	0	3	100	625	6	23	Swed W coast
Average %	48	33	11	3	0	6	100				
outgoing cargoes											
Amsterdam	2	7	11	40	37	3	100	905	8	85	Netherlands
London	0	5	1	39	51	3	100	893	8	32	Britain & Ireland
Hull	0	2	0	37	56	4	100	405	4	15	Britain & Ireland
Bordeaux	0	5	9	47	35	4	100	243	2	12	France
Marseille	1	4	7	45	38	4	100	443	4	23	France
Rouen	0	9	8	53	27	2	100	417	4	21	France
Lisbon	1	2	1	46	48	3	100	961	9	53	Portugal
Oporto	1	1	1	55	39	2	100	411	4	23	Portugal
Gothenburg	19	29	12	18	12	10	100	1,897	17	88	Swed W coast
Average %	3	7	5	43	38	4	100				

NOTE: Percent shares greater than or equal to 35 % are marked with grey shades.
SOURCE: EXTRACTS FROM TABLES IN A PROVISIONAL VERSION OF THE STR ONLINEDATABASE, ROUGHLY COVERING THE PERIOD 1769–1792. (HTTP://WWW.LET.RUG.NL/~WELLING/SONT/).

inhabitants. Almost 30 % of Stockholm's traffic in both directions concerned "urban market goods", a product category which was dominated for the most part by a few western European ports, such as Amsterdam, London and Bordeaux. Apart from Gothenburg, there was an extensive, although heavily unbalanced, traffic to and from several other west coast towns as well. Thus, Marstrand, with its c. 6 % share (more than 600 cargoes), was a relatively important port of departure, and this could also be said about Halmstad (394 cargoes, 3.7 %), Uddevalla (216 cargoes, 2 %), and Kungälv (156 cargoes, 1.5 %). Altogether eight smaller west coast towns delivered no less than 1,172 cargoes (11 %) to the capital city.[22] On the other hand, the outgoing traffic from Stockholm to the smaller west coast towns was much weaker; only 267 cargoes (2.4 %).[23] The product structure of Stockholm's traffic with the smaller Swedish west coast ports differed significantly from the city's traffic through the Sound with both Gothenburg and foreign destinations. Metal wares and forest products were insignificant in the traffic with small ports on the Swedish west coast. Perhaps, like Gothenburg, most of these towns had direct access to Swedish staple products, and therefore little need for this kind of import from Stockholm. Stockholm's dependence on imports from the Swedish west coast becomes obvious when the commodity structure is more closely examined. Of the 1,172 incoming cargoes from the smaller ports on the Swedish west coast no less than 1,001 (85 %) carried food, of these cargoes 956 (82 %) were fish cargoes, and of these fish cargoes no less than 583 (50 %) involved herring. This extensive fish traffic was a characteristic trait of the Gothenburg traffic as well. Gothenburg delivered, with 751 fish cargoes, almost as much as the other west coast towns together. However, relatively speaking, the fish cargoes were less important in Gothenburg's traffic to Stockholm than other imports. It amounted to 47 % of the city's outgoing traffic; much less than the other west coast towns' 82 % share. Herring had, with 443 cargoes, a significant share of the town's traffic, although in relative terms much smaller than the other west coast towns (28 % for Gothenburg compared to 50 % for the other towns). Thus, Stockholm's fish imports mainly came from the Swedish west coast towns, and it was dominated by herring, which amounted to no less than 1,026 cargoes, that is 37 % of the total incoming cargo traffic from the west coast towns, and 60 % of the fish cargoes alone.[24] Like Stockholm's need for urban

---

22 The ports were: Båstad, Fiskebäckskil (not a town), Halmstad, Kungälv, Landskrona, Marstrand, Strömstad and Uddevalla.

23 The ports were Båstad, Ängelholm, Halmstad, Kungälv, Marstrand, Uddevalla and Varberg.

24 Other important kinds of fish imported to Stockholm were *torsk* (cod), *mackerel, cabeljau* (dried cod), *vittling* (whiting), *drizzle/långa* (dried ling), and *lax* (salmon).

market goods, this incoming traffic of fish was a reflection of the large city's role as a consumer market.

5 Conclusions

The geographical range of Stockholm's traffic through the Sound with foreign countries in the 1770s and 1780s was oriented mainly towards four destinations: the Dutch Republic, Great Britain and Ireland, France and Portugal. Amsterdam, London, Bordeaux and Lisbon were Stockholm's main ports of call. This structure, however, does not provide a complete picture. A small, but noticeable share of the cargo traffic was directed towards or departed from distant ports in the Mediterranean and the Americas.

When it comes to the structure of the products involved there were a few basic patterns that characterized Stockholm's traffic through the Sound. First of all, metal wares and forest products played a dominant role in the city's outgoing cargo traffic. Especially iron, copper, pitch and tar had played an important role in Sweden's export trade as far back as late medieval times. They peaked as export products in the seventeenth century, but still played an important role in the eighteenth century. However, in the course of time some changes in the composition of the products occurred, tar and pitch in particular were supplemented with planks, boards and masts. Secondly, as a major urban center in Swedish society, Stockholm was heavily dependent on the import of foodstuffs, which becomes equally clear in the pattern of Stockholm's traffic with foreign ports. Salt, wine and other foodstuffs came from specialized ports in France, Portugal, Spain and Italy. A third, significant pattern involved Stockholm's demand for a variety of consumer goods, in which textiles had a considerable share. To a large extent, these needs were satisfied by London and Amsterdam. These basic patterns in Stockholm's incoming cargo traffic reflect the city's needs and demands as a place of consumption. Similar patterns were reproduced in the cargo traffic between Stockholm and the Swedish west coast towns as well. Stockholm's domestic traffic through the Sound was characterized by its dependency on food products (mainly fish). At the same time, this domestic traffic was also characterized by a relatively balanced exchange with Gothenburg. The latter patterns were similar to the relations between Stockholm and the large western European ports of London and Amsterdam. Eighteenth-century Stockholm was the center of a vast shipping network, and as such the focal point of Sweden's economic activities. In its relation with the large urbanized western European ports, the city appeared to have had a semi-peripheral status within an emergent world-system. Thus, as a northern port city far away from the densely populated regions of Western Europe, Stockholm's traffic through the Sound reflected the international position of Sweden, as well as the city's own position as the leading port of the Swedish realm.[25]

The digital registration of the toll registers has, without any doubt, opened up new paths for research into maritime transport structures and international trade patterns. The present effort to dig deeper into Stockholm's traffic through the Sound in the 1770s and 1780s has clearly emphasized this possibility. STRO has made it possible to reconstruct trade patterns, transport routes and economic biographies in detail, but it can also be employed as a tool for the in-depth analysis of commodity structures, the geographical range of trade connections or the day-to-day chronological analysis of historical events.

Moreover, the new and easy access to the data captured in the STR will not only improve our possibilities for writing economic history, it will also stimulate asking new types of research questions. Ecological perspectives might be applied to the registered data. For example, the trade cycles of grain and vegetables and the fluctuations of shipping seasons for various ports could be analyzed with reference to possible effects of climate variations.[26] The fluctuations in the traffic of such products as fish and fur might indicate the historic effects of large scale hunting and fishing on wildlife stocks.

As a source of cultural or language history the Sound registers are equally interesting. We now have easy access to a full-scale commercial terminology covering several hundred years of European history, and we will have the possibility to analyze the changes of taste and habits in various parts of Europe in detail, ranging from the Baltic to the Mediterranean Sea.

Last but not least, STRO has significant potential for local history as well. The registers provide us with so many places and so many individuals that, through this new source, might be placed in a wider context. Individual cities will be seen in their connections to the international markets, and it will be possible to identify and follow individual persons and skippers; in lucky instances, one might be able to follow them in their activities from year to year and from season to season. Shipmaster dynasties emerge in these sources of their commercial praxis, and parts of their economic networks might be

25 For this broad description of Stockholm's position in the Swedish and European shipping and trade networks see, for instance, the books mentioned in notes 8 to 10 above.

26 For similar studies see Jevrejeva, "Severity" and Leijonhufvud, Wilson and Moberg, "Documentary data."

mapped out. Still, with the strategy chosen, we will not lose the direct connection to the original sources, since the scanned registers are accessible on the internet. The possibility to go from the quantitative data to the original source text and back again is a confirmation as strong as any of the importance and value of this project.

CHAPTER 3

War of Hunger: Supplying the French Republic during the Revolutionary Wars (1793–1795)

Pierrick Pourchasse

In February 1792, William Pitt ventured to promise fifteen years of peace by reducing British military spending. However, one year later, in March 1793, he said that war was not only inevitable but, given the current circumstances, necessary for the survival of Great Britain and Europe.[1] The victories of the young French Republic at Valmy and Jemmapes, the French occupation of the Austrian Netherlands in the autumn of 1792, the trial of the king of France, Louis XVI, and his execution on 21 January 1793 had totally changed the attitude of the British authorities towards the Revolution.[2] The French Republic had become a threat to the stability of Europe and to the safeguard of British interests.

Following the execution of Louis XVI the British government informed François Chauvelin, Ambassador of France in London, that he must leave the United Kingdom before 1 February 1793. France responded immediately by a declaration of war on Great Britain and the Dutch Republic. In turn, George III declared war on France on 12 February. Optimism reigned in the British government at the beginning of the conflict. The king and his advisers believed that the war would be very short. According to Pitt "certainly, everything will be finished in one or two campaigns."[3]

The British government immediately decided to set up a blockade of French ports to paralyze the naval forces of the enemy. A military blockade of the naval ports was quickly accompanied by an economic blockade of all French ports. The British authorities tried to cut off all of France's trade relations. A war against its trade was also a war against its economy and a means of weakening the enemy's finances and, thus, of reducing its military capabilities. For Pitt the blockade of France was an absolute priority. He knew that a financial crisis was coming and was convinced that the Revolution could not survive a

1 Dziembowski, *Les Pitt*, 388. William Pitt the Younger (1759–1806) was prime minister of Great Britain from 1783 to 1801 and from 1804 until his death in 1806.

2 Black, *British foreign policy*, 406.

3 Dziembowski, *Les Pitt*, 407.

 | DOI:10.1163/9789004371781_005

long war. On 8 June, new measures, known as the Instruction of June 1793, prohibited all transport of foodstuffs to France and allowed privateers and British warships to seize all shipments to France. The first article of the Instruction reads as follows:

> That it shall be lawful to stop and detain all ships loaded wholly or in part with corn, flour or meal bound to any port in France; and to send them to such ports as shall be most convenient in order that such corn, meal or flour may be purchased on behalf of his Majesty's government, and the ships be released after such purchase, and after a due allowance for freight or that the masters of such ships on giving due security, to be approved of by the Court of Admiralty, be permitted to proceed to dispose of their cargoes of corn, meal, or flour, in the ports of any country in amity with his Majesty.[4]

The British decision to block grain shipments to France was an attempt to starve the French people. The British authorities justified it in several ways. First, the war was triggered by a government not recognized by its neighbors in a manner contrary to international law. Second, the supply of cereals to France was organized by an illegal government so that the supplies themselves were illegal too. Finally, the blockade would force the enemy to make peace quickly for financial reasons. As Grouvelle, envoy of France in Copenhagen put it: "our enemies show their barbarism and insolence by saying aloud that there is no other way to reduce us (this is their expression) than by starving us. This is the execrable plot they organized against us requiring terrible reprisals on our part."[5] Thus, the British blockade had two goals: weakening French finances and diverting the French population, threatened with famine, from revolutionary ideas. For its implementation, Britain organized a coalition of the main European countries. In February 1793, Russia put an end to its economic relations with France. In April, the King of Sardinia signed an agreement with England and on 25 May, it was Spain's turn. In July, the Kingdom of Naples joined the coalition, Prussia and the Emperor of Germany in August and Portugal in September. All of them promised to prevent the supply of France with food, particularly cereals.

Meanwhile France had more and more difficulties in providing its population with food. Even if the harvest of 1792 had not been bad, the political uncertainties and the inflation prevented the distribution of grain. Farmers

---

4 MAE, supplément Danemark, microfilm 5988, Letter of Grouvelle (8 June 1793).

5 MAE, supplément Danemark, microfilm 5988, Letter of Grouvelle (19 March 1793).

and speculators postponed selling their grain hoping to make a good deal. At the time of the declaration of war, imports became necessary. The revolutionary authorities were forced to import grain to reduce tensions in the markets. The situation became even worse when the harvests of 1793 and 1794 turned out to be especially bad. Hunger riots might threaten the survival of the revolution. The political discourse of the time suggests that the blockade worked perfectly. But is that true? The STR offer the possibility to test this and may help us to understand the political realities of the blockade.

1 The Danish Policy

The neutral countries of Northern Europe, which made navigation in wartime one of the bases of their prosperity, did not accept the British instructions. Denmark wanted to pursue its activities, especially its grain deliveries to revolutionary France. Prime Minister Bernstorff drew up a very clever policy towards the members of the coalition. He knew he could maintain the Danish neutrality while expanding the country's maritime activities because of the strategic position of Denmark:

> The general system of the King is the most perfect and impartial neutrality but he cannot entirely reconcile himself with one of the belligerent parties in opposition to the other [...] There is a wide difference between neutrals and distant powers, who have not been provoked, and those that have been offended [...].
>
> Denmark is a maritime and commercial power. It has therefore particular measures to pursue especially with respect to a nation with which it is connected by a trade treaty, which requires the most careful management. Its prosperity does not solely depend upon peace but also on the opinion that it shall not be interrupted and that there exists nothing which can have this effect; the King cannot allow himself to destroy this opinion.[6]

The King of England called for Denmark to participate in the war against France, "in the success of which any civilized nation must necessarily have the greatest interest."[7] The British request was supported by Prussia, Austria,

6 *A Collection of State Papers*, 325–326, The Answer of his Excellency, the Count of Bernstorff, Copenhagen, 1 June 1792.

7 Rigsarkivet, Danica, Microfilm 71 (PRO F.O.22 17).

the Dutch Republic and Russia. To intensify pressure on the Danish authorities and show their determination to obtain a favorable response to their wishes the coalition sent a fleet of 23 ships of the line and seven frigates, which anchored, near the island of Møn, not far from Copenhagen in the summer of 1793.[8]

Prime Minister Bernstorff reacted in an original way and published a letter in French to the Danish people and the international community explaining the Danish position in the newspaper the *Altonaischer Mercurius* on 28 July 1793. The first words of introduction were directed to all Europeans:

> The rights of the people are unchangeable; their principles do not depend on circumstance. An enemy at war may take revenge upon those who forget them. There may be a harmful reciprocity that saves the entirely honest rights but a neutral Power at peace may not form or experience such compensation. Its safeguard is in its impartiality and its Treaties. The renouncing of its rights will not be pardoned when this is in favor of one of the belligerent parties. This rests on the universal rights of the people that knows no distinction. This is neither judge nor party.[9]

When the British captured neutral ships the compensations and allowances they provided generally met the requests of the shipowners who, consequently, did not risk a lot by supplying France. The French authorities pressed Sweden and Denmark to sign an agreement to strengthen the position of neutrals against the coalition. This agreement included French promises of subsidies, but the subsidies the neutral powers subsequently requested were never paid.

Therefore, Denmark decided to take advantage of the circumstances and decided to bypass the blockade and supply French ports. Two things were necessary to realize this. First, the formal ports of destination of the relevant vessels should not be French ports. The ships therefore carried documents indicating that they were going to deliver their goods in Spain or Portugal in particular Bilbao and Lisbon.[10] Letters provided evidence that traders in these countries were waiting for the goods. Second, formally the goods had to belong to Danes. All documents of purchase and loading therefore clearly specified that all transactions were carried out by Danish traders.

---

8 Jespersen e.a., *Revanche og Neutralitet*, 427.

9 Werner, *En Dansk Storkøbmand*, 23.

10 AN, F/11/223, Report signed by J.C. Bechmann, Swedish merchant living in Bordeaux (18th November 1793): '… différents ports de la Baltique où je ferai les achats en grains qui s'expédieront simulées comme pour Barcelone, Bilbao, Cadix, Lisbonne, port à port … sous pavillon suédois ou danois.'

Some traders specialized in grain deliveries to France. One of the largest Danish merchants to participate in this business was Pierre Peschier. He was a Huguenot born in Switzerland who specialized in the grain trade from the ports of the Baltic, Denmark and Hamburg. He was also a businessman working for Ernst Schimmelmann, the Danish Minister of Finance. Peschier had many connections with agents of the French government, with traders from Hamburg and Altona, and with Swiss bankers. It is difficult to reconstruct this network because we have no records of his activities even though we often encounter his name.

Due to the disorganization of the French administration, it is not possible to determine the activities of the French ports during the revolutionary period. We have little documentation on the arrival of grain from Northern Europe. However, a document from the French agent in Copenhagen, Delamarre, includes a list of ships coming to France to deliver grain in 1794. STRO allows comparing this list with the declarations at the Danish customs. This comparison yields a lot of information on the strategy implemented by the neutrals and on the shipments delivered in France.

Table 3.1 lists the ships loaded in the Baltic destined to France according to Delamarre. STRO provide additional information on the passages of these vessels, including the port of departure, the port of destination and the quantity of grain delivered by the ships.

TABLE 3.1 Ships loaded with grain bound for France in 1794 according to Delamarre and identified in STRO

Date	Ship (Delamarre)	Captain (Delamarre, STRO)	From (STRO)	To (STRO)	Unit	Quantity
4-Aug	Le Gustave	Olof Nordstrøm	Copenhagen	Lisbon	Tonde	880
6-Aug	La Catherine et Sophie	Paul Christensen	Copenhagen	Lisbon	Last	66
10-Aug	La Dorothée Margretha	Herm. Christ. Fries	Dantzig	Bilbao	Last	41
6-Aug	La Fortune	Bane Pet. Pauelsen	Copenhagen	Lisbon	Tonde	2,090
3-Aug	Anna Cecilia	Peter Möller	Pillau	Lisbon	Last	100
9-Aug	Birgita Maria	Anders Andersen	Copenhagen	Lisbon	Tonde	2,530
7-Aug	Jacob Zacharias & trois sœurs	Nicolaj Heiss	Copenhagen	Lisbon	Tonde	2,948
6-Aug	Les Trois sœurs	Lars Ohnhamer	Dantzig	Bilbao	Last	42

TABLE 3.1 Ships loaded with grain bound for France in 1794 (*cont.*)

Date	Ship (Delamarre)	Captain (Delamarre, STRO)	From (STRO)	To (STRO)	Unit	Quantity
9-Aug	Le Neptune Frederic Gustave Le Finland	Paul Nilson	Copenhagen	Corogne	Tonde	1,540
6-Aug	Nicolay Martha	Jens Petersen	Pillau	Bilbao	Last	70
6-Aug	Ensger Louise	Boye Petersen Sen.	Copenhagen	Bilbao	Tonde	2,200
6-Aug	Ellens Dorothea	Reinerts Wattne	Pillau	Bilbao	Last	110
9-Aug	Elous	Swen Nilson	Copenhagen	Lisbon	Tonde	796
9-Aug	Nythaab	N.J. Lindqvist	Copenhagen	Lisbon	Tonde	796
9-Aug	Louisa	Jon Anderson	Copenhagen	Lisbon	Tonde	753
10-Aug	Enighed Minerve Les Deux Dames	Jens Thuesen	Pillau	Bilbao	Tonde	1,247
6-Aug	Haabet	Rasmus And Dunas	Copenhagen	Bilbao	Tonde	731
6-Aug	Fredericstadt	Harald Billosen	Pillau	Bilbao	Last	34
6-Aug	Anna Sophie Hoppet	Christ Pet Ronne	Copenhagen	Bilbao	Last	90
9-Aug	Cathrina Ingeborg Hoppet	Svend Hofgaarg	Copenhagen	Lisbon	Tonde	1,540
9-Aug	Marie Louise	Dirck Reinders	Copenhagen	Bilbao	Tonde	1,430
11-Aug	Margretha Anna	Rincke Boysen	Copenhagen	Cadix	Last	135
13-Aug	L'Iris	Peter Johanson	Pillau	Lisbon	Last	85
10-Aug	Delia	Lars Dahl	Dantzig	Lisbon	Last	120
10-Aug	Adjutor	Caspar Fasmer	Dantzig	Lisbon	Last	95
10-Aug	Den Flyvende Engel	Ole Morck	Copenhagen	San Seb.	Tonde	1,655
8-Aug	La Résolution St Mathieu	Frid Christ Fricht	Copenhagen	San Seb.	Tonde	1,290
10-Aug	Charlotte Christine	Lorentz Lorentzen	Copenhagen	San Seb.	Tonde	1,161
9-Aug	Gubben	Peter Janson	Copenhagen	Lisbon	Tonde	1,034
11-Aug	Die Bruder Lieblikbe	Joachim Meyer	Copenhagen	Lisbon	Last	70
16-Aug	Carlskrona	Joh. Erikson	Copenhagen	Lisbon	Last	50
10-Aug	L'Amitié	Boy Boy Schwendsen	Copenhagen	Lisbon	Tonde	2,967
15-Aug	La Marie	Joh. Otto Tengmarck	Copenhagen	Lisbon	Last	80
13-Aug	La Ceres	Joh. J. Bagge	Pillau	Lisbon	Last	90

TABLE 3.1 Ships loaded with grain bound for France in 1794 (*cont.*)

Date	Ship (Delamarre)	Captain (Delamarre, STRO)	From (STRO)	To (STRO)	Unit	Quantity
6-Aug	Anna Sophia Catharina	Hieronimus Paap	Copenhagen	Lisbon	Tonde	1,320
18-Aug	L'Amitié	Christ. Cartensen	Pillau	Lisbon	Last	74
26-Aug	Karen	Niels Schou	Copenhagen	Lisbon	Last	63
16-Aug	Providentia	Severin Jensen	Pillau	Lisbon	Last	122
16-Aug	Forsoget	Jacob Nissen	Pillau	Lisbon	Last	107
16-Aug	La Ceres	Thomas Knudt	Pillau	Lisbon	Last	84
	Gevalia	Joh. Paderborn	Copenhagen	Lisbon	Last	133
20-Aug	De Tvende Broder	Ulrich Angel	Copenhagen	Cadix	Tonde	1,505
24-Aug	Margaretha Mathilda	Johannes Rye	Copenhagen	San Seb.	Last	60
18-Aug	L'Industrie	Jess Sorensen	Copenhagen	Cadix	Tonde	2,472
18-Aug	Kronprinz Frederic La Sophie	Aaron Fore	Copenhagen	Gênes	Tonde	6,772
13-Aug	La Dame Cornelia	Thore Gousel	Dantzig	Bilbao	Last	83
21-Aug	Die Hofnung	Christ. Conrad Fisher	Dantzig	Lisbon	Last	97*
20-Aug	Le Patriote	Ingerbrecht Bugge	Pillau	Lisbon	Last	82

NOTE: Swedish ships freighted by Danish traders are marked in grey.
SOURCES: AN, F/11/223 AND STRO

The comparison between the two sources shows that many ships sent to France according to Delamarre's list were destined to Spain and Portugal according to STRO. The neutral vessels carried false papers to cross the North Sea and their masters intended to deliver their goods to the new Republic.

2 "To Starve the Rebels"

The British were aware of the intentions of the neutral parties and took their measures. The frigates of the Channel fleet commanded by young officers had orders to cruise and paralyze the supply of food to France. To find out the truth about cargoes and destinations the British examined neutral ships thoroughly. The questions to be asked separately to the captain and crewmembers were listed on a preprinted document and were put in a way as to confuse smugglers.

The examination was divided into 34 points with about 150 questions. An additional examination of 20 points and about 50 questions was employed for vessels from Northern Europe. The questioning was extremely accurate. The additional interrogatory numbers 14 and 15, for example, read as follows:

> 14: Do you know, have you heard of, or do you not believe, that Mssrs. De la Marre, Duveyrier, and Castera, French Commissioners or Agents at Copenhagen, have, in the Course of the last Year, and up to the Present Time, Freighted a very great Number of Danish, Swedish, Hamburg, and other Ships; and have Dispatched them from the Ports of Denmark and Sweden, and Northern Ports, with Cargoes of Provisions, and Naval and Military Stores, on Account, and for the Supply of France, under Fictitious Papers, in respect as to the Property of such Cargoes, and Fictitious also as to the Destination? How many of such Ships have been Freighted to them, and what were their Names, and the Names of the Masters of such Ships, or any of them, to the best of your Knowledge, Information or Belief?
>
> 15: Do you know, or have you any Connections in Trade with Mr. Elick Backman, or Messrs. Tournier, Merchants at Gotenburg, Mr. Sieveking, Messrs. Dennas et Lubbert, Mr. Ernst, Mr. Parish, Mr. Amberg, Mr. Chapeaurouge, Mr. Olivier, Messrs. Pierre Boué et fils, Mr. Jacob Burmester, senator Rucker, senator Klevicker, senator Poppe, senator Westphal, senator Adami, Henry Westphal, Mr. Gabe, Mr. Mackelers, Pierre, Springhorn, Mr. Glasshoff the younger, Jan David Bredermann, Mr. Wippe, Mr. Wiper, Mr. Wilcke, Jacob Hahn, Pierre Jansen, Henry Hansen, Henry Doltz, all Merchants at Hamburg; Mr. Otto Matthies, Matthias Matthies, Jan Ernst Matthiesen, Henry Kuper, Bohne Hansen, Mr. Theden, Mr. Tandau and Mr. Beekers all Merchants at Altona; the French Agents Albite, Honnore, Delamaire et Ceteraij residing at or near Altona; Messrs. Hansen, Merchants at Randers; or Mr. J Gummer, Merchant at Stockholm, or any, or either, and which of them? Do you know, have you not heard, or do you not believe, that some one or more of the Persons abovementioned, or some other Person or Persons, and who in particular, not mentioned by Name in the Ships Papers, had some and what Interest in, or control over, or connection with, the Cargo of the Ship in question, either directly or indirectly? Can you take upon Yourself to Swear positively that no one of such above named Persons, or any other Person or Persons not mentioned in the Ship Papers, had any such Interest in, Control over, or Connection with the Cargo in question.[11]

11 The National Archive (Kew), High Court of Admiralty, HCA 32/543.

The interrogation process looked like a police investigation. The questions were repeated and overlapping in various forms to confuse the shipmaster and his crew. Then the reports were analyzed, the answers compared and a decision was quickly made. In case of doubt, the vessels were seized. Generally, the British services were fully aware of the workings of smuggling and knew when the merchandise belonged to the French.

As shown in the interrogations, the British were familiar with the traffic and the merchants who organized the supplies to France. Thus, "the Fournier brothers from Gothenburg were known and recorded in England to be in charge of the French supplies and all their shipments that were encountered by the British Navy were conducted to England."[12]

To obtain this information the British authorities had an intelligence service in France as well as in the northern European grain-exporting countries. At the Convention assembly, Fabre d'Eglantine compared these agents to "vampires", which obey the orders of the "infernal genius" of Downing Street – that is to say William Pitt – whose mission was to destabilize the Republic by all means.[13] The French revolutionaries were worried: "The rumor gets around that there is in Paris a lot of English agents guided by Pitt in charge of monopolizing 'gros sols' (coins in silver). They buy up to one hundred percent and spy on all that happens in the Republic; they were housed in large hotels they rent in the Faubourg Saint-Germain or in country houses around Paris not to be discovered."[14] Thus former police officer Claude Antoine Rey, Lieutenant General of Police of Lyon until 1789 who emigrated to London in October 1792, organized with the help of two assistants an intelligence service whose activity was paid by the British government. In May 1793, he worked with four principal agents and subalterns in Paris and different provinces. He had informers in Brest, Toulon, Granville and Lyon, his hometown. The chief of the network who received the correspondence and whose name is not known, resided in Basel, Switzerland. Very quickly, this organization became too expensive for Great Britain's finances and it was suspended during the summer of 1793 but Rey had laid the foundations of a genuine system to spy on revolutionary France. Subsequently networks of emigrants in Switzerland collected news from France through a structured organization of agents and were the main source of information for the British government.[15] Nevertheless, as noted by Edmond Dziembowski "in 1793, the capacity of the Secret Service was very

12 Document of the 8th July 1794 as quoted by Rice, *Documents*, 170 (Report to the Convention).

13 Dziembowski, *Les Pitt*, 423.

14 Quoted by Blanc, *Les hommes de Londres*, 27.

15 Sparrow, *Secret Service*, 25, 31–57.

limited. If London had indeed spies in France these secret agents showed a lot of amateurism."[16]

Neutral shipmasters were soon aware of the British interrogations and were warned of what to expect when questioned. They could, therefore, prepare their answers.

> They (the English) went as far as to interrogate them under oath before the Admiralty officers. The object was to make them say everything they knew, had or even believed regarding the operations being carried out in Denmark, Sweden or Hamburg to supply food and other resources to the Republic. Some printed examples of the instructions issued by the English Admiralty are circulating here, of the questions to be put to the ships' captains. The Spanish Inquisition and the tyranny of our former police force could not have imagined anything more insidious or more revolting than these questions.[17]

The hunt seemed to be a success: 423 Danish ships have been identified as taken by the British during the years 1793, 1794 and 1795 and this list is not exhaustive.

3 An Erratic Blockade

The British did not apply the blockade permanently. The instructions of June 1793 were cancelled in August 1794 and then reinstated in the spring of 1795. Consequently, the number of prizes varied in the course of time.

Financial reasons dominated these changes of policy. The blockade was very costly to the British government as shown in the following document sent by the Admiralty to the commanders of the Navy:

> ... among the captures of neutral ships [...] there appears to be many cases where such ships are not laden with military stores or provisions, and where there is no ground to support the suspicion of enemy property, which has occasioned much expense and inconvenience to government [...] the only ground on which they ought to be stopped is a reasonable

16 Dziembowski, *Les Pitt*, 423. Clive, "The Home office," 532: "At the close of the eighteenth century the home office was a tiny organization, consisting of less than two dozen individuals."

17 MAE, Danemark, Letter by Grouvelle to the Convention, 3 floréal an II (22nd April 1794).

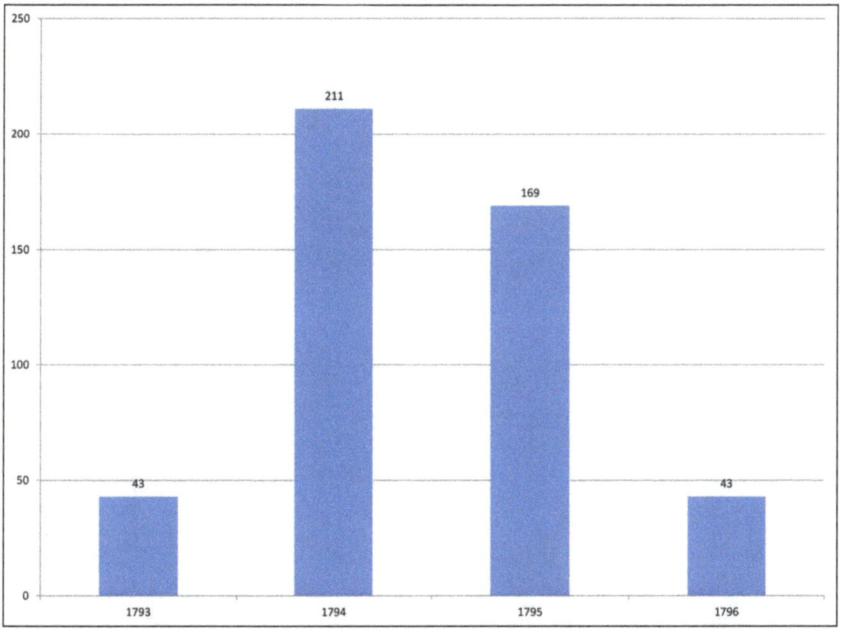

GRAPH 3.1 Number of neutral ships captured by the British
SOURCE: RIGSARKIVET, DANICA, MICROFILMS (PRO, HCA, 32-194 TO 32-907)

> suspicion of there being enemy property; and [...] in all those cases the captors must take at their own risk the proof of such suspicion ...[18]

This document reveals that the prizes were not always justified and that the British Admiralty did not want to pay the price of compensation and allowances that were not relevant. Accordingly, privateers who could not provide factual evidence justifying their decision would be charged the amounts due to neutral vessels.

In addition to the compensation paid to the owners of seized neutral ships and cargoes the blockade itself cost the organizing power a lot. On one hand, it was necessary to maintain the vessels that monitored the enemy coast continuously. They were light units, which had speed rather than firepower and were usually not suited for other types of military action. On the other, the blockade and the standing off jeopardized the vessels and the crews and led to shipwrecks and unexpected encounters with the enemy.

Finally, it appears that, probably for financial reasons, orders were carried out with varying conviction. In June 1793 a letter from the Danish Consul in

18 Quoted by Hill, *The Prizes of War*, 20.

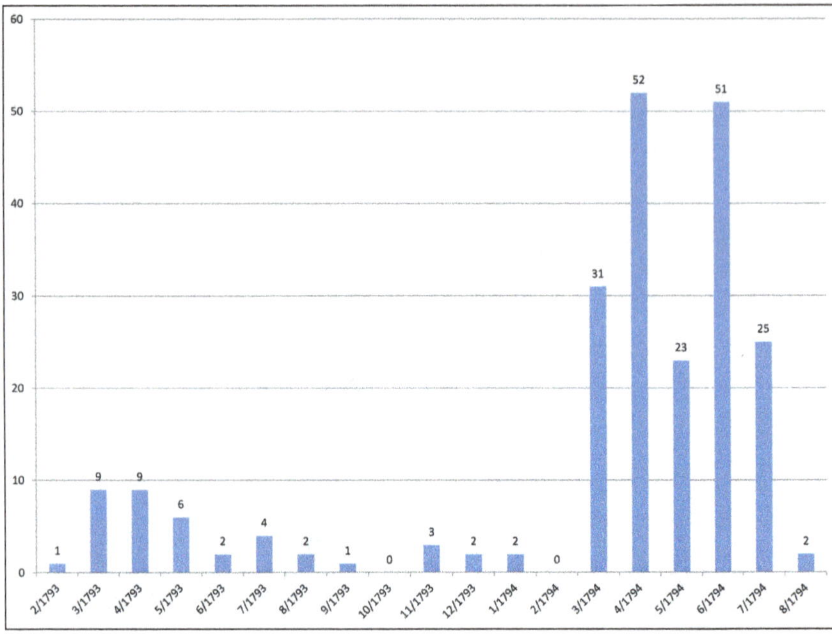

GRAPH 3.2 Number of neutral ships captured by the British (February 1793–August 1794)
SOURCE: RIGSARKIVET, DANICA, MICROFILMS (PRO, HCA, 32-194 TO 32-907)

Bordeaux noted that "currently the English let neutral vessels loaded with grain to France go since two Danish vessels and one from Hamburg just arrived in our port after being checked rigorously at sea."[19] In May 1794, in Genoa, a city which supplied France, a captain of a Danish ship arriving from Bergen with stock fish declared that he had been inspected and that, when he was asked where he was bound for, he had replied that he was going to Genoa after which the British had "wished him a safe journey."[20]

So many ships passed through the British blockade that it is difficult to evaluate the traffic to France. STRO are perhaps the only source that can give us relevant information. As we saw earlier, it appears that most of the ships registered here as going to Bilbao or Lisbon went to a French port. A first search

19 Rigsarkivet, Kommercekollegiet, 1817, Letter of von Hemert (29 June 1793) to the Kommercekollegiet.

20 Rigsarkivet, Kommercekollegiet, Journalsager 1158, Letter of the Danish consul at Genoa (10 May 1794) to the Kommercekollegiet.

in the archives of Bilbao confirms this impression.[21] Very few neutral vessels entered the Spanish port loaded with cereals in these years.

Moreover, it was forbidden to load a ship in France if it had not first brought in foodstuffs. As STRO provide information on passages to and from the Baltic, it is possible to reconstruct the journeys of ships going to France. This work is difficult because many of the relevant shipmasters tramped before returning to the North. However, for some ships it can be done.

Peter Lausteen (Illustration 3.1) probably discharged his cargo in Bordeaux and not in Lisbon as stated in the Sound customs since we find him on his way from Bordeaux to Copenhagen with Aquitaine wine on 5 May 1795 (Illustration 3.2).

Based on such findings it is possible to draw up statistics and compare passages through the Sound to Bilbao and Lisbon with the British prizes (Table 3.2).

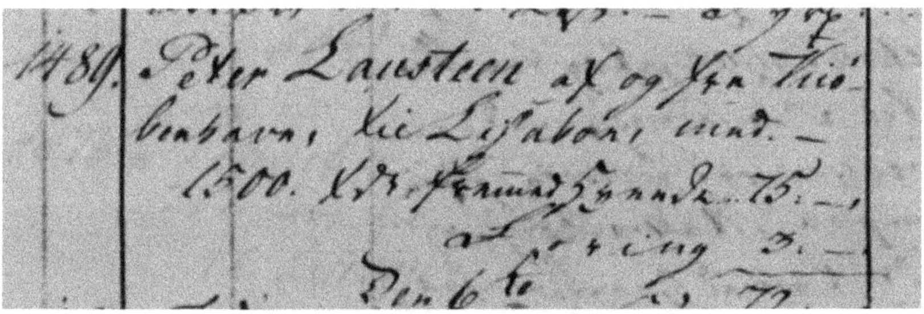

ILLUSTRATION 3.1 "Peter Lausteen af og fra Kiøbenhavn til Lisabon med 1500 tdr fremmed hvede," 5 November 1794
SOURCE: STRO

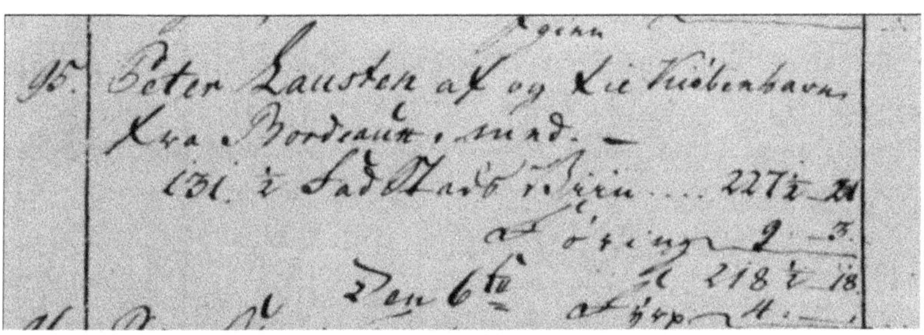

ILLUSTRATION 3.2 "Peter Lausten af og til Kiøbenhavn fra Bordeaux med 131 ½ fade Stadt Vin," 5 May 1795
SOURCE: STRO

21 We plan to verify precisely the arrival of neutral ships in Bilbao and Lisbon. The archives of these two cities contain documents concerning their maritime traffic. The work will be carried out in the near future.

TABLE 3.2 Number of Danish ships departed from Copenhagen loaded with grain and seized by the British in 1794

Journey	Sound (STRO)		British prizes (PRO)	
	1794	1795	1794	1795
Copenhagen-Ostend	1	23	0	9
Copenhagen-Dunkirk	0	36	0	12
Copenhagen-Le Havre	2	14	0	5
Copenhagen-Rouen	1	0	0	0
Copenhagen-Bordeaux	17	10	3	2
Copenhagen-Bayonne	0	3	0	2
Copenhagen-San Sebastian	4	0	0	0
Copenhagen-Bilbao	28	4	7	1
Copenhagen-Oporto	1	0	0	0
Copenhagen-Lisbon	47	7	10	1
Copenhagen-Cadiz	5	0	1	0
Copenhagen-Barcelona	3	6	0	0
Copenhagen-Genoa	4	0	1	0
Copenhagen-Leghorn	3	0	0	0
Copenhagen-Port à port	1	0	1	0
Total	**117**	**103**	**23**	**32**
%			**19.7**	**31**

SOURCES: STRO AND RIGSARKIVET, DANICA

The comparison shows that the chance of being caught by the British was very low in 1794: one in five for the ships loaded in Copenhagen and one in ten for the ships coming from other Baltic ports (see Table 3.2). The strategy implemented by the neutral traders seems to have worked perfectly and the risk to be taken was relatively low.

The situation changed completely in 1795. With approximately the same number of ships coming from the Baltic, the chance of being taken had multiplied since 1794 by 1.5 for ships coming from Copenhagen and by three for ships having departed from other Baltic ports. Of the ships destined to Ostend, which was under French control in 1795, 40 % were taken by the British (see Table 3.2). Neutral traders and shipowners gave up their strategy of concealment that had worked so well in 1794. This change was the result of a purely economic calculation. In 1795, the British suffered from an agricultural crisis and needed grain. If a neutral ship bound to France was seized by the Navy, the merchandise was bought, the freight was paid and the unloading was carried out very quickly. Therefore, there was no benefit in concealing the destination of the cargo. Nevertheless, although a great number of Danish vessels were brought into British ports, almost two-thirds of the Danish ships passing the Sound arrived in French ports to deliver their precious cargo of grain.

The French archives have only a few accounts of the quantity of grain delivered in the French ports. The information we have collected involves only 36,000 tons for the years 1793, 1794 and 1795. However, if we use STRO, and consider that all the passages listed as destined for Ostend, Bilbao or Lisbon were in fact destined for French ports, we can state that France received more than 90,000 tons of grain from the Baltic in the three years from 1793 to 1795, excluding supplies from the Elbe river and other markets west of the Sound (Table 3.3).

TABLE 3.3 Number of ships passing the sound loaded with grain probably destined to France but partly registered with other destinations, 1793–1795

From	1793	1794	1795
To Ostende			
Copenhagen		3	48
Memel		1	
		4 ships 403 tons	48 ships 6,907 tons
To Bilbao			
Copenhagen	19	22	3
Königsberg	8	1	
Dantzig	12	16	
Memel	2	1	
Libau	8		
Pillau	9	14	
Riga	1		
Rostock-Wismar			6
	59 ships 7,153 tons	54 ships 28,205 tons	9 ships 784 tons

TABLE 3.3 Number of ships passing the sound loaded with grain (*cont.*)

From	1793	1794	1795
To Lisbon			
Copenhagen	5	54	9
Königsberg -Memel	9	9	
Dantzig	10	30	2
Libau	4	3	
Pillau	16	35	
Riga	2	6	3
Other	5	13	14
	51 ships	150 ships	28 ships
	7,631 tons	13,220 tons	4,977 tons
To France			
Bayonne	1		6
Bordeaux	3	24	5
Nantes-Lorient		2	3
Le Havre-Rouen	1	3	17
Boulogne- St Val.-Dieppe			4
Dunkerque			55
France		1	4
	5 ships	30 ships	94 ships
	580 tons	3,805 tons	19,365 tons
Total	15,364 tons	45,633 tons	32,033 tons

SOURCE: STRO. WE HAVE CONVERTED THE "LASTS" AND THE "TONDE" AS MENTIONED IN THE STRO IN TONS FOR MORE CONVENIENCE.

In this table, we have not included the ships declared to be destined for San Sebastian, Porto or Cadiz although we suspect that many of them went to French ports, too. Further work needs to be done in the Spanish archives to confirm this assumption. It is in any case clear that large amounts of grain arrived in France from the Baltic. According to the figures of

Charles Carrière, these imports could feed the entire French population for nine days.[22]

The British blockade was obviously not very efficient. The Danes delivered their wheat and rye, the Americans their flour and rice, and cereals from all regions of the Mediterranean could be found in the warehouses of Marseilles, too. The government efforts to import grain were successful, as is illustrated by the 6,076 tons of wheat purchased in Denmark by the agents Delamarre, Duveyrier and Castera. At the climax of the crisis in the autumn of 1794 and during the spring of 1795 grain ships arrived in great numbers in the French ports. Ostend, Dunkirk and Le Havre sent thousands of tons of grain to Paris, the main concern of the revolutionary authorities. The words of Charles Carrière in conclusion of his work on the supply of Marseilles can be applied to the whole of France during the years 1793–1795: "That there was a problem of grain and flour in Marseilles during these 18 months, that local officials had hard times, that popular concern was obvious, all that was certain. But it was also certain that the supply was sufficient […]. The real reason of the stability of prices was the maximum […], but for the quantity and quality of supply, in truth, it is in the direction of the sea we have to look. The decisions of the Convention and its representatives, energetic as they were, would have been nothing without the port. Thanks to it and despite the maritime war Marseilles was saved from famine."[23] We can say that the sea saved the French Revolution.

4 Conclusion

The British authorities presumed that the starving French people would inevitably reject revolutionary ideas. The British seemed firmly committed to implementing their strategy of starvation but in fact, they allowed many ships to reach France. The neutrals were able to organize their traffic without problems and France received huge quantities of grain. The gap between political rhetoric and the facts seems enormous. The blockade was primarily a psychological weapon to show determination on the part of the British or, for the French, to emphasize the inhumanity of the enemy. In practice, the British blockade was impracticable and did not prevent France from being supplied.

22 Carrière, *Le problème des grains*, 164, note 2.

23 Carrière, *Le problème des grains*, 184. The law of the « Maximum » gave a price to all goods and this price could not be exceeded.

However, the British strategy had the additional effect of raising the prices for grain. The consequence was an increase of French financial difficulties so that the British achieved another important goal. This strategy, however, backfired. In 1795, the British traders had to buy grain at a high price to satisfy local demand.

PART 2

Comparisons in Context

CHAPTER 4

Dutch Trade and Spatial Integration between the Baltic and Spain, 1700–1778

Ana Crespo Solana

1 Introduction

Between the sixteenth and eighteenth centuries, commercial relations between Northern Europe and Spain were shaped by a variety of factors. Since the Middle Ages, production and market areas with direct access to the Baltic Sea were connected to ports in the South of the Iberian Peninsula, which facilitated access to both their direct hinterlands and the Mediterranean. With the decline of the Hanseatic League and the opening of new Atlantic markets, especially from the sixteenth century onwards, the traditional commercial networks evolving around market places like Bruges would relocate from Flanders to Holland. Merchants fled the southern provinces to escape the areas directly affected by the war against the Habsburgs. The Dutch took over most of the trade between the Baltic and the Iberian Peninsula late in the sixteenth century and continued to dominate it for most of the seventeenth century, although they faced fierce competition from the English, who attempted to gain a significant position in Baltic trade. During the seventeenth century and throughout the 1740s, Dutch merchants had to compete with merchants from Hamburg as this port greatly increased its volume of trade with southern Spain, mainly with Cadiz. Faber states that, despite all this competition, the Dutch had the best trading privileges granted by the Hispanic Monarchy between 1550 and 1700. After an "*achteruitgang*" (decline) between 1650 and 1760, Dutch trade recovered as a new era of growth was seen between 1760 and 1780.[1]

Until about 1700, political factors destabilized trade between the Dutch Republic and Spain, because of the continuous state of war in which both the Spanish Monarchy and the Dutch Republic were involved during most of the early modern period. War affected trade through the Habsburgs' military interventions (a number of commercial embargoes between 1585 and 1648), frequent

1 The research leading to the results presented below has received funding from the People Programme (Marie Curie Actions) of the EU 7th Framework Programme (FP7 2007–2013) under REA grant agreement n° PITN-GA 2013-607545.

 | DOI:10.1163/9789004371781_006

assaults by Dunkirk-based corsairs and the English penetration of the Baltic whenever England was granted diplomatic alliances by the Spanish Crown. These circumstances damaged Dutch trade with Spain. However, the demand for key products, such as weapons, wheat, timber for shipbuilding and textiles, increased.[2] Striking evidence collected by Unger and Allen seems to show that during the seventeenth century, when war and cooperation went hand in hand, Dutch businessmen ranked among the leading proponents of the spatial integration of northern European port cities with their southern counterparts.[3] One of the main routes in this system connected Amsterdam and Cadiz. It developed during the first half of the seventeenth century and rose to importance during the Twelve Years' Truce (1609–1621), when the King of Spain granted the Dutch permission to trade freely in Cadiz and in other Spanish ports. This development led to a considerable migration of merchants from the Spanish Netherlands and the Dutch Republic, determined to make a career in Andalusia.[4]

A number of studies have examined the presence of the Dutch merchant community in Spain's economy and society. Members of this community played a central role as exporters and distributors of the many different products to which they had access through well-established production and distribution networks. In the present article, the production and distribution networks between the Baltic, Scandinavia and Northern Europe, on one hand, and the southern Iberian Peninsula, on the other are analyzed based on the case of the Amsterdam-Cadiz connection and several other routes between the Baltic and southern Spain in the eighteenth century. For this purpose data on routes, ships and merchandise from comprehensive, specialized literature and archival sources were compared. These data were processed in a database on Hispanic Atlantic commerce, which is currently available as part of the CrespoDynCoopNet Data Collection stored in the CSIC's digital repository. In addition, a project is underway for the integration of the data from this database with the data in STRO.[5]

2 The Dutch and Spain – A Brief State of Play

Despite the almost constant state of war between 1580 and 1648, Hispano-Dutch commerce was the main way by which cereals, timber for shipbuilding, and

2 Alcalá-Zamora and Queipo de Llano, *España*, 122–128; Crespo Solana, "El comercio holandés," 45–76.

3 Unger and Allen, "The Depth and Breadth," 1–18.

4 Crespo Solana, "Legal Strategies," 181–213.

5 Cf. *CrespoDynCoopNet Data Collection* (accessed January 2014); Sound Toll Registers Online (accessed 27.04.2014).

manufactured products collected by the Dutch were exchanged for olive oil, wine, salt and American silver. The latter was obtained particularly in Seville and Cadiz as it was unloaded from the ships arriving from Spanish America. By the mid-seventeenth century, the Spanish-Dutch trade volume was significant and although its structure varied because of the increasing demand for colonial produce in the Baltic area, the basic scheme of these connections remained largely unchanged.[6] This commerce, facilitated by maritime connections, spanned the entire Baltic Sea, North Sea and Atlantic Ocean area. In the North, this maritime commercial space included the Scandinavian Peninsula, Finland, Russia, Poland, Prussia, and Denmark. The abbreviation Scando-Baltic, coined by Sven Lilja, is most useful when referring to this area.[7] Vital trade routes linked this area inextricably to the Mediterranean region. For Dutch merchants, the Baltic Sea and the Mediterranean Sea were fundamentally complementary. A host of merchant ships carrying produce from the Baltic Sea area and the rest of Northern Europe on behalf of Dutch firms would enter the Mediterranean Sea bound for ports in Italy and Asia Minor. This business, known as "*Straatvaart*," or Strait Navigation, as it passed the Strait of Gibraltar, was linked with American trade via Cadiz. Dutch ships engaged in the *Straatvaart* also called at Malaga, for cargoes of wine, fruit and grocery products, and Alicante. From the late sixteenth century, more than 200 Dutch vessels operated regularly in the Mediterranean and called at ports in Italy, Cyprus and Turkey. During the Twelve Years' Truce, an annual average of 100 ships from the Netherlands arrived at Spanish ports, mainly Bilbao, Malaga and Cadiz, and continued their journeys into the Mediterranean.[8] The United Provinces maintained, at the height of their commercial empire, a network of relationships across the whole of Europe, which enabled them to acquire vital market information and foresee the best opportunities to move merchandise across all areas. Hispano-Dutch commercial cooperation saw its golden age after the peace treaties of 1648. Later, this relationship consolidated because of the privileges the Spanish Crown granted to the Dutch merchant community in Spain as of 1673. The treaties of 1648 and 1673 were explicit in terms of commercial cooperation and navigation. Signed in The Hague, these two treaties were designed to be advantageous to private merchant interests while also ensuring that the Dutch had free access to the Andalusian regional market and to colonial exports. Stipulations were ambiguous because the Dutch were not allowed to trade directly with Spanish America but were permitted to become involved in colonial re-export trade from Andalusian

6 Steensgaard, "The Growth," 151.
7 Lilja, "Peoples, towns and states," 24–46.
8 Israel, "The phases of the Dutch Straatvaart," 1–30.

factories.[9] With the Treaty of The Hague of 1673, the Dutch Republic succeeded in securing preferential treatment from Spain, a situation that would last until 1778 when internal politics in both Spain and the Dutch Republic, and fierce competition from England and France, jeopardized Hispano-Dutch relations.[10]

For a long time, Amsterdam and Cadiz were the two key centers in the system of commercial exchange between the Scando-Baltic area and Spanish ports in Spain, the Mediterranean and the Indies. The connection between the two cities was in the hands of Dutch traders with businesses in Spain and America. This trade connection was consolidated in the course of the seventeenth century. Cadiz became the headquarters of the Spanish colonial trade with America in 1680. This convinced most foreign commercial firms involved in the Indies Trade to leave Seville and set up office in Cadiz. Since 1717, all fleets and galleons bound for *Nueva España* and *Tierra Firme* were to be arranged in Cadiz. This may explain why Cadiz hosted numerous colonies of foreign merchants; almost 22% of these foreigners came from the Low Countries.[11]

In Cadiz, the majority of Dutch immigrants joined an organization called the Ancient and Noble Flemish Nation and therefore enjoyed the protection and privileges attached to that citizenship. The Nation was a powerful corporation of citizens who were subject to the King of Spain.[12] A population analysis conducted on a total of 699 wills registered in Cadiz between 1700 and 1800 shows the following geographical distribution of the origins of the various groups of immigrants by province: Holland and Zeeland – 24%, North and South Brabant – 29%, Flanders – 41%, other northern provinces – 4% and other southern Flemish and Walloon provinces – 2%. These figures are most likely misleading, however, as people claiming Flemish origin in their wills could have well used that general term rather than risk disclosing information on their actual origin. There is clear evidence suggesting that many immigrants from the Northern Provinces claimed to be Flemish in order to hide their Protestant roots. Between 1700 and 1760, an estimated total of more than 600 families from the Low Countries lived in Cadiz. After 1740, migration decreased considerably. The number of members in this merchant colony did not decrease, however, as new generations born to families, members of which had married in Spain, sometimes in mixed marriages, would take over

9 Herrero Sánchez, "La Monarquía Hispánica," 105–110.

10 Crespo Solana, *El comercio marítimo*, 24–31.

11 Crespo Solana, *Mercaderes atlánticos*, 104–120.

12 See for an extended explanation: Crespo Solana, "A Network-based Empire," 139–159.

their parents' businesses or at least pursue the same commercial activities.[13] A great number of these merchants acted as consignees for members of the *Directie* – or *Sociëteit* – *van de Levantse Handel* (*Societeit van de Kamer der directeuren van den Levantsen handel en de navigatie in de Middelandtsche zee*), an organization representing the interests of private merchants doing business with the Mediterranean area, established on June 25, 1625, with local offices in Amsterdam, Rotterdam, Hoorn and Middelburg. This society harnessed the common interests of many Dutch firms involved in port-to-port trade from Cadiz and along the coast to the ports in Asia Minor. However, the "*Straatvaart*" convoy also stopped at a number of ports on the Atlantic coast and then loaded goods from the Baltic to be shipped to the Mediterranean.[14] It is no surprise that the Seville consulate was established at a time when other Dutch consulates were set up as well, in Livorno in 1612, Aleppo (1613), Venice (1614), Genoa (1615) and Algiers (1616).[15] This was part of the strategy of the relevant Amsterdam firms to boost their trade with the Mediterranean ports by expanding operations to ports like Cadiz, Alicante, Malaga, and Mahon.[16]

Most Dutch migrants to Cadiz became active in commerce and finance, including the money deposit market, or worked as partners and consignees of Amsterdam and Middelburg firms. Spanish sources give little or no information about the migration of the temporary labor force involved in secondary trading and financial activities that arrived in Cadiz within the specific framework of a *dienstcontract* or 'service contract', which was signed either in a Dutch city or on board of a ship bound for Spain.[17] This migration was part of a social context where young, single men born into families of traders would temporarily leave their homes as free agents, merchants who operated both in their own countries and abroad. These agents were not necessarily working for their country of origin. Their main driving force was the accumulation of wealth and power by operating outside the hierarchal chain of command of the state institutions. Free agents and their self-organized network played an important role in the expansion of the Dutch and Spanish trade.[18]

13 Crespo Solana, *Mercaderes atlánticos*, 113–130.

14 Van Royen, "The first phase," 69–102.

15 Nationaal Archief, Den Haag (NA), *Inventaris van het Archief van de Directie van de Levantse Handel en de Navigatie in de Middellandse Zee (1614) (1625–1826), (1828)*, Inv. Nummer 1.03.01. 173 (onwards Levantse Handel: LH).

16 NA, LH, 173 and SAA, DOHR, 444. Crespo Solana, *Mercaderes atlánticos*, 147.

17 Crespo Solana, *El comercio marítimo*, 40.

18 Ebben, Fagel and Vermeir, Eds., *Agentes e Identidades*, 11.

Some agents were members of merchant families that had immigrated to the Dutch Republic from the southern Low Countries.[19] Others were Jews. Most of them would end up in Spanish port cities as partners of 'Flemish' or other local merchants under the condition of a *dienstcontract*.[20] This type of contract would enable them to set up an office or warehouse to do commercial business.

Despite the success of Dutch direct trade with several American ports, the Dutch presence in Cadiz rose during the second half of the seventeenth century. Materials from the *Archivo Provincial de Cádiz* show that Dutch migration to Cadiz was much larger than Dutch migration to its own American enclaves, which was – demographically speaking – a complete failure as a colonization project.[21] Dutch migration to Cadiz increased between approximately 1680 and 1740. The Dutch colony had more than 40 or 50 families,[22] and the Flemish Nation consisted of almost 600 families (see above).[23] Cadiz played a substantial role as the Dutch gateway to America at a time when Mediterranean trade was in crisis.

The analysis of the commercial connection between the south of Spain and the Scando-Baltic space provides very interesting insights into the mechanisms that facilitated maritime and spatial integration between these two regions. Cadiz was a nodal point connecting several market areas where the Dutch did business. It had a very specialized function in what D.W. Meinig described as a "geographically fragmented 'empire'" formed by a network of strategic nodal points along critical trade routes.[24] In a recent article it was stated that "[t]he city of Cadiz was crucial in these merchant networks because it connected Atlantic routes and market areas. Cadiz was a factory-port used by Dutch convoys for storing and re-distributing products as well as for obtaining cash to fuel their businesses along the routes linking Southern Europe, the Mediterranean and Spanish America. The Dutch presence in Cadiz therefore is

19 As it has been stated by Briels, *Zuid-Nederlandse immigratie*, 33.

20 Crespo Solana, *El comercio marítimo*, 42. An example of a "dienstcontract" in SAA, NA, 11250/109, 25/5/1739, Dienstcontract of the merchant Johannes Ignatius Wijman, from Cádiz, with Herman van den Bree.

21 The failure of Dutch demographic colonisation in America, especially in the Caribbean, has been stated by Emmer, "The Dutch Atlantic," 31–49.

22 Archivo Histórico Provincial de Cádiz (onwards AHPC), Notarial Archives (NA). The notarial offices most widely used by Dutch and Flemish traders were the notaries numbered 5, 9, 15, 19 and 23.

23 Crespo Solana, *Mercaderes atlánticos*, 103–157.

24 Meinig, *The Shaping of America 1*, 62.

indicative of the importance of cross-imperial, cross-cultural trade in the early modern Atlantic".[25]

3 Baltic and North European Connections with Southern Spain

Economic history in the Netherlands has rarely focused on Dutch trade with the southern Iberian Peninsula or on the central, market-connecting role of the Dutch in this business as buyers, sellers and skippers. It is commonly accepted in Spanish historiography that the Dutch acted on their own initiative as a dynamic driving force of the Dutch maritime trade with the Iberian Peninsula.[26] Jonathan Israel gave quantitative details of Dutch economic relations with Spanish ports in the Iberian Peninsula, especially between 1606 and 1661, which he called "the Dutch period of the Spanish Monarchy."[27] It is a fact that Spain was not the Republic's most profitable market, even though it is uncontested that Spain was essential to Dutch trade as a key logistic area. After the peace treaties, the pre-existing commercial structure between the Netherlands and Spain benefited from the new prerogatives agreed with the Spanish Crown and strengthened the link between the Iberian coast, the Mediterranean, the Baltic and, indirectly through the ports of Seville and Cadiz, America, too. The Baltic trade was an asset to the Dutch when trading in southern Spain. Long before the war against the Habsburgs was over, in 1593, Dutch trade firms were involved in the distribution of grain in southern Europe and the Mediterranean. They opposed the States General, which forbade this trade with the enemy. They were happy to take the risk rather than abandon a profitable commercial activity.[28] Besides, Dutch ships used in the Levant trade would always call at ports in southern Spain on their way into or out of the Mediterranean.

The first Dutch consulate in Spain was set up in Seville on August 22, 1615. Sanlucar de Barrameda was second on May 28, 1648, and in 1649, the Canary Islands followed suit. The Seville consulate developed into mainly a *comptoir* of the *directeuren van den Levantsen handel en de navigatie in de Middelandtsche zee*. In 1630, the Directors of the *Levantse Handel* opened an office in Cádiz. At that time, Dutch trade with Mediterranean seaports was well developed and fleets would usually stop at Cadiz and moor at La Carraca, where a shipyard

25 Crespo Solana "A Network-based Empire," 139–140.
26 Crespo Solana, *Mercaderes atlánticos*, 143.
27 Israel, *The Dutch Republic*, 139.
28 Van Tielhof, *"The Mother of all Trades,"* 36.

was built at a later stage.[29] In the 1630s, each year about 200 ships averaging 300 tons each and carrying cargoes worth three million guilders sailed to Spain, Portugal and the Mediterranean. In Dutch shipping, southern Europe was the third largest destination in Europe after the Baltic Sea and the England-Scotland-Ireland area.[30]

A *"Description of the city of Malaga"* dated 1587 states that Dutch ships would load wine, figs and other dry fruits, fabrics from Granada, Baeza and Cordova – including silk – after having unloaded their cargoes of French and Flemish fabrics, Flemish wood and table boards and even silk from Calabria and Sicily. Malaga was a very active port from where merchandise from Cadiz, other Mediterranean ports and Amsterdam was redistributed to other areas.[31] The Dutch increased their activities in Malaga during the Twelve Years' Truce having been regular goods suppliers to this city for many years. On one occasion, in 1623, the Spanish authorities seized a number of Dutch vessels in the port of Malaga, which led to a massive outcry from local traders and authorities when they saw they could not retrieve their goods loaded in Dutch hulls. Trade also increased in Alicante during the Truce. Here, the turnover of salt, wool and spices rose considerably and Alonso Cortejo was appointed as consul of the Dutch merchants.[32] From 1625, the *Directie van de Levantse Handel* collected data of the Dutch ships sailing from Amsterdam to Cadiz after connecting with Baltic and other northern ports. There are not many empirical data that bear witness of direct connections between Baltic Sea ports and Spain prior to 1670. There is, however, plenty of solid information for the years after 1670. In STRO, there is some information on this connection, indicating the ports of Danzig, Vyborg (Vijborg, in Spanish documentation) and Riga as the most popular.[33]

The areas and ports most frequented by the ships freighted in Amsterdam on their way to Cadiz and Mediterranean ports were Stockholm, Fredikshamn, Vyborg, St. Petersburg, Narva, Riga, Windau, Libau (present-day Liepaja), Memel, Königsberg (present-day Kaliningrad), Danzig, Kolberg, Stettin, Anklam, Rostock, Norrköping, Pernau (Pärnu), Lübeck, Gothenburg, Jutland and Norway. Both STRO and the CrespoDynCoopNet Data collection show this. Hamburg was another relevant connection within the Dutch "port à port" trade; this port gave access to Spanish wool and wine, which was subsequently distributed to Baltic ports. Bilbao was for centuries the main Spanish

29 Crespo Solana, *El comercio marítimo*, 32–37.

30 Bruijn, "Scheepvaart," 138–139.

31 Archivo Real Academia de la Historia (RAH), Manuscritos 9–6114 "Descripción de la ciudad de Málaga."

32 Montojo Montojo, "Guerra y paz," 349–378.

33 Some examples: www.soundtoll.nl, records 489909 (28-8-1748), 490767 (30-10-1743) and 492972 (30-4-1743).

port for the export of wool. Some wool was also shipped from Cadiz, but the amounts and frequency were both low. Finally, it should be emphasized that the Amsterdam-Cadiz connection was linked with other geographic areas, including various Mediterranean ports and the Caribbean. In Spain, Dutch ships made stops in Alicante, Barcelona, the Canaries, Cartagena, Ceuta, Gibraltar, Malaga, Sanlucar and Seville, Barcelona and Mallorca. They also called at Dunkerque, Hamburg and Calais. In the Mediterranean, the most popular ports were Marseille and Livorno, home to a Dutch trading colony since the seventeenth century.[34]

Some of the relevant ships sailed under English or French flag, but this was a common practice in certain wartime periods and regardless, the ships were bound for Dutch merchants in Cadiz or were sailed by a Dutch captain.[35] The information collected from the Amsterdam fleets compared with the Dutch ships arriving in Cadiz, according to notarial documents from the city, show that there was a series of Baltic ports closely related with commerce in Cadiz via the *Straatvaart* route. One possible reason was that most of the ships that were bound for ports on the Iberian Peninsula and the Mediterranean were transporting grain, wood and other products from the Baltic and northern Europe. Juan Baptista de Roo, a 1725 consignee from Cadiz, commented that it was common for ships arriving from the Baltic to receive immediate instructions to redirect to the Strait of Gibraltar[36] without unloading. Previously, in a letter to the Directors of the *Levantse Handel*, the Consul of Cadiz, Philip Renard, listed the ships arriving in the port of Cadiz, among which there were vessels transporting goods from the Baltic that had previously stopped in Riga, Narva and Danzig.[37] The main Baltic ports related to this route appear in map 4.1.[38] There are also some non-Baltic ports, which unintentionally provided a special, function as a stopover for these convoys when collecting merchandise for transportation to Cadiz, like Hamburg, or Bergen in Norway. Hamburg was an international center for the trade in colonial products (especially sugar) that were controlled by Jewish merchants with close links to Amsterdam. Hamburg was also a financial center.[39]

Map 4.1 shows the main ports and the different routes; made visible by means of the local SIG prototype cartographic geo-visualizer in which information about the passages to Cadiz as found in STRO was included.[40]

34 Engels, *Merchants*.
35 www.soundtoll.nl, record 585108 (28-7-1726), Shipmaster Willem Otterlong, from Cadiz.
36 AHPC, 16/3763, fols. 351–353. Cádiz, 21 October 1725.
37 NA, LH, 173. Letter of Philip Renard, Cádiz, 13 February 1746.
38 AHPC, notarias 9 and 15.
39 Newman, "Hamburg," 57–93.
40 See Table 7.

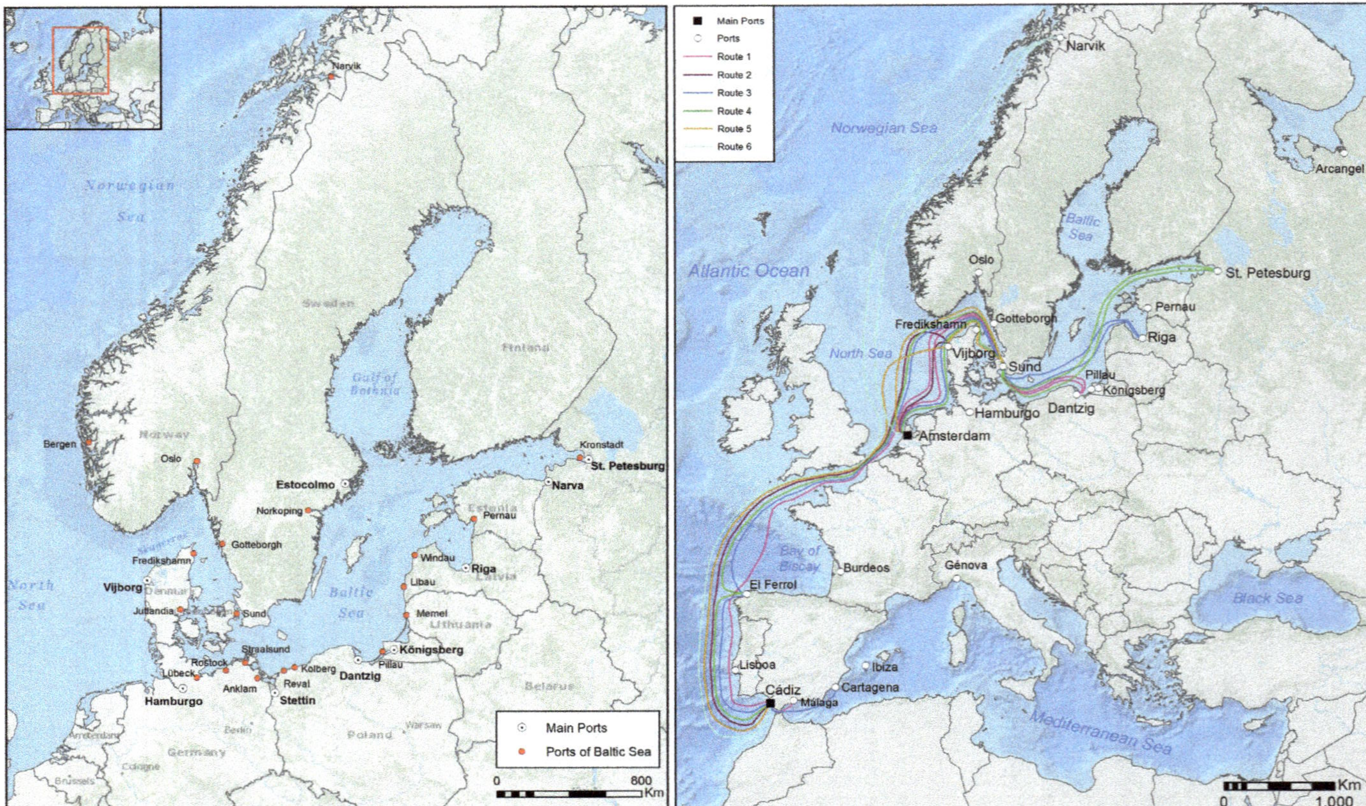

MAP 4.1 Baltic and northern European ports connected with Cadiz (1670–1778)
SOURCES: *CRESPODYNCOOPNET DATA COLLECTION*, HTTP://HDL.HANDLE.NET/10261/23894 (ACCESSED JANUARY 2014) AND THE SOUND TOLL REGISTER ONLINE: WWW.SOUNDTOLL.NL (ACCESSED 27.04.2014).

In STRO, the geographic name 'Cadiz' appears in various spellings (Cadix, Caditz, Cadim, Cadis, Cadiz) in more than 4,000 entries. The information contained in STRO is complemented by the so-called *Straatvaartlijsten* (*Straatvaart* lists) in which the ships under Dutch flags arriving in Cadiz are registered. According to these lists, throughout the second half of the seventeenth and for most of the eighteenth century, all convoys (which averaged approximately 130 to 150 ships each) would, after having called at Cadiz, sail through the Strait of Gibraltar to several Mediterranean ports.[41] Despite ongoing warfare in the area, Dutch merchants were always reluctant to stop sending ships to Asia Minor, especially to Smyrna and Aleppo. The political scenario was hostile due to fierce competition from the English and the continuous threat of the Barbary pirates, and the Dutch began to pull out of this trade from the 1680s onwards. Some isolated data appear to show that since the 1690s, Genoese traders became masters of the maritime trade between Spain and Italy as they took advantage of the rivalries and competition among the northern European nations.[42] One of the characteristic features of the trade and navigation between Cadiz and Amsterdam late in the seventeenth century was the gradual decrease in importance of the Mediterranean markets as they were replaced in the minds of the Dutch merchants settled in Cadiz by American markets, which looked more appealing and potentially profitable.

The War of Spanish Succession (1701–1714) and the Great Northern War (1700–1721) caused significant alterations in the evolution of the Dutch trade in Cadiz as the Scando-Baltic area became very unstable and the English stepped up their competition in the Baltic trade.[43] Despite a downturn in their connections between North and South in these early years of the eighteenth century, the Dutch eventually rose again. The Directors of the *Levantse Handel* continued to provide the institutional context of Hispano-Dutch commercial relations. They set up a comptoir or agents' office that also operated as a Dutch consulate. The Dutch consul of Cadiz and his officers, including a vice-consul, were responsible to the Directors of the Levant Trade for checking all Dutch ships arriving from the Dutch Republic. As a Dutch consulate, representing the Directors, this comptoir performed civil and commercial duties for Dutch businessmen settled in Cadiz. Le Moine de L'Espine and Isaac Le Long refer to the consulate in the description of Cadiz in their book *De Koophandel van Amsterdam*, published in 1780: "There is this small Spanish city in the heart of Andalusia with this very famous port, Cadiz, across the bay from el Puerto de

41 Crespo Solana, *El comercio marítimo*, 106–110.

42 Heeringa, *Bronnen tot de Geschiedenis*, 51–53.

43 Crespo Solana, "El comercio holandés," 45–77.

Santa Maria where many merchants live and have their businesses. Fleets and galleons regularly depart from this bay, and this traffic is fueled by the many firms in the hands of Dutch, English, French, Italian or other foreign families. In addition, each nation has its own consulate. Companies and agents all contribute to the consulates overheads in proportion to their volume of trade".[44]

4 Merchants and Merchandise

The merchandise traded through the Amsterdam-Cadiz connection in the eighteenth century did not differ significantly from that traded in the previous century. There is evidence of an increase of the turnover of colonial commodities. The Amsterdam colonial re-export trade saw a significant increase between 1681 and 1731. The next period of growth began after 1730 with an increase of the sugar, coffee, and tobacco and pepper trade.[45] Cadiz came second after Amsterdam as a depot for American and Asian commodities as the number of VOC ships calling at Cadiz increased over the years.[46] The main products arriving from northern Europe in the ports of Andalusia were still herring and other salted fish, cereals, timber and metals. Fabrics from Ghent and Antwerp were traded, too. Amsterdam provided an Atlantic gateway for a good part of the production of Brabant and Flanders. The increase of the colonial redistribution coincided with an increase of raw materials like iron for industries such as shipbuilding. In the first half of the eighteenth century, Vyborg timber and Swedish steel appeared in the southbound trade flow. From Swedish ports the Dutch mainly exported iron in 1694 and 1695, with still more profitable times to come in the first half of the eighteenth century.[47] Further exports from the Baltic include timber, staves, iron, animal skins, wheat, linen and canvas.[48] In STRO, we find Spanish wine, Alicante wine, cannonballs and other products from the Mediterranean and the Indies, which were stored in Cadiz by the consignees of the *Levantse Handel*, such as pepper, Campeche wood and cocoa. In addition, Dutch traders in Cadiz had an almost complete monopoly on the cocoa supply to the Iberian ports.[49]

44 Le Moine de L'Espine and Isaac Le Long, *De koophandel van Amsterdam*, 646. Translation by the author.
45 Posthumus, *Nederlandse prijsgeschiedenis*.
46 Steensgaard, "The Growth," 105.
47 Lindblad, *Sweden's trade*, 56.
48 See, for example, www.soundtoll.nl, record number 416481, 25-10-1759.
49 Archivo General de Indias (onwards AGI), Arribadas 12. "Memorial del comercio del cacao", 11 May 1728.

A crosscheck between the CrespoDynCoopNet Data collection and STRO shows that Cadiz appears 1,387 times as departure port and 2,926 times as a destination port between the middle of the seventeenth century and 1820. The different stops the Dutch vessels made in Baltic ports before arriving in Cadiz make clear that there are a series of ports in the Scando-Baltic region, which had close ties to the south of Spain. Table 4.1 shows these ports – where ships having departed from Amsterdam called at before arriving in Cadiz.

Moreover, the combined analysis of CrespoDynCoopNetData Collection and STRO shows that the economies in the regions linked to the routes served by Dutch convoys experienced fluctuations from 1700 because of war. Data for the period 1702–1713 compiled by Ormrod show that Dutch trade in the Baltic fell in much the same way as English trade.[50] Apparently, Baltic economies built strong financial links with the Atlantic especially in relation to the trade in colonial products (mostly cacao, tobacco and cinnamon, which appear in STRO as well as in notarial documents from Cadiz). In addition to information on shipping, the notarial sources of Amsterdam and Cadiz offer information on the nature of trade and the commercial firms' reaction to crises and war. Cadiz and the other port cities where the relevant firms held office were very badly hit by the hasty departure of some of the major firms in troubled times. The all-important timber trade for the shipbuilding industry was very seriously affected by the Russian blockade of certain northern ports like Narva, from where timber was exported to the Iberian Peninsula. Many documentary

TABLE 4.1 Main shipping routes from Amsterdam to Cadiz via the Baltic (1650–1770)

Route	Port 1	Port 2	Port 3	Port 4	Port 5
1	Amsterdam	Danzig	Cadiz	Malaga	
2	Amsterdam	Viborg	Cadiz		
3	Amsterdam	Riga	El Ferrol	Cadiz	Cartagena
4	Amsterdam	S. Petersburg	El Ferrol	Cadiz	
5	Amsterdam	Sund	Viborg	Cadiz	
6	Amsterdam	Narva	Cadiz		

SOURCES: CRESPODYNCOOPNET DATA COLLECTION, HTTP://HDL.HANDLE.NET/10261/23894 (ACCESSED JANUARY 2014); CRESPO SOLANA, *EL COMERCIO MARÍTIMO*, PP. 80–120; CRESPO SOLANA, CRESPO SOLANA, "EL COMERCIO HOLANDÉS", PP. 45–77.

50 Ormrod, *The Rise of commercial empires*, 60.

sources indicate that Dutch ships destined for Spain were carrying Baltic timber.[51] Dutch trading companies made agreements with the Spanish Crown regarding the provision of resources for naval construction and even managed to control the provision of timber products in certain historical periods.[52] Several Dutch companies were appointed shipbuilders' suppliers for the *Casa de la Contratación* or the *Intendencia de Marina* in Cadiz. The War of the Spanish Succession was detrimental to the Amsterdam-based *Weduwe (Widow) Wittebol & Co.* In 1699, their correspondents in Cadiz – Laurenzo Overbeecq & Co. – left for the Republic because of uncertainty and the decline of shipping caused by the increased difficulty in reaching Baltic ports.[53] Other firms, however, continued providing shipbuilders' supplies to the Spanish navy for the entire next decade.[54] Despite the concern caused by the War of Spanish Succession, several companies were founded in Amsterdam to conduct trade in Cadiz and their contracts envisaged future business trips. In April 1702, Jan Wesseling and Jacob Smit set up a firm with that purpose – the second company they created. Jan Lijnslager and Cornelis Rost did the same thing.[55] Other traders, like Pieter de Yperen and Jacobus Cramer left Cadiz after a short stay.[56] Despite the difficulties caused by the War of Spanish Succession, the role played by the merchant communities in Cadiz was crucial to the survival of commerce after 1710. Commercial firms from the Dutch Republic and from northern Europe, for example Sweden and the Hanseatic cities, succeeded in continuing and even invigorating this trade in times of war. These companies were part of wide networks spread over the Baltic and Scandinavia and needed the precious metals that arrived in Cadiz. The strategy employed by these firms was consistent: a colony of merchants would settle in a port; a high-profit-margin product would be set ready to be exported; Dutch port-to-port shipping would ensure success.

The Dutch merchants in Cadiz stored merchandise delivered by Dutch ships arriving from ports such as Danzig or St. Petersburg and sent Spanish products to Baltic ports in exchange. In 1703, for example, Harmen Warsinck, a wine merchant from Amsterdam, gave Paulus Nieman from Danzig a blank proxy to collect the merchandise, which had been stored in Cadiz, and to

51 Sogner, "Norwegian-Dutch Migrant Relations," 45.

52 Some relevant information is provided by: Cooper, *The Decline of Spain*, 459.

53 NA, *Archief van Nederlandse Gezanten en consuls tot 1810*, *Archief Schonenberg*, "Ingekomen brieven van particulieren", 26.

54 Crespo Solana, *La Casa de la Contratación*, 199.

55 SAA, NA, 7190/85–87 and 3356/1457.

56 SAA, NA, 5291/1589.

send it to Danzig together with a cargo of assorted Spanish wines.[57] Between 1702 and 1708, Dutch firms in Cadiz endured hardship, but in 1708, several of them re-started. In July the *Kaantor* of Melchior de Ruuscher and Rodrigo Mels was opened at Puerto de Santa Maria.[58] In 1707, a warship under captain Floriszoon Cruijtman acted as a merchant ship with a cargo loaded at Sanlúcar de Barrameda and bound for Amsterdam in the name of Pieter de Clercq.[59] In November 1708, another firm was established under Christian Duisberg and Gilberto de Bruijn and began to trade actively in Cadiz.[60] The reactivation of the Baltic connection became evident in 1709 despite the fact that two big wars were being fought at the time.

In the 1720s, new reasons were added to the Dutch interest in maintaining the Cadiz connection. While trade with Mediterranean ports dwindled to 31.5 % of the total connections, trips to America became more and more important and reached up to 62.3 % of total trips by means of a number of legal subterfuges between authorities in the Spanish Board of Trade (*Casa de la Contratación*) and local merchants in connivance with the Flemish Nation in Cadiz. Concurrently, shipping grew again as the Amsterdam Admiralty had made the Spanish Crown aware of certain rules for an unimpeded flow of traffic.[61] Merchant ships required passports or licenses granted by the Admiralty College as approved by the States General in a *Placcaat* from 1727. This *Placcaat* had been established to regulate Dutch commerce at various ports after the wars in the Mediterranean and as a result of the collaboration between the States General and Spain as part of the Quadruple Alliance after 1718.[62] This *Placcaat* also regulated the "visit" paid by the Spanish authorities to ships calling at Cadiz and requesting help and provisions at the La Carraca shipbuilding facilities in the bay. The passport or license issued by the Admiralty College also guaranteed that no smuggling took place.

Most ships that sailed from Amsterdam to Cadiz via the Baltic Sea called in the Baltic at Danzig, Vyborg, Riga, St. Petersburg and Narva. Most of the relevant routes were used to supply the Spanish Armada – Vyborg was a standard port for the collection of wood. Furthermore, in El Ferrol and Cartagena, along with Cadiz, were the main shipyards of Spain. Here the main supplies of wood for the construction of ships arrived by sea. Routes numbers 1 and 6 in the table

57 SAA, NA, 6678/331.
58 SAA, NA, 5905/521.
59 SAA, NA, 7214/1009.
60 SAA, NA, 5000/1223.
61 Crespo Solana, "Legal Strategies," 187.
62 Van Koningsbrugge, "Tussen Mars en Mercurius," 51–86.

are the ones for which most data are available, and which seem to have had the most maritime traffic (see table 4.1).

Despite a brief fall in shipping late in the 1720s, traffic within the Amsterdam-Cadiz connection saw a dramatic increase owing to the recovery of Spanish trade with the Indies and the ensuing prosperity enjoyed by Cadiz as the head port of the Hispanic trade in the Atlantic. The peak years of this growth in trade were between 1740 and 1760.[63] From 1770 onwards,[64] shipping rose again as is shown by the *Straatvaart* lists and STRO. The latter also show a sharp increase in navigation to Cadiz for the years from 1770 through to 1820. This coincided with very high activity in the Bay of Cadiz because of the trade conducted by neutral nations ("*comercio de neutrales*") as has been demonstrated by Antonio García-Baquero and Marina Alfonso Mola.[65]

5 Final Reflections

Daniel Defoe once said that Dutch maritime trade was characterized by collecting goods from various regions to resell them to other producers and sellers after having transported them via various routes. His criticism and satire stemmed from Anglo-Dutch competition. The Dutch method of trading was the most useful for nations like Spain that were in England's empire-building networks. In this article, the information contained in databases about the commercial maritime connections between various geographical areas connected by the Dutch fleets that arrived in Cadiz was evaluated. It was made clear that Cadiz was a commercial hub connected with America and the Mediterranean, and was home to many Dutch commercial companies. This allowed, prior to various Hispano-Dutch trading agreements, Dutch ships (especially the convoys managed by the *Directeuren van de Levantse Handel*) to arrive in Cadiz from various ports of departure, among which the Scando-Baltic ports played an important role. Combining two complex databases – STRO and CrespoDynCoopNet – offered such a huge amount of information about the dynamic of these complex maritime connections that it simply cannot be addressed in this short article. The information we have at our disposal, however, will doubtlessly be the subject of significant future research.

---

63 Crespo Solana, "Legal Strategies," 190.

64 SAA, NA, 15707/446, Amsterdam, 3.3.1777, documents of Arnoldus Johannes van Brienen and co. about the ship "De Vrouw Catharina," to Riga, Ferrol and Cadiz.

65 See: García-Baquero González, *El Libre comercio*, 45; and Mola, "El comercio marítimo," 255–299.

CHAPTER 5

Trade through Lübeck Instead of the Sound – Route Choice in Early Modern Hamburg's Baltic Trade[1]

Yuta Kikuchi

1 Introduction

In early modern Europe, when commodity distribution was strongly hindered by a large number of political, economic and natural obstacles, and the infrastructure as well as the traffic flow was inadequate, transporting goods was an uncertain venture. This situation was especially evident in Germany, known then as the Holy Roman Empire, which consisted of numerous states. Naturally, several repeated debates arose among historians about the predominant trade routes and modes of transport (i.e. land, river or sea) in the distribution of goods.

Opinions on the importance of the various trade routes differ considerably. Some scholars emphasize the predominance of waterborne traffic, including transport by sea, river or canal.[2] According to them, there was a general shift from overland to seaborne transport from the Middle Ages to the early modern period. Other scholars holding a different perspective emphasize the importance of overland trade.[3] One limitation of this discussion is that both types of scholars have treated the dilemma between overland and waterborne routes as if they were competing with each other for the dominant route while paying little attention to the interrelation of the two methods. Comparing the

---

1 The major part of the evidence presented here was assembled from archival sources and my dissertation: Kikuchi, *Hamburgs Handel*, 210–226, and the following articles in Japanese (English titles are given here for the articles and the journals): Kikuchi, "Hamburg's overland trade," 27–51; Kikuchi, "Hamburg's seaborne trade," 109–126.

2 Walter Großhaupt, for example, suggests that, in long-distance trade, people used river and sea routes whenever possible. See Großhaupt, "Waren," 225–226. According to Peter Kriedte, the 'worse the condition of the roads, the greater the importance of the canal network. [...] Roads often only provided the link between two canals'. Kriedte, "Trade," 102.

3 One of the most prominent contributions is a series of works by Manfred Straube, who demonstrated the essential role played by Leipzig's fairs in commercial traffic in early modern continental Europe. See Straube, "Zum Warenaustausch," 22–36; Straube, "Leipzig und Sachsen," 239–244. Also, see the contribution by Astrid Schmidt-Händel on the isatis trade of Erfurt by land: Schmidt-Händel, "Landtransport," 197–212.

 | DOI:10.1163/9789004371781_007

importance of various trade routes to describe shifts in commercial flow is, of course, one of the principal subjects of economic history. However, considering the uncertainty in transporting commodities, such treatment might not always be adequate to understand the functions of each trade route. Moreover, it is noteworthy that trade is always at risk of being interrupted by several obstacles. Therefore, assuming a complementary relationship is appropriate between all available routes: on each occasion, merchants and transporters chose what, in their opinion, was the best available route to reduce the risks. Hermann Kellenbenz highlights legitimately that, despite the evident predominance of waterborne transport, overland transport was sometimes preferred to avoid the risks of shipwreck or piracy, which were not uncommon in pre-modern society.[4]

This perspective was most likely applicable to the North Sea-Baltic trade in the early modern period. It is generally agreed that mediaeval Hanseatic trade between the North Sea and the Baltic, which happened mainly via the overland route between Lübeck and Hamburg, gradually shifted to a seaborne route through the Sound beginning in the fifteenth century. Accepting the claim that there was a significant shift in trade flow from the overland to the seaborne route, we assume that the former did not completely lose its function, but rather continued to play some role in the East–West traffic. Although several detailed studies have appeared on the Baltic trade of various European states and regions in the early modern period, very little has been written on trade between Hamburg and Lübeck. Thus, there is scope for further investigation. Focusing on the trade flow from Hamburg to Lübeck and on to the Baltic in the seventeenth and eighteenth centuries, a period in which this former Hanseatic trade route is rarely mentioned in the literature,[5] this paper explores how a trade route was chosen given various – mostly unfavorable – conditions. It is assumed that trade routes were chosen under the conditions of a multiplicity of choices, flexible complementarity and long-term continued existence of different trade routes. My assumptions are supported by empirical research on trade flows between Hamburg, Lübeck and the Baltic, consisting mainly of quantitative information from the toll account books kept in Hamburg and Lübeck, and partially on other materials such as merchant correspondence.[6]

4 Kellenbenz, "Das Verkehrswesen," 121.

5 There are some exceptions suggesting the importance of land traffic between Hamburg and Lübeck, for example, Kellenbenz, *Unternehmerkräfte*; Kellenbenz, "Landverkehr," 124; Newman, "Hamburg," 69; Harder-Gersdorff, "Avoiding Sound Traffic," 237–261.

6 Staatsarchiv Hamburg (Hamburg), 111–1, Senat Cl. VII, Lit. Ea Pars 1 (Zollbücher); 371–2, Admiralitätskollegium; 415–2 I, Amt Bergedorf I; 621–1, Firmenarchiv; 622–1, Familienarchiv; Archiv der Hansestadt Lübeck (Lübeck), Zulageherren.

For a strict analysis of the function of each type of trade route, 'land trade' was assessed primarily by analyzing the land route via Oldesloe, and 'river/canal trade' separately by analyzing the waterborne route via Lauenburg (See Map 5.1). Moreover, seaborne traffic was analyzed as well, based on data from STRO. The following discussion is divided into two chronological stages: the first is prior to the beginning of the Great Northern War and the second is thereafter. The results of the analysis show a marked difference in the functions of trade routes before and after this period.

2 Trade Flow before the Beginning of the Great Northern War

At the beginning of the 17th century, while trade with Western Europe was growing steadily, Hamburg was faced with a great difficulty regarding her trade with the Baltic. Because of a political dispute with Denmark over administrative matters, King Christian IV obstructed shipping of Hamburger through the Sound.[7] Beginning in 1603, Hamburg citizens were no longer able to enjoy the toll privilege they had been granted in 1560 on the grounds of the treaty of Odense. They now had to pay more than other communities to transport their goods and ships through the Sound. Around the same time, overland trade was restricted because of a discord with Lübeck on the Hanseatic commercial policy.[8] In 1605, Lübeck restricted the passage of products from the Baltic through the city to Hamburg.[9] Citizens of Hamburg were now required to unload their goods in Lübeck and offer them for sale to Lübeck citizens for a certain length of time.

In this way, Hamburg's trade with the Baltic by both sea and land was seriously hindered. Nevertheless, the merits of transporting by land continued to prevail. English merchant Rawstorm, who needed to export kerseys from Hamburg in 1607, suggested transporting them from Lübeck to Danzig, reporting to his partner in London that 'I am credibly informed that that way is both speediest and safest and the charge all one'.[10] The reason for exporting them to Danzig lay in the decreased demand for them in Nuremberg, which as the center of woolen production in the German inland would have been a difficult

7 As the Duke of Holstein, he demanded allegiance from the city. Regarding the dispute, see Loose, *Hamburg und Christian IV*.

8 Lübeck disapproved of Hamburg's openness to foreign, non-Hanseatic traders as it was expected to erode the monopolistic position of the Hanse and Lübeck in North Sea-Baltic trade.

9 For this discord, see Baasch, "Die »Durchfuhr« in Lübeck," 109–152.

10 Fisher, *Letters*, 205.

place to sell unfinished woolen textiles. Here it is noteworthy that the overland route offered its own advantages over the seaborne route. The fact that this was considered the 'speediest' form of transport was undoubtedly because of its short distance. Travel by land via Oldesloe requires a journey of only around 55 km between Hamburg and Lübeck, while between Hamburg and the Sound amounts to ca. 950 km. Furthermore, the travel itself was less risky, since there was no danger of privateering.

This advantage played a crucial role during the Thirty Years' War, which brought European trade by both land and sea into a state of chaos. Hamburg and Lübeck were exceptions and were spared of serious warfare, resulting in an increased trade between the two cities. Table 5.1, based on the toll records levied in 1630 or 1637 in Hamburg on goods exported from the city by land or on the Elbe clearly shows more trade transactions with Lübeck compared with other cities. Especially striking is the observation that cloth (Laken) was exported to Lübeck in addition to wine and sugar. After the English Merchant Adventurers Company settled in Hamburg in 1611 after several removals of their staple market in northern Germany, the city became a center for the finishing and distribution of old English draperies. The data show that the main destination for the re-export of English cloth was the Baltic Sea region, linked via Lübeck. The amount of trade in such cloth was considerable because it accounted for the transport of old draperies (klæde =Laken) from Western Europe to the Baltic through the Sound at that time.[11] On the other hand, export to the German inland, which had been significant before the war,[12] had now declined. The trade flow to the area had shifted to the Baltic Sea region via Lübeck. In this regard, trade through Lübeck experienced a so-called war boom.

11 See Bang and Korst, *Tabeller*, vol. 2A.

12 Especially, the line between Hamburg and Nuremberg was important, favoured from the turbulence of Antwerp commerce in the latter half of the 16th century. See Unger, "Nürnbergs Handel," 1–85, especially 24–30; Baumann, *The Merchants Adventurers*, 11–12, 301–308; Sakuma, *Die Nürnberger Tuchmacher*, 161–164.

TABLE 5.1 Export of cloth, herring, sugar and wine from Hamburg by land and river in 1630 or 1637

Region	Cloth, pieces (Laken)	Herring	Sugar			Wine
		Loads (Last)	Barrels (Fass)	Barrels (Fässlein)	Barrels (Tonne)	(Pipes)
Lübeck <37>	7,381	133	171	59	90	2,423
Cities in Schleswig-Holstein <37>	1,542	50	4	3	10	141
Baltic cities <37>	1,159	7	3	3	8	70
Lüneburg <30>	834	849	181	39	8	290
Region around Lüneburg <30>	514	116	6	9	2	265
Altmark <30>	8	186	–	–	–	114
Brunswick and Hanover <37>	265	12	–	–	1	43
Magdeburg <30>	78	137	37	17	0	271
Other Saxon cities <30>	78	17	37	17	0	77
Leipzig <37>	940	0	50	3	–	17
Thuringia <37>	-	19	2	–	–	2
Frankfurt (Oder) <30>	151	166	20	9	9	643
Brandenburg <30>	10	471	2	1	5	154
Other cities in Kurmark <30>	71	280	7	2	3	205
Southern Germany <37>	167	10	29	13	–	0
Hamburg's surroundings <30>	74	3	–	–	–	28

SOURCE: STAATSARCHIV HAMBURG (HAMBURG), 111–1, SENAT CL. VII, LIT. EA PARS 1 (ZOLLBÜCHER) NR. 3G, VOL. 8, 11, 12. SEE ALSO KIKUCHI, 'HAMBURG'S OVERLAND TRADE', PP. 44–45.

For import trade via the land route, no quantifiable data are available. As mentioned above, the passage was strongly restricted by Lübeck. Nevertheless, Hamburger merchants attempted at getting supplies of Baltic goods via Lübeck, as can be deduced from the number of petitions they submitted to the city council of Lübeck.[13] Passage could be arranged through negotiation, and large transactions thus became possible. In 1634, for example, the request of Hamburger merchants to send 560 ship-pounds of copper through Lübeck was granted.[14]

At that time, copper was becoming one of the most significant commodities transported from the Baltic to the West through Hamburg.[15] The trade in Hungarian copper, which had once dominated the European markets, now faced severe difficulties due to the political disturbances that had been ongoing since the end of the 16th century, and the Thirty Years' War pushed it into a critical decline.[16] For Hamburg, this meant changing its supplier. Instead of importing from Hungary, the city bought copper from Sweden. The firm of Paler and Rehlinger in Augsburg, which had witnessed impressive trade in Hungarian copper through the agency of a Hamburger merchant named Emanuel Jenisch, shifted its business gradually into financial transactions in 1620s.[17] Jenisch was compelled to send Swedish copper in place of the Hungarian commodity to Spain.[18] Note that Hungarian copper could be shipped from Danzig via Lübeck

13 The existing petitions during the seventeenth century list the following articles: 25 barrels of butter from Denmark (1604), salted and dried salmon (1606), copper from Sweden (1606), 40 slices of bacon and 2 barrels of butter from Denmark (1607), salmon and other fishes from Denmark (1608), 50 ship-pounds of wax from Danzig (1608), 45 last of rye from Danzig (1630), 35 last of rye (1630), 560 ship-pounds of copper from Sweden (1634), 40 last of rye (1644), 400 last of grain (1644), 60 ship-pounds of cannonballs (1644), Swedish cannons (1672), iron (1673) and fatty products (1694). Archiv der Hansestadt Lübeck (Lübeck), ASA Externa, Deutsche Territorien, Nr. 5374 (Hamburger Gesuche um Durchfuhrerlaubnis), Nr. 5397 (Hamburg an Lübeck: Bitte um Ausfuhrerlaubnis); Staatsarchiv Hamburg (Hamburg), 111–1, Senat Cl. VII, Lit. Ec Nr. 12 (Lübeckische Zölle), Vol. 1b, Vol. 4. In addition, iron, feathers, train oil and tar were also named. See Baasch, "Die »Durchfuhr« in Lübeck," 116.

14 Staatsarchiv Hamburg (Hamburg), 111–1, Senat Cl. VI, Nr. 1a. Vol. 1, Fasc. 10 (Schreiben der Stadt Lübeck 1601–1717), Lübeck an Hamburg 1634.

15 Particularly in trade with Spain and Portugal, copper was the fourth most important traded material, next to textiles, grain and wax. In 1632–34, for example, a total of ca. 1,157,000 mark textiles, 1,054,000 mark grain, 827,000 mark wax and 264,000 mark copper were exported from Hamburg to Spain and Portugal. These figures are estimated from the toll account books of the admiralty of Hamburg: Staatsarchiv Hamburg (Hamburg), 371–2, Admiralitätskollegium F3 (Verzeichnis der dem Admiralitätszoll unterliegenden, auf Seeschiffen ein und ausgehenden Waren, geordnet nach Kaufleuten [Maklern] mit Angabe der Schiffer und der Zollabgabe), Bd. 1 and 2.

16 Vlachovič, "Produktion und Handel," 624–627; Vlachovič, "Die Kupfererzeugung," 166.

17 See Hildebrandt, ed., *Quellen und Regesten*.

18 Staatsarchiv Hamburg (Hamburg), 211–2, Reichskammergericht, S150.

to Hamburg.[19] As discussed below, copper leaving Lübeck was transported by land, not by river.[20]

Hamburg had access to the Baltic not only through land routes but also through rivers and canals. The Stecknitz canal connected Lübeck with Lauenburg, which is connected to Hamburg by the Elbe. At a glance, this seems to be a very useful infrastructure system; however, this route takes twice as long as the overland route via Oldesloe. Let us now consider the function of this water route. The record of the Elbe-toll, which was analyzed in Table 5.1, does not imply the significant role of the waterway in the export from Hamburg. Only a small amount of wine and fish was transported via Lauenburg. Nils R. Nissen proved that transporters engaged in shuttle shipping on the Stecknitz (so-called Stecknitzfahrer) often did not load return freight from Hamburg.[21] For imports from the Baltic, however, the canal was of great use. According to the Elbe-toll accounts, large amounts of Baltic products were shipped from Lauenburg to Hamburg: tar, pitch and different types of timber.[22] Other commodities were seldom listed on the account books. Here it is notable that all these articles are categorized as so-called 'bulky goods' – low-price commodities treated on a massive scale. For such cumbersome items, mass transportation by water carriage was more suitable. This logic explains why copper, which was an important part of land trade, did not feature among the waterborne imports from Lauenburg. Copper was at that time valued as highly as wax,[23] and according to its price–weight relationship it was economically not feasible to transport it via the longer route by river. In view of these facts, we may plausibly conclude that people changed their trade routes according to the nature of the commodities they were shipping. The same logic applies to exports. Relatively heavy goods, such as wine and herring, were transported from Hamburg by river, but English old draperies were transported by land instead.

19 See Kellenbenz, *Unternehmerkräfte*, 83–84.

20 One concrete example of such transport is a complaint of Hamburg against Lübeck in 1606 about the prohibition against the passage of copper sent by way of Oldesloe. Archiv der Hansestadt Lübeck (Lübeck), ASA Externa, Deutsche Territorien, Nr. 5386 (Behinderung des Hamburger Ostseehandels durch Lübecker Durchfuhrverbote 1606).

21 Nissen, "Neue Forschungsergebnisse," 8–9.

22 The amounts are as follows. Tar and pitch: 265 last from Lauenburg, 284.5 last from other German cities; Deals: 14,372 pieces from Lauenburg, 46,505 pieces from other German cities; Clapholt (Klappholz): 47,280 pieces from Lauenburg; Pipeholt (Pipenholz): 274,280 pieces from Lauenburg, 1,290 from other German cities. Staatsarchiv Hamburg (Hamburg), 111–1, Senat Cl. VII, Lit. Ea Pars 1 (Zollbücher) Nr. 3g, Vol. 1.

23 According to the toll account books of the admiralty of Hamburg (see note 15), both commodities were estimated at 200 marks per ship-pound.

Which area in the Baltic Sea region was most connected to the Hamburg–Lübeck trade? The annotation 'dänisch Gut (Danish goods)' or 'Stralsunder Gut (Stralsunder goods)' noted on the toll account books for some cloths exported to Lübeck in 1637 indicates that part of the re-exported cloths was destined for these areas.[24] Copper was derived mainly from Sweden, as we have already seen. Danzig, Königsberg, Riga and the Scandinavian region including Gotland can be regarded as sources of timber and timber by-products, such as tar and pitch.[25]

In the period after the Thirty Years' War, no sources provide quantifiable information on overland trade. With the gradual recovery of inland trade, the relative importance of the Hamburg–Lübeck trade seems to have declined; however, surviving evidence assures us of its continued existence. The toll account books of Lübeck, which unfortunately include no place names, suggest the transport of cloths and colonial products such as sugar and tobacco from Hamburg.[26] The amounts of these goods, however, appear to be fairly small. As a whole, there is no evidence suggesting the significance of the land trade as in the earlier period.

Let us now examine the seaborne trade between Hamburg and the Baltic. For a few years after 1621, when the 12–year peace treaty between Spain and the Netherlands had expired, trade experienced a temporary upturn since the Dutch trade was oppressed by Spanish embargoes, while Hamburg profited from the ability to display neutral flags.[27] A recession soon arrived, however, when trade was oppressed by commercial restrictions levied by the Governor of the Habsburg Netherlands. Under these conditions, no notable commodities passed through the Sound either to or from Hamburg. In contrast to the land trade, which retained its position as a main traffic artery since the Middle Ages, seaborne trade from and to the Baltic no longer played any role, unlike that in other northwest European countries.

---

24 Merchants of Copenhagen imported cloth from Hamburg via Lübeck to Denmark. See Jørgensen, "Denmark's Relations," 78. Stralsund maintained trade during the Thirty Years' War, and after the grain supply from the Pomeranian hinterland had been cut off by the war, the trading of cloth from Hamburg became important. See Olechnowitz, *Handel und Seeschiffahrt*, 114–124.

25 See Harder-Gersdorff, "Lübeck, Danzig und Riga," 124, note 64; Sjöberg, "Gotlands Handel," 105; North, "The Export of Timber," 1–14.

26 Archiv der Hansestadt Lübeck (Lübeck), Zulageherren, Nr. 2–5.

27 See Kikuchi, "Sound Toll Registers online".

3 Trade Flow from the Great Northern War until the End of the Century

During the period from the beginning of the Great Northern War until the end of the 18th century, there was rapid growth in Hamburg's seaborne trade with the Baltic in the export branch after the war. Moreover, although the overland trade may have lost its former predominance, probably as early as the last half of the 17th century, as we have supposed above, it played a complementary role to the seaborne trade, for example, during wartime when traffic on the sea was interrupted, or due to various other factors.

The first complementary function of the land trade in the 18th century was witnessed during the Great Northern War, when the seaborne trade of Hamburg with the Baltic was almost extinct. Graph 5.1 illustrates this shift. This graph is based on the revenue of the Elbe-toll collected at Esslingen (today Zollenspieker), the first toll-station from Hamburg going upwards, that is, from ships going to Lauenburg/Lübeck.[28]

The sharp upsurge of toll revenue in 1717–21 is related to the war. In 1716, the main theatre of war moved from Russia and Poland to Sweden and Norway, that is, to the entrance of the Baltic. Therefore, overland trade developed as an alternative to seaborne traffic. The types of commodities exported by this route cannot be defined accurately because of unclear declarations of freight in the toll account books, but it was evident that the main commodities were wine and sugar. The land route must have been used more often than usual, and probably earlier than the canal route. Hamburg wrote in 1705, as an answer to a complaint from citizens of Lübeck, who had to pay a toll for goods from France, that the toll revenue of Hamburg would be short without this measure, because Hamburg's incoming tolls for the seaborne trade were reduced due to the war. These goods were brought not by sea but by land to Lübeck.[29] In 1714, considering the Danish oppression at the Sound, Hamburg's Chamber of Commerce asserted that they would now have to send all goods via Lübeck.[30]

After the war, trade faced a rapid recession, and from the 1730s to the 1750s, it showed gradual but very moderate growth. Therefore, we may not estimate the volume of the overland trade too highly in this period. [31] On the contrary,

28 The toll account books also include transportation revenue to other cities on the Elbe. For comprehensive analysis of this source see Kikuchi, *Hamburgs Handel*, 210–226.

29 Pitz, *Die Zolltarife*, 457, Nr. 319.

30 Staatsarchiv Hamburg (Hamburg), 111–1, Senat Cl. VII, Lit. Kc Nr. 5 (Commercium mit Dänemark), Vol. 2, fol. 3v.

31 The passage restriction in Lübeck, which had depressed the trade flow from Lübeck to Hamburg (see p. 3 and note 8), was lifted in 1728; however, this did not seem to stimulate

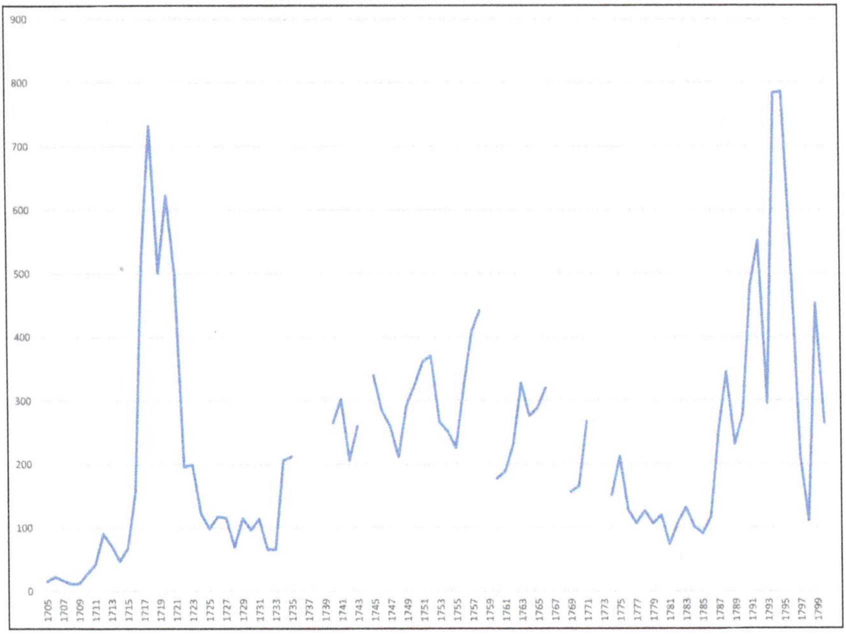

GRAPH 5.1 Elbe-toll revenue from exports to Lauenburg and Lübeck (in Marks)
SOURCE: STAATSARCHIV HAMBURG (HAMBURG), AMT BERGEDORF I, 415-2 I, PARS. II, SECTIO. III, VOL. 1F (EINNAHME UND AUSGABE BEIM EßLINGER ZOLL, REGISTER DER FÄHRGELD UND ZOLLEINNAHME ZU EßLINGEN), FASC. I, NR. 10–28; FASC. II, NR. 1–124; FASC. III

seaborne trade showed significant growth from the 1730s, especially in the export of colonial products, as shown in Graph 5.2. Around this time, we see a general development of Hamburg's intermediary trade with colonial products, especially sugar. Mainly shipped from France to Hamburg, a vast amount of raw sugar was traded, and highly advanced sugar refineries were built.[32] The refined sugar was exported to the city's hinterland, the central European inland and the Baltic region.

Interestingly, the Danish oppression at the Sound lasted as before, or rather, it was reinforced. In 1737, it was reported at the city council of Hamburg that the 'old tariff' would be applicable to the freight of Hamburg citizens during navigation in the Baltic, not while anchoring in Hamburg, but while

the trade between the two cities, at least in exports from Hamburg to Lübeck. As discussed below, exports from Hamburg to the Baltic during this period began to flow on a larger scale via seaborne trade.

32 See Petersson, "Zuckersiedergewerbe," 53–81.

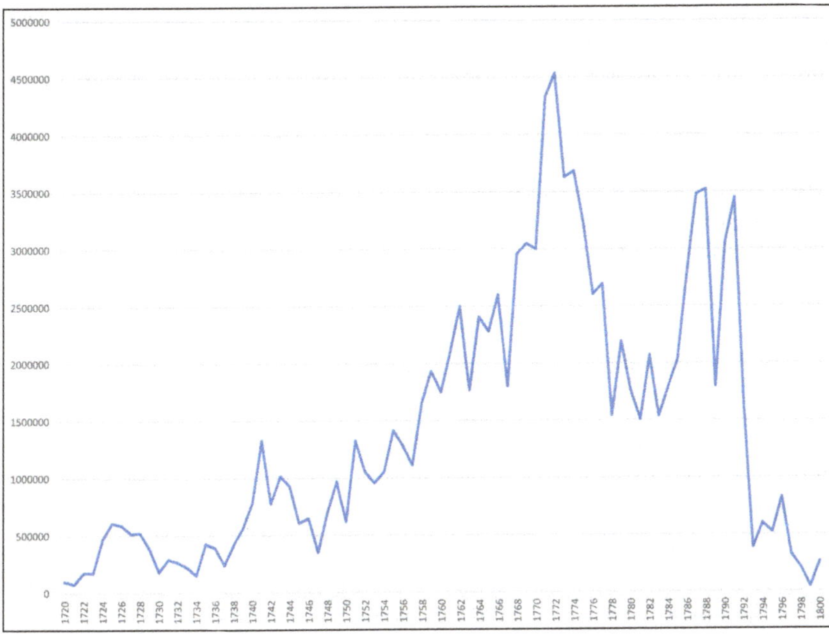

GRAPH 5.2 Seaborne export of colonial products from Hamburg to the Baltic through the Sound, 1720–1800 (in pounds)
SOURCE: BANG AND KORST, *TABELLER OVER SKIBSFART OG VARENTRANSPORT GENNEM ØRESUND 1661–1783 OG GENNEM STOREBÆLT 1701–1748*, VOL. 2–4 (COPENHAGEN AND LEIPZIG), 1930–1953; SOUND TOLL REGISTERS ONLINE, HTTP://WWW.SOUNDTOLL.NL. SEE ALSO KIKUCHI, "HAMBURG'S SEABORNE TRADE," P. 122.

sailing from a foreign place to the Baltic, or vice versa.[33] The 'old tariff' remains unclear, but we can suppose with certainty that this refers to the tariff imposed before the peace treaty of Christianopel in 1645, through which Denmark fixed a new toll tariff at the Sound. Under the old tariff, one had to pay 20–25 percent more toll than usual.[34] With reference to the amount of the Sound Toll, it was confirmed that the freight of Hamburg citizens without passing the city on the Elbe was actually subject to the toll under the old tariff. The extra charge to ships and freight of Hamburg citizens remained as before.

How, then, can the growth of seaborne export shipping be accounted for? The examination of the Sound Toll registers provides some explanations. First,

33 Staatsarchiv Hamburg (Hamburg), 111–1, Senat Cl. VII, Lit. Ec Nr. 4, Vol. 7k (Excerpta Dei Archivarii von Som, den Oresundischen Zoll betr. 1736–1742), Q1.

34 See the list of both tariffs (written in 1766) in Staatsarchiv Hamburg (Hamburg), 111–1, Senat Cl. VII, Lit. Kc Nr. 5 (Commercium mit Dänemark), Vol. 7, fols. 14r–23v.

not only the shipmasters of Hamburg but also a number of foreigners, especially the Dutch, and later, beginning in the 1770s, shipmasters from various other regions such as Sweden, Denmark, Schleswig-Holstein, Mecklenburg, Pomerania and Prussia, brought colonial products from Hamburg to the Baltic. Their share in the total voyages from Hamburg to the Baltic in 1731–1800 amounts to an average of 84 per cent.[35]

Second, Hamburger merchants often loaded their goods onto foreign ships to avoid the extra charge levied at the Sound on the ships from Hamburg. Although it is not possible to estimate the exact amounts of goods that were shipped in this way due to the inaccuracy of the sources, many records of foreign shipmasters sailing from Hamburg carrying freight belonging to the city's merchants ('Hamborger gods' [Hamburg goods]') are identified in STRO.[36]

Third, Hamburger merchants, though burdened by the obstacles at the Sound, managed to engage in the export trade while refraining from importing products from the Baltic. For Hamburg's intermediary trade, the import of Baltic products to the city, especially that of foodstuffs and raw materials, was impractical. There was low demand for these products in Hamburg's German hinterland. Re-exporting via Hamburg to the western markets by sea, that is, 100 km up the Elbe and then returning seawards, was uneconomical, because unlike sugar, which had to be refined in the city as described above, Baltic products could be transported directly to the final destinations without passing Hamburg. Yet according to the old tariff, the toll was higher on the freight of citizens of Hamburg transported directly from the Baltic to the western markets. Thus, Hamburger merchants mainly concentrated on the export business to make the maximum profit under these disadvantaged circumstances.

In STRO, examples of such voyages can be confirmed. For instance, in 1749–56, Claus Piel, shipmaster of Altona, often made the round-trip voyage between Hamburg and St. Petersburg carrying Hamburg goods, but when he sailed from St. Petersburg to Marseille on 21 August 1749, from Stettin to Amsterdam on 30 July 1750, and from St. Petersburg to Livorno on 18 August 1756, he shipped no goods belonging to Hamburger merchants.[37] The same is true for many, including Geritt Simons of Norden and Foppe Bouwessen Backer of Altona.[38]

35 Bang and Korst, *Tabeller*, 1.

36 Since the special charge was levied on Hamburger goods at the Sound, the annotation 'Hamburg goods' was often recorded in the toll books.

37 Sound Toll Registers Online, http://www.soundtoll.nl, passage ID 249 (15. 6. 1749), 313 (21. 8. 1749), 109 (30. 5. 1750), 247 (20. 7. 1750), 204 (12. 6. 1756), 320 (18. 8. 1756). No extra charge on Hamburg goods was levied for these three voyages.

38 Of course there are exceptions. Some shipmasters transported Hamburg goods without visiting the city on the Elbe. The reason for this is unclear, but probably varies from case to case.

Fourth, the greater a shipment of treated commodities, the larger the transportation vehicle. By the 18th century, colonial products were no longer considered costly commodities, but rather bulky goods because of their large quantities. Thus, they were transported on ships rather than wagons. This was a reason for using the seaborne route instead of that by land despite the greater distance.

Considering the Treaty of Gottorp between Hamburg and Denmark in 1768, which resolved the long political conflict in exchange for a large monetary payment from the former, the city was finally excused from the restriction that had lasted for over 150 years.[39] As a result, the seaborne export trade from Hamburg to the Baltic grew rapidly and reached its peak in 1772.[40]

Now let us turn to the question of whether the overland trade had completely lost its importance in the intermediary trade of Hamburg. The development of seaborne exports was checked in the mid-1770s, and the following stagnation continued until 1783.[41] This period corresponds with the American War of Independence. Due to ongoing conflicts between the European sea powers, the import of colonial products from Western Europe to Hamburg was tightened, thus reducing re-export to the Baltic. However, in this period only, there was a temporary but notable trade in these commodities from Lübeck by land, though exchange along this route normally flowed in the opposite direction. Table 5.2, using the example of sugar transport, shows this unusual movement. This phenomenon ceased after the war ended.

Considering that Lübeck was only a stop in transit, where did the sugar come from? The toll account books of Lübeck suggest that the source was Denmark. In addition to its colonies along the Indian coast, Denmark also controlled some Caribbean islands. Copenhagen was thus a distribution center for colonial products in the Baltic Sea region.[42] During this time, trade in colonial products was the leading sector in the commercial relationship

39 In article 10 of the treaty, the Danish king agreed to treat Hamburg equally well as he treated other nearby nations such as the Netherlands, thus abolishing the extra charge. For the contents of this treaty, see the printed original text: *Vergleich, welcher zwischen dem Hochfürstlichen Gesamt-Hause Holstein und der Kayserlichen Freyen Reichs-Stadt Hamburg zu Gottorff am 27ten May 1768 geschlossen* [...] *worden*, printed by Jeremias C. Piscator (Hamburg, 1768).

40 Note that exports inland from the Elbe were, contrary to the booming exports to the Baltic, strongly stagnated. That was due to the Prussian trade restriction against Hamburg. Frederick the Great tried to restrain the inflow of commodities from Hamburg to his territories in order to protect Prussian industries. As a result, the goods flow was redirected from inland German areas to the Baltic. See Kikuchi, *Hamburgs Handel*, 221–225.

41 See Graph 5.2.

42 Rasch, "Kopenhagen," 58–64.

TABLE 5.2 Transportation of sugar from Lübeck to Hamburg, 1778–92 (in barrels)

1778	1779	1780	1781	1782	1783	1784	1786	1787	1788	1789	1790	1791	1792
3,710	1,523	1,794	2,220	1,740	2,725	791	35	234	71	6	0	0	126

SOURCE: STAATSARCHIV HAMBURG (HAMBURG), 371–2, ADMIRALITÄTSKOLLEGIUM F12 (VERZEICHNIS DER ZU WASSER UND ZU LANDE ANGEKOMMENEN WAREN MIT ANGABE DER KAUFLEUTE [MAKLER] SOWIE DER HERKUNFT UND DER MENGE DER WARE [CONTENTBUCH]), BD. 2–15.

between Lübeck and Denmark.[43] A particularly favorable situation arose during the American War of Independence, when, with England and France engaged in a bitter struggle, Denmark as a neutral country was able to expand her commercial interests.[44] According to the toll book for 1780, a total of 925,250 pounds of sugar and 85,400 pounds of syrup were imported from Copenhagen to Lübeck.[45] In addition, in 1781–83, a significant quantity of coffee was also imported from Lübeck to Hamburg,[46] which was sourced from Copenhagen.[47] By the end of the war, the supply of sugar from Lübeck to Hamburg diminished rapidly. From the mid-1780s through 1792 (the end of the record), there was only an occasional supply and only in very small quantities.[48]

Furthermore, the import of tobacco from Lübeck was also frequently recorded in the toll account books. Friedrich Justus, a tobacco merchant of Hamburg, who imported tobacco from Copenhagen via Lübeck in 1776, wrote, to his customer that, in spite of the war in America, he was very well supplied with the commodity and could manage to stabilize the price.[49]

43 Rasch, "Die Beziehungen," 23.

44 Baxa and Bruns, *Zucker*, 64.

45 Archiv der Hansestadt Lübeck, Zulageherren, Nr. 22.

46 A total of 855 barrels and 2890 sacks were imported in 1781; 1034 barrels and 4789 sacks in 1782; and 2168 sacks and 5775 barrels in 1783. Staatsarchiv Hamburg (Hamburg), 371–2, Admiralitätskollegium F12 (Verzeichnis der zu Wasser und zu Lande angekommenen Waren mit Angabe der Kaufleute [Makler] sowie der Herkunft und der Menge der Ware [Contentbuch]), Bd. 2–15.

47 Archiv der Hansestadt Lübeck, Zulageherren, Nr. 23.

48 Archiv der Hansestadt Lübeck, Zulageherren, Nr. 24. In this year, only 1600 pounds of sugar were imported from Wismar and 100 pounds from Amsterdam. Along with sugar, the supply of coffee from Lübeck to Hamburg also ended in 1784 along with the end of the war. See the toll books cited in Table 2 and note 46.

49 Staatsarchiv Hamburg (Hamburg), Firmenarchiv, 621–1/54 (Friedrich Justus), Kopiebücher 12c, fol. 708. For imports from Copenhagen via Lübeck see for example fols. 675, 677, 680, 684, 702.

Here we see one of the functions of the overland trade. Whenever traffic by sea became difficult, the overland route served as an alternative. A similar phenomenon has been observed in the growth of trade and transport by canal during the Great Northern War. The second upturn in this type of trade at the end of the century (See Graphs 5.1 and 5.2) can be explained in the same way: seaborne exports to the Baltic faced stagnation while overland exports grew, and consequently, most ships from Hamburg went to the Baltic loaded with ballast. A glance over the Sound Toll registers identifies several such ships, which were then destined directly to the western markets with foodstuffs and raw materials. The predominance of ballast shipping indicates that there was a shift in the pattern of seaborne trade from exporting finished products of the city to obtaining primary products for sale in other markets. Demand for these goods increased in Western Europe due to the French Revolutionary Wars. In response to this change, it may have been necessary to give up exporting goods to dispatch ships and instead complete each transaction as fast as possible, since finding customers in the Baltic region was not always fast and easy.[50] Thus, goods exported from Hamburg were no longer shipped by sea. To compensate for this, the overland route provided another channel.[51]

Another aspect of the complementary role played by the overland trade route is observed in imports from the Baltic. As mentioned above, trade flow from the Baltic by sea did not usually pass through Hamburg since that route required more time and greater cost. Grain was shipped by this route, but only occasionally. Imports on this route played no significant role. This was not the case for the overland route: analysis of the admiralty toll account books in 1778–92 reveals that various Baltic products were constantly being shipped from Lübeck, including hemp, flax, linseed, linen, sailcloth, leather, Russian leather (Juchten), fur, skin, ash, wool, fish, train oil, tallow, feather, saltpeter, mats, copper, iron, tar, and pitch; in addition, on a temporary basis, colonial products such as sugar and coffee were shipped, as well as tea and cotton fabrics (calicoes).

Just as in the seventeenth century, there was a sharing of roles between land and canal trade. In fact, merchants at the time intentionally divided their usage between these two modes of transport. In 1714, Hamburger merchants mentioned this traffic to Lübeck, stating that 'gross goods are usually transported

50 Harder-Gersdorff, "Seehandel," 67.

51 In addition, the stagnation of exports to the German inland recovered to some degree in the 1790s because of the easing of Prussian trade restrictions, resulting in a partial conversion of the trade flow. Kikuchi, *Hamburgs Handel*, 225–226 and 232.

on water'.[52] Analysis of the admiralty toll account books in 1778–92 indicates this tendency fairly clearly on a quantitative basis: transport on the Stecknitz-canal consisted almost exclusively of bulky goods such as iron, tar and pitch. In other words, almost all ship cargoes from Lübeck via Lauenburg contained these commodities. The toll account books include no information about timber transport; however, it is reasonable to consider that timber was mainly shipped on the canal. Of the yearly average of 41,273 iron bars imported by water from Lübeck/Lauenburg in 1778–92 were 37,385. Therefore, the proportion of waterborne trade for these items amounts to 90 per cent. For tar and pitch, the yearly average of total import was 487 last and 345 last (so 70 per cent) came from Lübeck/Lauenburg on ships.

4 Factors Influencing Route Choice

As we have seen, the logic by which bulky goods were transported more often by ship applies to the relation between sea and land as well as that between road and river. Therefore, the sea route, although requiring a much greater distance, was typically chosen for colonial goods. However, when the seaborne route became difficult for one reason or another, such as war, the commodity flow was diverted to the overland route. In a discussion of route choice, however, it is not enough only to consider the price–weight relationship and political situation. Various other factors also influenced the decisions of merchants; in this section, we deal with this topic.

Seasonality was one such factor. The waterborne route was not available all year round, as the sea and rivers were frozen in the winter. The Sound Toll registers show that passage through the Sound almost completely ceased in the winters, while the toll account books on the land trade reflect a relatively busy traffic from Lübeck during the same months. Lorenz-Meyer, a wine merchant from Hamburg, wrote to a customer in Kolberg/Kołobrzeg in March 1741 that the wine he had ordered was sent by land because the season did not allow the use of the water route.[53]

In connection with the seasonal availability of trade routes, one also must consider the seasonality of commodity supply and the locations of the cities that served as suppliers or distribution centers. For example, the voyage to

52 Staatsarchiv Hamburg (Hamburg), 111–1. Senats Cl. VII, Lit. Ec Nr. 12 (Lübeckische Zölle), Vol. 1b, fol. 34r.

53 Staatsarchiv Hamburg (Hamburg), Familienarchiv, 622–1/65 (Lorenz-Meyer), Kopiebücher A1, fol. 48.

St. Petersburg, which lies at the vertex of the Gulf of Finland, took a great deal of time. In addition to the time it took to traverse the physical distance, delays caused by unexpected weather and the time required for loading and unloading at the port, those transporting the ships and goods of Hamburg citizens had to consider the fact that strict visitation at the Sound had lasted very long before the political reconciliation between the city and Denmark.[54] Winter ice often hindered traffic on the Gulf of Finland, and because water gradually flowed ice-free by April, the purchase of Russian commodities took place mostly in May and June, when merchants and their representatives came from the interior of Russia. Therefore, merchants typically preferred the seaborne route for exports from Hamburg in spring. In a memorandum on the subject of Russian trade in 1764, the Hamburger merchants highlighted that commodities were dispatched directly, that is, by sea, to St. Petersburg in spring, and by way of Lübeck or Kiel in summer and autumn.[55] In the Sound Toll registers, we see exports most frequently in May. The land trade through Lübeck saw a seasonal increase in the transportation of Baltic products as the city was able to receive the primary products of the Baltic Sea region first after the harvest. In 1712, Hamburger merchants commented that, for trade to the Baltic, the overland route was used more often in the winter, due to the danger of the passage through the Sound and because various products from the Baltic Sea region such as hemp and flax were shipped first to Lübeck in this season.[56] Thus, the method of commodity dispatching depended strongly on seasonal as well as geographical factors.

If no ships were available, goods were transported by land. The merchant Lorenz-Meyer in Hamburg wrote to his customer in Stettin/Szczecin that he would send wine via Lübeck because the ship he expected to use to transport the goods had already left and there might have been no more ships making the journey.[57] For transport from Lübeck and on to other destinations, merchants had to consider whether a ship would be available there as well.[58]

---

54 This was reported in Hamburg in 1742. See Staatsarchiv Hamburg (Hamburg), 111–1, Senat Cl. VII, Lit. Ec Nr. 4, Vol. 7k (König. Dänisch. Norwegische, auch Schleswig-Holsteinische Zölle), Q20.

55 Baasch, *Quellen zur Geschichte*, 334–335.

56 Staatsarchiv Hamburg (Hamburg), 111–1, Senat Cl. VII, Lit. Ec Nr. 12 (Lübeckische Zölle), Vol. 1b, fol. 34r.

57 Staatsarchiv Hamburg (Hamburg), Familienarchiv, 622–1/65 (Lorenz-Meyer), Kopiebücher A1, fol. 147.

58 Friedrich Justus asked his partner in Lübeck whether the ship to Riga had already departed, and if so when the next ship would become available. Staatsarchiv Hamburg (Hamburg), Firmenarchiv, 621–1/54 (Friedrich Justus), Kopiebücher 12b, fol. 27.

5 Conclusion

In the first half of the 17th century, the evident predominance of land transport in the trade of Hamburg with the Baltic was confirmed. However, this position was subsequently lost, and after the 1730s, when the growth of Hamburg's intermediary trade set in, seaborne trade through the Sound sustained this development. Ships with larger capacities became an essential element in the trade of massive quantities of colonial products.

Therefore, the land trade seems to have taken a subordinate role. Nevertheless, as clarified, it remained indispensable for the maintenance of overall trade. Several obstacles prevented the sole use of the seaborne route for transportation, such as wars, sea ice and the unavailability of ships. The overland route was used in such cases. By providing an alternate route for situations in which seaborne transport was not possible, the land route made the incessant circulation of trade flow possible. Moreover, from an economic perspective, the overland trade had some advantages. The seasonality of commodity supply, connected with the fact that the sea was covered with ice in winter, made Lübeck a distribution center for the Baltic region even into the 18th century, thus maintaining trade flows to and from Hamburg. For Hamburg, this meant that the city could receive the products it needed from the Baltic without using the longer seaborne route. In other cases, these goods were transported directly from the Baltic to the western markets. There was also a division of roles between roads and canals. In essence, merchants had many factors to consider in choosing among the available seaborne, land and canal routes, as we have seen from concrete examples of their trade activity.

Therefore, the overland transport between Hamburg and Lübeck formed a subsystem of all trade between Western Europe and the Baltic. Our assumptions at the beginning of this chapter – namely, that merchants had a multiplicity of choices and that trade routes had complementary relationships and long-term continued existence – are thus justified.

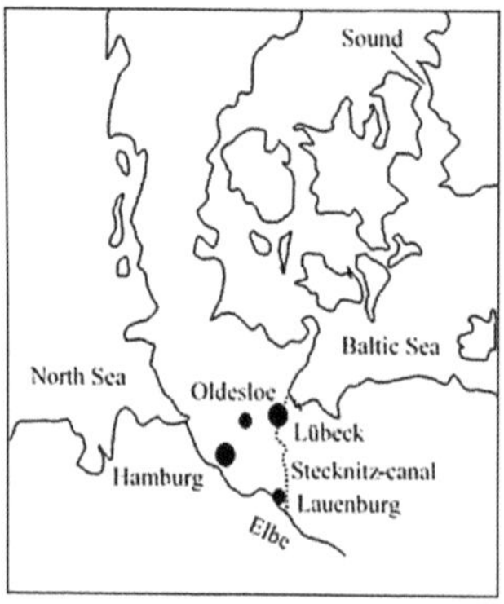

MAP 5.1 Hamburg's overland connection to the Baltic

CHAPTER 6

The Story of Two Straits: British Shipping to the Baltic and the Mediterranean in the Late Eighteenth Century

Katerina Galani

The geographic scope of this paper covers a virtual triangle that links Great Britain to the Mediterranean and the Baltic Sea. These two regions represent relatively similar case studies, as they are both closed seas with a narrow point of entry: the Strait of Gibraltar and the Danish Sound. Both seas were surrounded by powerful states in the eighteenth century, which negotiated and contracted with Britain in order to carry out trade. While the rise of overseas trade played a fundamental role in the economic development of Britain, and has thus inspired extensive research by economic historians, current debate on eighteenth-century shipping and trade has slowly drawn the attention from the Atlantic and colonial trade to the Baltic and the Mediterranean, from the new markets back to the old, European ones.[1] Despite the expansion into the colonial markets, intra-European trade was still the most significant in terms of value and volume throughout the eighteenth century. As Patrick O'Brien has stressed, 76% of European exports were directed within Europe during the 1790s, leaving only a small share in total economic activity to the trade with the periphery.[2]

In this light, the aim of this paper is to examine British shipping in the Mediterranean and the Baltic in the second half of the eighteenth century, offering a macroscopic view. Despite similarities between these two European markets, there were also pronounced differences that diversified British strategy for shipping and trade, particularly when the intermittent wars of the late

1 A brief overview of the current literature demonstrates a growing production addressing the Baltic and the Mediterranean trade and more specifically the British engagement therein. On the Baltic see Hutchinson, "The Norwegian and Baltic Timber Trade"; Rönnbäck, "New and Old Peripheries"; Evans and Rydén, *Baltic Iron*; Kaplan, *Russian overseas commerce*. See also Johansen, "Danish Shipping Service." On British trade in the Mediterranean see Galani, *British Shipping*; Galani, "Foreigners"; D'Angelo, *Mercanti inglesi a Malta*; D' Angelo, *Mercanti Inglesi a Livorno*; D'Angelo and Vassallo, eds., *Anglo-Saxons*; Gallant, *Experiencing Dominion*; Hamilton, De Groot and Van den Boogert, eds., *Friends and Rivals*.

2 O'Brien, "European Economic Development," 4, 16.

 | DOI:10.1163/9789004371781_008

eighteenth century disturbed the existing trade routes and alliances. In contrast to the far-off markets which procured exotic foodstuffs (coffee, sugar, cocoa, spices), both the Mediterranean and the Baltic, in close geographic proximity to the British Isles, furnished Britain predominantly with staples. The Baltic was almost the sole provider of naval stores; hemp, iron, timber, flax and tar were designated both for the naval and merchant fleets, upon which rested Britain's power and plenty. Their supply was inelastic despite several attempts to boost domestic production and find alternative resources, albeit of inferior quality, in America, Canada or Spain.[3] The high dependence of Britain on the Baltic market had economic and political implications during the Napoleonic Wars. Trade routes had to remain open at any cost, not just for the sake of commerce but also for the continuation of war and the maintenance of the fleet across all seas. Naval stores were coupled with significant grain imports mostly from Danzig, one of the greatest grain ports in Europe.[4] In addition to a considerable outward bulk trade, the Baltic was one of the biggest export markets for colonial produce and British manufactures.[5]

Geographic and environmental factors impinged decidedly on navigation in the Baltic. The duration of a passage e.g. to Sweden was relatively short, thus allowed several round voyages per year. Nevertheless, the Baltic trade was seasonal, limited usually from March to November. Winters were particularly heavy with storms, while ice completely blocked the northern ports and could damage ships or detain them in foreign ports for long spells, until the melt of the ice.

Navigation in the Mediterranean was less problematic with milder winters, while a long-established network of agents settled in the Mediterranean ports facilitated trade.[6] The different polities that surrounded the Mediterranean created a jigsaw with uneven and unique pieces, ranging from Western nation-states to multiethnic empires, with branches extending to Northern Europe, the Black Sea and the Middle East. The complicated political environment of the Mediterranean influenced British policy regarding shipping and trade in the region. These circumstances fostered diversity in business practices and required flexibility and adaptability to exploit the conditions of trade with each contracting party. British free traders, who mostly operated in the Western

---

3 Davey, "Securing the Sinews," 166–172.

4 Davis, *The Rise*, 218–219.

5 Mitchell and Deane, *Abstract*, 311.

6 While British communities of traders in the Mediterranean (e.g. Livorno, Messina, Minorca, Malta, Smyrna, Aleppo) have been thoroughly researched, it seems that British settlements in the Baltic ports have drawn less attention. There are however recent exceptions. See for example Karttunen, *Making a Communal World*.

parts, coexisted with the monopolistic Levant Company, which conducted trade, under favorable conditions, with the Ottoman Empire in the eastern Mediterranean.[7]

In terms of commodities, imports from the Mediterranean included raw wool and cotton, silk, dyes for the British textile industry and foodstuffs, such as grain, olive oil, wine, fresh and dried fruits (oranges, lemons, currants). British exports were primarily manufactured goods, i.e. woolen cloth dispatched in large quantities to the southeastern markets, and colonial re-exports. Dried and salted fish from the North Atlantic arrived in bulk in the Mediterranean and were directed to major redistribution hubs such as Livorno, Genoa and Malta.

Despite their idiosyncratic characteristics, both markets were integral parts of the British commercial network, each one covering specific needs in supply and demand. It is no coincidence that both seas became principal theatres of armed conflicts during the Napoleonic Wars, only to prove their economic and political significance to Britain.[8] Until 1807, the outbreak of war seemed to have had minor effects on British trade. When Napoleon targeted Britain's economic infrastructure by obstructing trade with the continent, an economic embargo was implemented on both European fronts, blocking the access of the Mediterranean coastline in the south and the influx of British goods to the European inland through the Baltic ports in the north.

The Berlin Decree and the Treaty of Tilsit in 1807, which united Russia and France against Britain, officially closed the Baltic to British ships. With the exception of Sweden, the sole British ally in the area until 1810, the rest of the adjacent countries (Denmark-Norway, Prussia, Russia) joined the Continental System transforming the Baltic into a hostile sea and jeopardizing British shipping and trade. The protection and survival of trade, which was indispensable and irreplaceable for Britain, was assigned to the Baltic fleet from 1808 until 1812, when the political alliances in the region changed once again: Napoleon attacked Russia ushering in the end of the embargo.[9] Given the circumstances, the continuation of trade was a challenging task that required recourse to alternative means: vessels were organized in large convoys, escorted by the Baltic fleet. The adverse weather conditions during the winter months, however, compelled the fleet to return to Britain every year; it was unsafe to remain

7 Wood, *A History*; Epstein, *The Early History*.

8 Galani, *British Shipping*, 4–6; Schneid, *Napoleon's Conquest*, 63–77; Knight, *Britain against Napoleon*, 17–18, 22; Kent, *War and Trade*.

9 For the Baltic fleet under the commandment of Sir James Saumarez, see Voelcker, *Admiral Saumarez*.

stationed in the Baltic, in close proximity to the enemy and disconnected from the home base due to storms and ice.[10]

In the Mediterranean, the attempt to inflict economic warfare was more complex as the sea could not be entirely closed to British ships. Firstly, Gibraltar, the gateway to the sea, was in British hands functioning as a naval base, which secured safe crossing into the Mediterranean. Furthermore, while the northern coastline succumbed to Napoleon closing the ports to British ships, in the southern and eastern Mediterranean the Ottoman Empire and its allegiant African Regencies continued bilateral trade with Britain. As in the Baltic, a sizeable Mediterranean fleet ploughed the sea protecting trade and engaging in several battles with the enemy.[11]

From a British perspective, the key objective was the continuation of trade in the Mediterranean, a traditional supplier of staple products like grain, olive oil and fruits and a keen importer of manufactured goods. Equally, the region was crucial in intercepting French expansionism in Southern Europe, Africa and Asia. The outbreak of the Revolutionary Wars and the occupation of Mediterranean ports and islands by Napoleon inevitably reintroduced the Mediterranean into the British political agenda. The maintenance of the Mediterranean market was vital not only to support British maritime supremacy against France but also to preserve a valuable supplier of grain to feed the industrialized masses at home and the military forces at the theatres of war.[12] The need to protect sea routes became imperative particularly after Napoleon's expedition in Egypt in 1798. This was regarded as a decisive step towards the French permeation into India, further menacing the British interest in the region.[13] The British political design for the Mediterranean was radicalized compared to the previous centuries and established a network of insular bases with a combined naval and maritime presence.

Despite the embargo at the northern and southern front, the official statistics on trade (Table 6.1) show the limited effectiveness of Napoleon's economic policy. Trade routes might have been disrupted but trade did not cease. Comparing the two markets, the Baltic seems more affected especially in 1811, when all the Baltic nations had joined the blockade, while the Mediterranean trade appears to be resilient, especially the exports which rose considerably in 1809 and 1811.

10 Davey, *War*, 81–2.

11 Knight and Wilcox, *Sustaining the Fleet*, 220–222; Rodger, *The Command of the Ocean*, 616.

12 See Hobsbawm, *Industry*, 112–131 for the significance of grain trade from the eastern Mediterranean and the Black Sea to Britain and Western Europe.

13 Duffy, "World-wide War," 196–7.

TABLE 6.1 Great Britain's external trade; official values (000£)

	North	Europe	South	Europe
	Imports	Exports	Imports	Exports
1795	4,106	10,045	2,566	2,412
1797	4,897	9,185	1,277	1,587
1799	7,292	7,939	1,842	2,099
1801	7,235	14,442	2,274	3,545
1803	5,346	11,372	3,527	3,968
1805	7,137	13,026	2,872	2,440
1807	5,154	9,412	2,819	3,278
1809	5,660	13,666	3,935	10,055
1811	2,652	2,358	1,685	12,606
1813*	–	–	–	–
1815	4,986	19,860	3,244	9,071
1817	4,897	16,988	3,100	9,529

NOTE: The values for 1813 are missing.
SOURCE: MITCHELL, *BRITISH HISTORICAL STATISTICS*, P. 495

While the official statistics offer a clear, yet incomplete, picture of trade during the war-years, they do not convey information about British shipping in the Baltic and the Mediterranean. This paper aims to co-examine the effects of warfare on British maritime activity in these two European markets, thus raising the employment of British merchant vessels in hostile waters, among the enemy fleet and privateers, as one of the key issues.

The impact of the economic warfare on the belligerent parties during the Napoleonic Wars has been long debated.[14] Evidence, presented here, from the Baltic and the Mediterranean seem to corroborate the rather limited effect of Napoleon's Continental System to British shipping. It is noteworthy that in both cases neutrality was a fundamental precondition for unhindered trade, placing in an advantageous position those who were not caught in the rivalries.[15] Neutral carriers, either local or external, benefited from the rising freights and entered the market to claim a share.[16] In the Mediterranean, it was

14 Heckscher, *The Continental System*. See also O' Rourke, *The worldwide economic impact;* Crouzet, *L'Économie Britannique*.

15 Galani, "Caught between Empires".

16 Andersen and Voth, "The Grapes of War"; Galani, "The Napoleonic Wars."

local carriers such as the Greeks of the Ottoman Empire, neutrals to the Anglo-French intermittent wars, who undertook trade from the Levant during the upheaval.[17] The Baltic seems to have followed a similar pattern. Hostilities and the fear of privateering drove the British to recourse to the local shipping market. The disruption of trade and the inelastic demand for Baltic imports increased substantially freight rates turning the Baltic into a profitable, yet dangerous, market. Local shipowners and mariners accommodated British interests and sustained the flow of trade in a mutually advantageous arrangement.[18]

1 Electronic Resources: A Macroscopic Approach

Examining maritime traffic in an extended area, in fact, a whole sea, is naturally a rather complicated endeavor and it is heavily dependent on the availability of data. The macroscopic study of shipping to a number of ports and over a long time span demands lengthy, uninterrupted and detailed archival series that allow quantification through the compilation of electronic databases. The comparative study of British shipping in the Baltic and the Mediterranean in this paper draws upon electronic databases that facilitate the quantitative and qualitative analysis of maritime traffic. With regard to British ships in the Baltic, all references to British ships crossing the Sound in the late eighteenth century were extracted from STRO. The Mediterranean, however, does not benefit from an equivalent comprehensive and systematic source. Due to the limitation of the available data, the existing literature has employed a number of different, sporadic sources to address British shipping in the late eighteenth century. In several cases, British maritime presence was inferred through French archives, although these were handled with caution, as the accuracy of the recorded data was suspect especially during the period of the Anglo-French conflict.[19] The primary sources that have been used so far ranged from customs ledgers to consular reports from ports, ship manifests, Mediterranean passes, sanitary records and admiralty records.[20] Therefore, data constraints have condemned

17 Galani, *British Shipping*, 293–309.

18 Ryan, "Trade with the Enemy," 128–132 and Ryan, "The Defence of British Trade," 463–4.

19 For instance, the size of the European fleets extracted from the French consular reports in Romano "Per una valutazione."

20 On specific ports, see for example Carrière, *Negoçiants Marsellais*, with port entries deriving from the sanitary records; Katsiardi-Hering, *Η ελληνική παροικία της Τεργέστης*, with data on ship movements drawn from consular reports in the state archive of Venice. For shipping between Britain and Malta from 1800 to 1815 see D'Angelo, *Mercanti Inglesi in Sicilia*, based on the custom ledgers from The National Archives. On a specific time span see

the eighteenth- and early nineteenth-century British shipping to a disconnected, patchwork study, which allows mere glimpses into the history of British engagement in the Mediterranean.

The state of knowledge and our understanding of British shipping is greatly supplemented by systematically employing the *Lloyd's List* as an historical resource. The *List* has the unique advantage of being an uninterrupted and unbiased archival source that provides a complete time series of British shipping around the world for more than two hundred years. The second half of the eighteenth century, covered in 25 volumes, is currently housed in the Guildhall Library, London. The comprehensive and consistent nature of the source, the distinctive layout of the paper, the uniform type of data recorded and the style in which data appeared did not change over the period under study. It should be underscored that *Lloyd's List*, a specialist publication that remains in circulation to the present day, was tailored to the needs of a shipping industry that was flourishing in the City of London in the late eighteenth century.[21]

In the City, in the absence of designated business offices, coffee houses turned into the ideal places for merchants and shipowners to conduct business, to collect information about vessels and cargoes and meet with merchants, shippers and underwriters to contract for insurance for their ventures.[22] Among the coffee houses, Lloyd's held a prominent position thanks to an organized network of correspondents reporting regularly on ship movements. Furthermore, *Lloyd's List* developed a close relationship with the Admiralty. The relationship was demonstrated especially throughout the years of war and offered an additional guarantee of the accuracy of the intelligence recorded. These traits explain the increasing impact of the *List* on the maritime community of the Metropolis.

Lloyd's List was published twice per week – on Tuesdays and Fridays – with a quarterly subscription of 3 shillings paid at the Bar of the Coffee House.[23] The first surviving issue dates back to 1740.[24] The front page of the publication contains auxiliary information about the regular mail services, the course of exchange in London and a number of port cities, the prices of gold and silver, of banks' stocks, bonds, annuities, lotteries etc. The *List* also included reports

Fayle, "The Employment." Fayle presents British ship movements in a number of various markets for a single year, 1792. Unfortunately, his sources are not discussed in his paper.

21 Kynaston, *City of London*, 3–8, 117–129.

22 Cowan, *The Social Life of Coffee*, 171–172.

23 Cameron and Farndon, *Scenes from Sea and City*, 5.

24 All earlier issues from 1734 appear to have been destroyed in the great fire of the Royal Exchange in 1838.

on sailors' casualties, damages, shipwrecks and prizes that were of a special interest to the shipowners and shippers.

Nevertheless, the principal information *Lloyd's List* disseminated was the circulation of ships in an actual list, the *Marine List*, from which the publication took its name. Each ship was recorded by its name and the name of its captain. The reports were organized in two categories: "British Ports" and "Irish and Foreign ports", based on the port where the vessel was recorded. The first group composes of a detailed register of all ships arriving at British ports from a number of ports of departure worldwide. On several occasions, ships' clearings (departures) were also recorded, although this practice was not always consistent. The second part of the list recorded sightings of British vessels abroad. Under the list of foreign ports, besides the Irish, one can identify ports of North America and Canada, the West Indies, the Baltic, the Mediterranean and the East Indies.

Due to its nature and consistency, the *List* was suitable for the construction of an electronic database, extracting from the plethora of data recorded in the thousands of its pages all references to Mediterranean ports.[25] These were recorded either as a) ports of report i.e. the port where the information about ship movements was collected or b) declared ports of clearing or arrival of vessels.[26] In the final product, which includes approximately 10,000 entries of ship movements, the extracted data originate from twenty-nine Mediterranean ports, including Spanish, French, Italian, North African and Levantine ports and entrepôts. In the database, each entry includes the date, the name of the ship and the captain, the port where it was recorded (e.g. the port of call), the port of its departure (e.g. the port from where the ship arrives) and – when stated – the port of its intended destination.

The information recorded in *Lloyd's List* does not include the vessel's flag, which would have allowed a direct, although not necessarily infallible, identification of British shipping. In the absence of such an indication, the only solid criterion that has been followed in the construction of the database is to infer nationality from the names of both ships and captains. Names that are obviously non-British, for example, Scandinavian, French or Greek, have been omitted from the database to allow an as accurate as possible identification of the British vessels. It is intuitive that vessels of British interest would

25 I have constructed a database for the purpose of my doctoral thesis. The database is not currently open to public access. For a detailed analysis on the source and the methodology of the electronic database see Galani, *British Shipping*, 64–80.

26 A typical entry in the database is for example: the ship *Mercury*, captained by Pearce entering Stangate Creek from Livorno on the 4th of January 1791 (*Lloyd's List*, no. 2261).

clearly be the primary objective of the collectors of intelligence on behalf of *Lloyd's* across the British and foreign ports. Comparative data, where they exist, for foreign ports of record, makes this particularly evident. Why would, for instance, a correspondent established in Livorno in the service of *Lloyd's* record only one ship on a single day, when it is most certain from the actual traffic of Livorno shows that many more called at the port on the given day?[27] The only reasonable explanation is that the correspondent was committed to report only British-owned vessels or, more broadly, vessels of British interest.

1.1 *Shipping to the Baltic and the Mediterranean*

British trade in the Baltic was a flourishing business in the eighteenth century as is shown by the number of passages recorded in the Sound Toll Registers. The Danish Sound gave access to a wide market with several nodes in the British trade network. St. Petersburg appears as the most frequented port, followed by Klaipeda, Riga, Gdańsk and Copenhagen. On the other leg of the voyage, London carried 30 per cent of the overall traffic. However, determined by geographic factors, the Baltic trade was largely a business of the northern and northeastern ports: the Scottish ports of Leith and Dundee, Hull, Newcastle, Liverpool, Yarmouth and King's Lynn shared, in principal, the rest of the trade.[28]

The topography of shipping was quite different for the Mediterranean. Once again, London stands out as the primary port of call representing 56 per cent of ship movements for the late eighteenth century. London in effect included a number of different ports on the Thames, where ships would anchor to load and unload their cargoes: the most common ports of call for ships arriving from the Mediterranean were Stangate Creek and Gravesend, representing 18 per cent and 33 per cent respectively of the overall traffic. In addition to London, the Mediterranean trade was more of a southern business: Portsmouth, Plymouth, Falmouth represent each around 10 per cent of the traffic. The northern ports were of trivial importance, while Dublin and Cork stand out from Ireland albeit with a minor overall percentage. On the other end of the journey, the most frequent ports for British shipping represent all parts of the Mediterranean:

27 Comparison is feasible for Livorno, as detailed evidence of the daily traffic is available from the Quarantine records of the port. From the *Lloyd's List* no. 10434 it is known, for example, that on the 8th October 1802 the correspondent from Livorno had reported only the ship *Jane*, captain Kelly, which had declared Leith as her port of departure. By cross-checking the same date (allowing as well a few days for the report to reach London) we see a number of deep-sea vessels entering Livorno, with American, Russian, French and Greek-Ottoman flags. Archivio di Stato di Livorno, Magistrato poi Dipartimento di Sanità marittima, F. 704/164v–165r.

28 This overview is based on processed data from STRO.

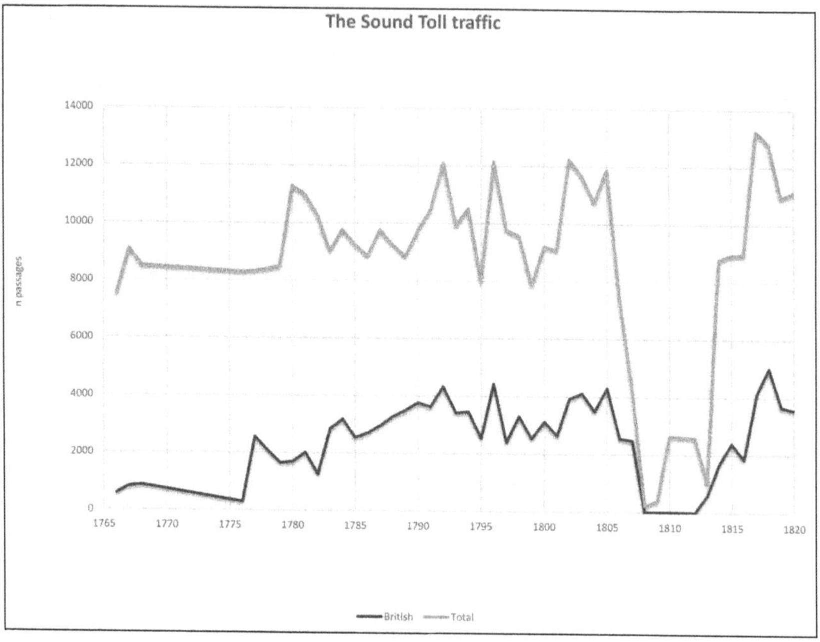

GRAPH 6.1 The traffic through the Sound (British and total passages), 1765–1820
SOURCE: STRO

from Gibraltar, to the Spanish coast (Alicante), to Malta and the Italian peninsula (Livorno, Messina), the Ionian Islands (Zante) and the Levant (Smyrna). During the Napoleonic Wars, in the early nineteenth century, there is a tightening of the British network around protected havens, such as Malta.[29]

Charting British vessels through the Sound offers a macroscopic view of British shipping in the region (Graph 6.1) and allows quantitative interpretations. Firstly, British passages accounted for approximately 30 per cent of the overall Baltic traffic in the late 18th century and demonstrated an upward trend during the last decades.

The decline of 1780–1783 may be provoked by the First League of Armed Neutrality during the American War of Independence.[30] The Baltic nations (Russia, Denmark-Norway, Sweden, Prussia) formed an alliance to protect neutral shipping from the Royal Navy, which indiscriminately searched neutral ships to restrict French contraband. This coalition was not proactively hostile to Britain and thus British trade soon picked up. The Second League of

29 Galani, *British Shipping*, 87–104. This overview is based on processed data from *Lloyd's List*.

30 Rodger, *The Command of the Ocean*, 347–348.

Armed Neutrality, in 1800–1801, also had only minor impact on British trade. However, as the Anglo-French wars were well under way, Britain considered the League as a coalition with France and thus attacked Denmark in the first Battle of Copenhagen, to ensure that the Danish Sound would remain open for the vital Baltic trade.

Since the outbreak of the Napoleonic Wars, until the treaty of Tilsit and the Continental System in 1807 British trade remained active. Despite the hostilities with France and its allies, the Baltic was used to distribute British exports to the Continent. The most turbulent period for British trade was marked by the second Battle of Copenhagen, which spurred a series of military actions at sea. From 1807 to 1812, when the Franco-Russian relations deteriorated leading to Napoleon's invasion to Russia and the coalition of Britain with Russia and Sweden, Britain was at war with the Baltic nations: ports were closed; trade routes were disturbed and Danish privateers targeted British ships, while Bornholm stood as their primary stronghold and prize market.[31]

An overview of the total traffic through the Sound drawn from STRO is quite revealing of the situation in the Baltic. It is evident that the outbreak of war caused a dramatic drop in shipping altogether. While thousands of ships crossed the Straits in the previous years, upon the imposition of the embargo only a few hundred (226 and 401 in 1808, 1809 respectively) registered at the Sound. Within this grim situation, British ships were inevitably hit harder by the economic warfare.

However, this does not seem to be the complete picture. Time of crisis requires flexibility and adaptability and therefore the British searched for alternative trade routes, exactly as they did in the Mediterranean at the same time. British ships entered the Baltic from the North Sea through a second passage to the Sound, the Great Belt, a traffic flow, which seems to escape the available statistical data. Although the Belt was much longer, largely uncharted for British ships and fairly dangerous to navigate, it was considered a safer passage, as vessels were not in such close proximity to the Danish coast and guns as they were at the Sound.[32]

Besides shifting routes, large convoys were organized and escorted by the Royal Navy for the protection of vessels. In addition, trade seems to have been carried on foreign vessels, mostly on local carriers, bearing false papers that concealed any link to the British market.[33] Despite the declared animosity, German, Scandinavian, Dutch and Russian ships were in fact licensed to carry

31 Ryan, "The Defense of British Trade," 444–448.

32 Davey, *War*, 77–81.

33 Ryan, "The Defence of British Trade", 443, 463–466.

Baltic products to Britain to circumvent the economic embargo and sustain the trade. Paradoxically, foreign, even enemy ships were protected by British naval convoys to the frustration of British shipowners, who were *de facto* expelled from the Baltic market. Shipowners at Hull, Scarborough, Newcastle and London condemned the ever-growing interference of foreigners in the British trade and sought to encourage the domestic shipping industry. They proposed that Bornholm and Ertholmene, a constellation of small islands in the Baltic, should be seized by the Royal Navy and transformed into a protected redistribution hub, with a maritime and naval function.[34] However, the heavy winters and the potential isolation of the garrison in the Baltic undermined the efficiency of such plan.

The proposal was in alignment with a broader British strategy of insular expansion, which had been implemented successfully in other seas. In the words of G. F Leckie, "we must therefore sometimes conquer, and if we are excluded for a time from the continent of Europe, form for ourselves an insular empire, complete in its parts and sufficient to itself".[35] In this light, Heligoland in the North Sea, off the German coast, was captured by the British in 1807 and was used as a naval base and a center of smuggling. But in fact, there is no greater example than Malta in the Mediterranean. During the Napoleonic Wars, in 1800, the British strategically occupied Malta as a naval and mercantile base.[36] Facing the Sicilian granary, Malta was the ideal place for the stationing of troops as well as an entrepôt for the conduct of trade across the Mediterranean. In fact, Malta held a large share of the eastern trade: silk, cotton, olive oil, dry fruits poured in from the Levant and were then re-exported to the British Isles.[37] The volume of imports was so large that the contemporaries noted that there were not enough warehouses to store them. Indicatively in 1812, trade in Malta alone represented 12.2 per cent of total British exports.[38]

The role of Malta in the British maritime network became increasingly important at the turn of the nineteenth century when British interests adjusted to the changing economic reality in the Mediterranean: the rigid monopoly of the Levant Company had to be loosened in order to preserve trade with the Ottoman Empire.[39] While local carriers, non-Muslim Ottoman subjects (mostly Greeks) had permeated the Levant Company carrying goods westward on behalf of British merchants, the Company's bylaws demanded that

34 Ryan, "Trade with the Enemy," 126–132.

35 Leckie, *An Historical Survey*.

36 Gregory, *Malta*, 212–225, 256–264.

37 The National Archives, CO 158/1, p. 19v–20; Crouzet, *L'Économie Britannique*, pp. 305–307.

38 Crouzet, *L'Économie Britannique*, 697.

39 Galani, *British Shipping*, 293–309.

all non-British vessels should first call upon Malta.[40] In the aftermath of the Napoleonic period, Malta was abandoned, as the island's occupation had served the special conditions of war.

The restructuring of trade routes appears far more successful in the Mediterranean than in the Baltic. The British network was tightened around a few protected islands: Malta, Sicily and the Ionian Islands. Strategically located on the crossroads of trade, they were hosting the garrisons and acted as redistribution centers. The continuation of British trade in the Mediterranean was attributed largely to the flexibility and adaptability to the new conditions. In the Baltic, on the other hand, the climatic conditions as well as the lack of friendly or neutral powers placed Britain to a far more difficult position.

Contrary to the regular trade, the victualing of the fleet, e.g. the transportation of provisions and ammunitions, as well as soldiers and prisoners could not be entrusted to foreign vessels. In order to meet the demand, the Victualing Board appealed to the open market rather than following the Spanish model of private monopoly or the French model of state concentration.[41] While private merchants and shipowners were profiting from the service, they provisioned the war industry. The State also benefited at more than one level, merging private with public interests. Contracting with individuals was reinforcing the State's bargaining power, while at the same time it sustained economic activity during wartime. The explicit Admiralty policy to organize centrally the victualing of the fleet from London was implemented in both the Baltic and the Mediterranean. In the former, it was a rather discontinuous, seasonal endeavor as the fleet returned to Britain over the winter months. In the latter, it appears smoother and beneficial: it promoted a second, war-induced, market for British shipowners to carry victuals and stores and sustained British shipping actively and productively despite the war.[42]

Graph 6.2 shows the trend of the passages of all vessels engaged in the Anglo-Mediterranean shipping based on data collected from *Lloyd' List*. These are one-direction voyages and not round-trips. The black column indicates only the arrivals, while the grey column includes the outbound voyages, displaying all passages.

The analysis is based on the homebound passages, as the coverage of British ports in *Lloyd's List* was more comprehensive. Clearings, which are included in the second column, are a compelling indicator of the dynamics

40 *By-Laws of the Levant Company, 1812*, 14.

41 Torres Sanchez, "The Triumph of the Fiscal-Military State;" Knight and Wilcox, *Sustaining the Fleet*, 5.

42 Galani, *British Shipping*, 104–115.

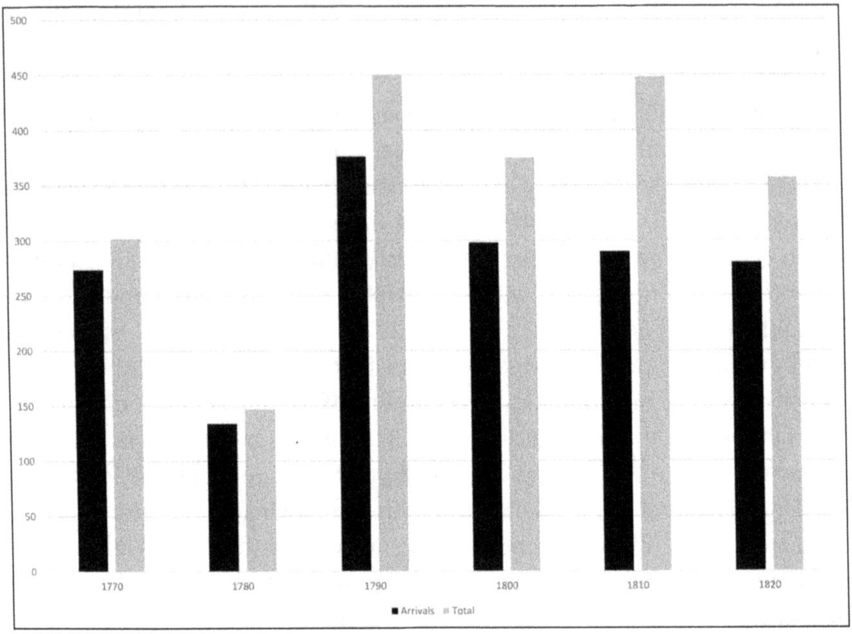

GRAPH 6.2 British ship movements related to the Mediterranean (entries and clearances); Data collected from British ports

SOURCE: PROCESSED DATA FROM THE AUTHOR'S *LLOYD'S LIST* DATABASE, 1770–1820

of the Mediterranean market among shipowners. Although inbound ships could reflect the return to home waters after a long voyage and sojourn in the Mediterranean, the number sailing off in a particular year should indicate the fear, or as it seems in this case, the lack of it, for shipping in the Mediterranean. The divergence between the two columns, which signifies the number of clearings, marks its highest value during the war. The 158 merchant ships recorded heading east of Gibraltar in 1810 suggest a vibrant shipping market. Beyond the general trend, a closer look in the years of war shows an increasing number of clearings that were recorded in *Lloyd's List* compared to the years of peace; in other words, more British ships were taking the risk of sailing to the Mediterranean disregarding the ongoing war.

It should be emphasized that the highest value in the figure (450 vessels) coincides with the eve of the French Wars in 1790, which ushered in an era of increased shipping activity in the Mediterranean. In the aftermath of the Napoleonic Wars, in 1820, there is a trend of stabilization rather than a steep decline. This comes in contrast to the existing literature, which describes an excess of ships that had been built during the war and were underutilized in the following spell, leading to an abrupt fall in freight rates at the termination of conflicts.[43] It seems that the figure in 1820 remains high, higher than the equivalent in the beginning of the period in 1770. This was due to the ascendant grain market of the Black Sea, which would attract ever more British shipping in the Mediterranean in the nineteenth century. In terms of economic geography, the Black Sea belonged to the "greater Mediterranean" and the sea routes by which grain was carried to Britain's industrial population, were inevitably traversing the Mediterranean, interwoven with its local trade and shipping.[44]

The lowest volume of shipping in 1780 is an indisputable proof of the interconnection among shipping markets, as developments in the Atlantic imposed a heavy cost on the Mediterranean. There was an increasing wartime demand for seaborne transportation to sustain the British forces in North America, which redirected resources from the Mediterranean. At the same time, at the height of the American War of Independence, the British mercantile marine was raided by the combined forces of Spain and France causing the loss of more than 50 vessels, with an estimated cost of £1.5 million.[45]

What is evident from the above is that the French and Napoleonic Wars did not have a negative impact on the number of the British merchantmen sailing in the Mediterranean. Contrary to the pervasive idea in the literature of a recession of the Mediterranean market due to economic and military warfare, the archival evidence shows no drop in the overall shipping activity.[46] On the contrary, *Lloyd's List* seems to indicate that the outbreak of war provided a fertile ground for profit maximization in the shipping business. Although war called for a shift in business strategies for British traders and shipowners, the data from the *Lloyd's List* demonstrate a significant rise in shipping between 1770 and the war period. It should be taken into account that the figure captures only the shuttle voyages between the British Isles and the Mediterranean ports. Intra-Mediterranean shipping eludes these statistics. However, archival evidence from the British emporium of Livorno shows a considerable participation in the internal Mediterranean shipping

43 Palmer, *Politics*, 1–2; Harley, "Ocean freight rates, 854; Stopford, *Maritime Economics*, 105–106.

44 Őzveren, "The Black Sea World," 61–5.

45 Hodgson, *Lloyd's of London*, 54.

46 Crouzet, *L'Économie Britannique*, 143–149 and Acemoglu, Jonson and Robinson, "The Rise of Europe," 546, 550. The authors contrast the volume of Atlantic and Mediterranean trade and demonstrate a great divergence after 1700. Atlantic trade is defined as the trade of West Europeans with the New World and Asia and encompasses colonial and slave trade. Andersen and Voth, "The Grapes of War," 5–27 compare the ascendant Danish fleet to the belligerent fleets operating in the Mediterranean.

market. This allowed both full employment for a longer period and an additional income for shipowners.[47]

Facing the military and economic challenges of the Napoleonic era, Britain had to protect shipping and trade in two crucial European markets, and at the same time support the fleet and wage war successfully. The applied policy involved a series of measures combining public and private interest: the readjustment of trade routes to avoid enemy vessels and blocked ports, the occupation of strategic points, most likely islands, to create a safe zone for the collection and diffusion of commodities and the support of military operations in an otherwise hostile market. Trade was protected further through the organization of convoys, though this was in practice an inescapable compromise: safety was weighed against the glutting of the market, upon the mass arrival of ships, and the subsequently reduced prices of British products.

Given the circumstances, the quest for allies was intrinsic for both war and trade. If the seas were closed to British ships, then Britain had to recourse to the assistance of foreigners. Neutral ships, either local or external carriers, were chartered to carry British trade.[48] In the Mediterranean, non-Muslim Ottoman subjects replaced the British in the ports of the Levant carrying products westwards to redistribution hubs from where British ships undertook the homebound journey. In effect, the permeation of foreign vessels eroded the long-established rigid monopoly of the Levant Company, leading to its invalidation long before it was revoked officially. In the Baltic, counter-intuitively, Britain employed not only foreign but even enemy vessels to ensure the preservation of trade to the detriment of British shipowners.

The trade statistics on the two markets capture the repercussions of war, and the Baltic seems to have been hit harder than the Mediterranean. While trade routes and networks were reshuffled, shipping followed a different course. The transportation and victualing of the Royal Navy in the Mediterranean and the Baltic was a considerable boost to shipping. Provisions were organized centrally for the different theatres of war and the Admiralty resorted to the private shipping market for the necessary carrying tonnage. The policy was common in the Baltic and the Mediterranean although its implementation did not bear the same fruits.

Based on the data from *Lloyd's List*, it seems that the transport service reinvigorated the Mediterranean market. Instead of a repressed maritime traffic, the number of passages increased during the years of war. Besides the traditional trade, a war-induced shipping market drew more vessels in the

47 Galani, *British Shipping*, 137–151.

48 Marzagalli, "American Shipping," Galani, "The Napoleonic Wars."

Mediterranean. Furthermore, the Victualing Board appealed to British merchants established in the Mediterranean for the *in situ* procurement of fresh provisions. Water, fresh meat, citrus fruits and biscuits were the main foodstuffs bought locally. This practice further encouraged intra-Mediterranean trade, which offered an additional income to British vessels and merchants. The example of a British merchant in Sicily illustrates the new reality brought in by war. The Liverpudlian John Woodhouse had settled in Marsala in 1773.[49] He was soon involved in wine trading, which was flourishing in the region. By 1794, the business had expanded and Woodhouse built his first winery integrating his business vertically from trade to production. It was during the war that the business thrived, as contracts were signed with the Royal Navy, and in particular Nelson's fleet in Malta, for the supply of wine to the fleet.[50] Sicily along with Sardinia, Gibraltar, Minorca, Malta and Cyprus were the main suppliers of fresh provisions.[51]

On the contrary, the Baltic fleet depended less on local provisions compared to the Mediterranean. In a harsh environment, surrounded by hostile nations, the fleet could not rely much on the local market but for livestock. The sole provider was Sweden, e.g. the ports of Karlskrona, Stockholm and Gothenburg, which did not always have abundant surplus to cover, on demand, the needs of the Royal Navy. Furthermore, the limited pool of suppliers weakened competition and local provisions cost dear. The so far available archival sources suggest that this intra-Baltic market did not greatly contribute to shipping. Navigation within the Baltic was a dangerous venture and there is evidence that local supplies were carried on warships rather than merchantmen.[52]

The shipping market in the Mediterranean seems to have better endured the adversities of war compared to the Baltic. The upsurge in shipping activity was driven less by the local market, which appears to have been susceptible to disruptions by war, and more by the market for provisioning the troops stationed in the Mediterranean. The rise in shipping was centered on ports with both commercial and naval functions, such as Malta, Sicily and the Ionian Islands.[53] Effective protection of these ports by the Royal Navy facilitated navigation and trade.

49 Bottari, "Relations between Sicily and Great Britain," 86–88. Woodhouse is to the present day related to the Marsala wine-trade.

50 For further examples of local contractors, see Knight and Wilcox, *Sustaining the Fleet*, 65.

51 McDonald, *Feeding Nelson's Fleet*, 63.

52 Davey, *War*, 193, 200–201.

53 Duffy, "World-wide War," 196–197; Mackesy, *The War in the Mediterranean*, 7–17, 105–113, 351–358.

The Baltic seems to have been a challenging market especially during the Continental System. Despite the obstacles, the re-organization of trade and shipping by the Admiralty was successful in accommodating the needs of the Baltic fleet. However, as the available material from the Sound implies, it does not seem to have encouraged the private shipping market to support maritime economic activity in the region during the war. The geographic and climatic conditions, the surrounding hostile nations and the lack of British bases across the sea hampered the circulation of vessels, products and troops and, most likely, deprived the British from the benefits of a war-induced economic activity in the Baltic. Even though Napoleon's embargo was implemented in both seas in similar ways, its effectiveness varied: geopolitics and the economic particularities of each market allowed for this diversification.

PART 3

Source Critical Arguments

CHAPTER 7

Cross-checking STRO with the French *Balance du Commerce* Data

Loïc Charles and Guillaume Daudin

1 Introduction

During the eighteenth century, Europe set the cultural, political and economic conditions for its entry in the industrial era. While the role of international trade has been considered for a long time as a minor factor in the industrial revolution, the focus of economic history has changed somewhat during the last two decades. The emergence of a global perspective in economic history has led prominent scholars to account for the important role of international trade in Europe's rise to dominance of other world regions.[1] However, whereas extra-European trade is comparatively well known and has been the object of recent syntheses,[2] intra-European trade has largely been neglected. The scarcity of works on foreign trade statistics of pre-industrial times is all the more unfortunate as external trade flows are the single economic data that most early modern states have collected with care. Indeed, the first attempts at measuring foreign trade regularly can be dated back to the late seventeenth century. From 1696 on, the English crown was able to collect a continuous series of customs data and release a yearly evaluation of the English balance of trade. The French royal administration created the *Bureau de la balance du commerce* in 1713. Its task was to produce a yearly document containing a detailed outline of French external trade as well as a calculation of its general balance. There was a pan-European movement towards the more extensive and better measurement of external trade throughout the eighteenth century, with various countries gathering the same kind of data through their central administrations. Annual series have been located for Sweden from 1732, Hamburg from 1733, the Austrian Netherlands from 1759, Milan in 1762, 1769, 1778 and 1791, Venice from 1769/1770 onward, Portugal in 1776–77, 1783, 1789,

1 Allen, *The industrial Revolution*; Nye, *War, Wine, and Taxes*; Pomeranz, *The Great Divergence*.
2 O'Brien and Escosura, eds., "The Costs,"; Roitman, Pétré-Grenouilleau and Emmer, eds., *A Deus Ex Machina Revisited*.

 | DOI:10.1163/9789004371781_009

and from 1796 onward, Spain from 1778 onward, and so on.[3] Research on trade of the British Isles is more advanced than for other countries. A recent book has renewed the research on Scottish trade in the eighteenth century.[4] A team coordinated by David Jacks, Kevin O'Rourke and Alan Taylor is currently gathering data on English and British trade from 1696 to the early twentieth century. The authors of the present chapter engaged in a project – TOFLIT18 – financed by the French National Research Agency (*Agence Nationale de la Recherche*). In the context of this project (https://toflit18.hypotheses.org), a database is developed that will contain information not only on the national trade flows registered in the *Balance du Commerce*, but also at the regional/port level.

Despite this spurt of recent interest in early modern trade statistics, of which the (re)discovery of the above-mentioned statistical series provides ample proof, economic historians consider them difficult to use. Issues of under-registration of trade because of smuggling and bad registration practices seem to make these data unreliable. One way to get around these criticisms is to compare two trade data sets and see whether they actually depict the same economic trends or not. Many of these data sources cover the same trade flows, registered by different authorities. Therefore, the information gathered by these institutions often differed: some, like STRO,[5] measure trade flows by quantity, others, like the French bureau of the balance of trade (further: FBT), by value.

Still, French Baltic trade as registered by the Danish authorities in the Sound should mirror reports of the French authorities. Previous studies have provided such a crosschecking, either between the Sound and other places,[6] between different countries,[7] or even between different sources in the same country.[8] Most of these studies present rather pessimistic results. This may be due in part to the rudimentary methods applied to the data. Even today, in the era

3 Charles and Daudin, eds, *18th Century International Trade Statistics*.

4 Rössner, *Scottish Trade*.

5 The authors thank Jan Willem Veluwenkamp and Ubo Kooijinga for sharing the Sound Toll Register online project, Werner Scheltjens for sharing his work on commodity names and units of measurement based on STRO, INED for funding some translations, and Alexandre Aubourg for stellar research assistance with units of measurement in the *Balance du commerce* database. This paper is part of the research project TOFLIT18 «Transformations of the French Economy through the Lense of International Trade, 1716–1821». As mentioned above, this project has been funded by the Agence Nationale de la Recherche (ANR-12-BSH1-0005-03).

6 Daudin and Pourchasse, "Cross-Checking"; Ojala and Karvonen, "Assessing the Reliability".

7 Rössner, *Scottish Trade*; Charles, Coenen, and Daudin, "Comparing Early Trade Statistics"; Moreira et al., "Comparing Trade Flows".

8 Rössner, *Scottish Trade*.

of modern and standardized statistics reconciliation between mirror trade flows is still an issue, so perfect correspondence between eighteenth-century data should not be expected. Accordingly, our objective is more general: we are looking for some common trends and structures that may be identified. At the very least, we believe that our exercise in comparison provides new information about the datasets and present directions for further research. A first, preliminary study on the subject, in which a number of goods was excluded because they were not translated from the original Danish, gave deceptive results.[9] For the present analysis, however, we have worked with an enhanced dataset based on STRO and a bigger set of flows from the French side. We do not expect a perfect fit of the information given by the two databases; we are barely looking for common elements between STRO and FBT. We have applied a comparative method to both datasets in order to better understand the nature of the information they contain and to assess how economic historians could use them meaningfully.[10] Another purpose of our work is to provide new tools and methods for the further development of comparative analyses of early modern trade databases.

In the next section, we briefly discuss the features of the French dataset compared to STRO. In the third section, we present the method we followed in order to have them talk to each other. In the fourth section, we critically assess the results of our comparative analysis.

2 The French Dataset

In France, a *bureau de la balance du commerce* was created in 1713.[11] The bureau was a small unit: in addition to its director, originally one of the directors of the General Farms (Fr. *Directeurs des fermes générales*), there were no more than four clerks for most of the period.[12] The *bureau* was initially put under the direct supervision of the Director of Trade, the most important official in the French

9 Daudin and Pourchasse, "Cross-Checking".

10 The data at the regional and port level, which is gathered in the TOFLIT18–project, is much more precise and closer to the kind of information given in STRO. Therefore, we are expecting to reach a much better fit for the two data sets in the future.

11 The following paragraphs are mostly based on Charles and Daudin, "La Collecte," 128–55. This is the most recent and detailed reference on the bureau, but additional information on the bureau and the data it produced can also be found in: Morineau, "La Balance," 170–233; Tarrade, *Le Commerce*; Dardel, *Navires et marchandises*.

12 In Ancien Régime France, taxes were farmed to private companies. The most important of them, which held a quasi-monopoly on taxes, was the General Farms company. It was in particular in charge of the collection of the various custom duties.

economic administration after the controller general of finances, who accommodated the bureau in his Parisian house. Until 1781, the bureau held the task of computing the data and presenting them once a year to the controller general and the Council of commerce in a synthetic form, the *Objet général*. There was no significant change in the structure until the beginning of the 1780s. Necker, the new controller general of finances, wanted the bureau to become a more general center of economic expertise. In the following years, its workforce rose steadily to seven in 1784 and more than a dozen in 1787. At that time, the bureau of the balance of trade was able to conduct wider economic surveys, most notably to prepare and, subsequently, evaluate the consequences the trade treaties France made with the newly born United States (1778), Russia (1785), and England (1786). However, the piling up of reforms and new tasks had a major negative effect: the bureau was overloaded and was no longer able to produce the French balance of trade within a reasonable time period. The French balance for 1782 was only released in 1786 and the balances for 1783 to 1786 were never completed.[13] The bureau disappeared in 1791, altogether with the Council of commerce and most of the Ancien Régime's former administration, swept away by the revolutionary government.

How did the bureau create the data set that was consigned in the *Objet general*? At the local level, some 230 General Farms bureaus gathered the information. They sent to Paris an extract containing a list of goods and their total quantities imported or exported at the end of each month. The bureau then treated these extracts: it added up the extracts by province (*généralités*) and proceeded to standardize the quantity units. Sometimes prices were recorded by the General Farms' employees, but not systematically. As the bureau wished to compute values rather than quantities, it sent to each province's chamber of commerce (or to the intendant when there was none) the list of goods asking the representatives of the merchants to provide price estimates or to check the price given by the General Farms local bureaus.[14] Economic historians have shown that prices included in the *Objet général* showed no systematic bias and were close enough to international prices (as given by the Amsterdam market price).[15]

13 Before 1782, usually it took less than two years to complete the *Objet général*.

14 It must be noted that the bureau asked an average price or "just value" and was not concerned with registering the short-term variations, see Nederlandsch Economisch-Historisch Archief, Pierre Bruyard papers, files 76–77.

15 See Morineau, "La Balance," 183–184; Tarrade, *Le Commerce*, 770–771; Dardel, *Navires et marchandises*, 20.

Up to 1745, the *Objet général* consisted of several folders (*cahiers*), one for each *généralité*.[16] In these books, goods were classified in alphabetical order with their respective value – the quantities were also mentioned for some goods. Each entry was disaggregated according to the geographical area or country of origin or destination of the goods.[17] From the year 1746 to 1751 included, the books were made according to each country instead of the regional entity (likewise, inside each book, the goods were listed by *généralité* instead of country). Finally, from 1752 to 1780, it took a stable design: the whole trade was listed alphabetically according to the name of the good, with an indication of its origin or destination; information on the *généralité* was not recorded anymore.[18] In the *Objet général*, the flows of trade were given only in value from 1752 to 1770, but quantities were also recorded systematically from 1771 onward.[19] Following the 1781 reform, some changes occurred and, among other things, the list of countries was changed. These changes, however, were marginal, at least for the issue taken up in this paper.[20]

The database used in this paper includes about 27 years, from 1750 to 1789 with occasional lapses, of French external trade. It includes a total of more than 150,000 flows – each flow being made of one specific type good described by an individual name, in a specific year, to or from a specific country. In the future, the dataset will be expanded in two ways. First, more years – especially revolutionary and post-revolutionary – (up to 1823) will be included. Second, we will include regional data, i.e. data on flows between French *généralités* and foreign countries.[21]

16 The number of the *généralités* or *Directions de Fermes*, since these two sub-divisions corresponded, has changed marginally across the eighteenth century, but it was 18 for most of the period.

17 Country is a short-hand term for geographical regions: If some of these regions actually account for countries such as Sweden, Spain or Portugal, others were in fact including several countries such as England (England, Ireland and Scotland) or Guinea (whole Africa).

18 However, we can recover some of this information by using provincial registers, which have been partially preserved for several maritime provinces or *généralités*, such as Bayonne, Bordeaux, Caen, Marseille, Nantes, Rennes and Rouen. All together these provinces accounted for more than 80% of French external trade.

19 Before 1771, information on the quantities can be found in the provincial registers, where they were systematically recorded.

20 For more details on these changes, see Charles and Daudin, "La balance," 143–154.

21 For more details on the state of progress of the project and the data to be included in the database in the near future, see http://toflit18.hypotheses.org/.

3 Methodology

STRO and FBT are sources of a very different nature, which makes a direct match impossible. On the one hand, STRO includes information that concerns ships and cargoes rather than flows. Moreover, the Danish authorities were registering the volume of the cargo rather than its value. On the other, in the annual statistics of the French *bureau du commerce* flows of trade are measured, not cargoes, and values are looked for rather than quantities of goods.

3.1 *STRO*

In order to match the two datasets, the data from STRO were modified.[22] Basis for these modifications was a text extraction file (under .csv) from STRO dated November 3rd 2013. Two files included all the necessary data: the "ladingen.csv" file (including 4.25 million single-merchandize cargo registrations) and the "doorvaarten.csv" (including 1.5 million passages). The 'taxes'-file was not used. The file "all_places_standard.csv" included all that was necessary for the treatment of place names, including an impressive standardization of 21,576 variations into 1,704 standardized names of places, 37 small and 15 big categories. Thanks to that, it was very easy to identify passages to or from France. From these data files, data on French trade with the Baltic between 1749 and 1795 was extracted to create a data set overlapping with the merchandize level-data from the FBT (1750–1789). This brought the number of cargo registrations down to 111,000.

The identification of goods was much more difficult than the identification of place names. With the assistance of a professional translator and several colleagues, the identification of goods was carried out. "Our" 111,000 cargoes included 5,218 different *products*. 24 appear more than 1,000 times, 163 more than 100 times, 602 more than 10 times. 3,217 were hapax used only once. These 5,218 different *products* were standardized into 470 Danish names; 2,535 product denominations (nearly 50%) were not identified, but they corresponded to only 3,018 cargo registrations (less than 3% of the total number of cargo registrations). The 470 Danish names were translated into 399 *marchandises* in French (and further normalized into 367 *marchandises normalisées*). The final operation was to classify these 367 categories into 17 Standard International Trade Classification (SITC)-based sectors (see Table 7.1). The identification process for the products involved in French trade with the Baltic between 1749 and 1795 led to the following results: 13,530 cargo registrations (12%) were not classified; most of them consisted of ballast (2,193), "varied goods" (5,722) and "provisions" (977).

22 All the STATA programming is available from the authors.

TABLE 7.1 Classification of goods (Standard International Trade Classification)

0: Foodstuff, various	0a: Foodstuff, European
0b: Foodstuff, Exotic	1: Beverages and tobacco
2: Raw materials	3: Fuels
4: Oils	5: Chemicals
6: Manufactured goods, by material	6a: Manufactured goods, linen
6b: Manufactured goods, wool	6c: Manufactured goods, silk
6d: Manufactured goods, cotton	7: Machinery and transport goods
8: Miscellaneous manufactured Goods	9: Other (incl. weapons)
9a: Species	

Another issue was how to measure the size of the trade flows. As mentioned above, the Sound Toll Registers do not include the value of goods. A first option is to use the information included about the value of the cargo toll paid since most of these were *ad valorem*. However, besides the value of each good, the amount of tax paid depended also on the nationality of the owners of the cargoes (there was an exemption for Danish owners during the period of interest) and the nature of cargoes (different kind of products were taxed differently). Hence, it turned out to be extremely complicated, almost impossible in fact, to calculate the value of the cargo using only the toll assigned to it. However, this variable may be used as a proxy, if only to check what kind of information it may give us.

A second option was to use the quantities given by the registers. In that case, the first issue was to provide some standardization of the units of measurement. 524 variations of units of measurement were present in the sample under study. Recent research on the conversion into metric equivalents of premodern weights and measures helped to unify several units and reduce their total number to 114 standardized names of units of measurement.[23] 3,852 cargo registrations were left without a recognizable unit of measurement: we treated them as "pieces". Acknowledging the difficulties of working with eighteenth-century units, the second step was to convert the 114 standardized names of units of measurement into a common metric equivalent.[24] All liquids volumes were transformed into weights by assuming a volumetric mass density

23 Scheltjens, "The Volume," 83–110; Scheltjens, "French Imports," 137–173.

24 In particular, the same word/unit (for example the 'last') might designate different metric quantities depending on the nature of the goods (e. g. a 'last' of stockfish does not equate a last of 'coal') and the region it refers to (e. g.a 'last' in Amsterdam does not represent the same quantity as a 'last' in Königsberg).

TABLE 7.2 Converting units of measurement

	Scheltjens's procedure	Using destination instead of departure	Using other information	Total
Weight	48,533	914	18,474	67,921
Number of pieces	8,023	469	21,832	30,324
Rigsdaler			10,613	10,613
Other	11		102	113
Total	56,567	1,383	51,021	108,971

of one. If identification failed, the destination was used to identify the unit of measurement instead of the origin. If that failed again, external information or the means and modes in the existing data were used to identify units of measurement.[25] Table 7.2 sums up the conversion procedure. It was not possible to convert 1,919 cargo registrations.

3.2 *French Balance of Trade*

Since it registers flows rather than cargoes, the French database is smaller than STRO. It is under STATA format and included around 150,000 observations in mid-August 2014. Only a limited part of these observations concern trade with the Baltic and identifying them is a bit tricky.[26] Before 1733, the only designation found in the French balance of trade reports is "Nord". It designates a region that comprises Sweden, Denmark, Hanseatic ports (mainly Hamburg, Bremen, Lübeck and Danzig), Prussia and Russia. Trade with Denmark is identified separately from 1733, trade with Sweden from 1734 and trade with Russia from 1744. The first difficulty is that some of this trade did not pass through the Sound, such as the trade with Archangel'sk, Hamburg, Bremen, Norway, Göteborg and, more generally, the North and Arctic seas. There is also a category "Allemagne" (Germany) which includes land trade only.[27] Therefore, it is not possible to identify trade with the Sound. After 1780, trade with Sweden, Denmark and Russia is still reported separately. "Nord" disappears and is replaced by

25 Including Johansen, *Shipping and Trade.*

26 See the discussion in Jeannin, "Les Marchés Du Nord," 47–74; Pourchasse, *Le Commerce Du Nord.*

27 On one document, the category is further specified as "l'Allemagne, la Lorraine et le Pays de Liège", see: Bibliothèque municipale de Saint-Brieuc, fonds Gournay, ms. 87, folder n° 2. Trade with "Allemagne et Pologne" is indicated as being only conducted by land in Archives Nationales (Paris), F12/1834B, "Tableau estimatif du commerce …".

"Quatre villes hanséatiques" (Hamburg, Bremen, Lübeck, Danzig) and Prussia. Trade with Prussia is indicated as being only by sea. Taking into account all trade flows that potentially went to the Baltic (i.e. Sweden, Denmark, Russia, "Nord", "Villes hanséatiques" and Prussia), the French data include 15,004 observations, covering 26 years between 1750 and 1789. Still, there is no way to differentiate trade with the Baltic from trade with Hamburg and Bremen – which was probably quite important. The only possible comparisons with STRO are for trade between France and Sweden (except Göteborg), Denmark (except North Sea and Norway ports) and Russia (except Archangel'sk). In the STRO dataset, this corresponds to the small categories "Sweden and Finland", "Estonia" + "Kurland" + "Livland" + "Russia around St. Petersburg" and the standard places "Stralsund" and "Greifswald" for Swedish Pomerania.

On the cargo designation side, the French database uses 3,320 designations for trade with the "Nord". This number was reduced to 1,761 after correcting spelling mistakes and homogenizing similar forms. Ten goods are mentioned more than 100 times: *Marchandises* (goods): 205; *Eau de vie* (spirits): 141; *Mercerie* (haberdashery): 139; *Merrain* (staves): 136; *Vin de Bordeaux* (Bordeaux wine) 136; *Indigo* (indigo) 123; *Planches de sapin* (fir planks) 111; *Mâts* (masts): 108; *Huile d'Olive* (olive oil): 106; *Fer en barre* (iron bars): 106. Fifty-nine goods are mentioned more than 50 times. All goods were classified into the same 16 SITC-based sectors that were used for the treatment of STRO (See table 7.1 above).

In the French statistics, a value expressed in *Livre tournois*, a monetary unit that would be transformed into the Franc during the Revolutionary era, was assigned to all trade flows. Only flows from thirteen years (1750, 1770–1777, 1779, 1780, 1782 and 1787) were recorded in quantities as well. About 80% of the flows for each of these years' record quantities, which makes 6,720 in total for the thirteen years. A large majority of these quantities are expressed in *livres* (pounds) (4,802 out of 6,720). Others are recorded in numbers (615), *muids* (a type of barrel) (241), *tonneaux* (another type of barrel) (178), *barils* (barrels) (156), etc. Using the name of the merchandize and the place of origin most of these units could be translated in numbers and metric measures using a variety of sources.[28] Some units of measurement were categorized as bundles when neither the corresponding weight, volume nor number of pieces could be found, e.g. baskets of glasses, crates of citrus, etc.

---

28 Including Wikipedia, Werner Scheltjens's work, http://www.genefourneau.com/mesures.html, http://www.cnrtl.fr/definition/millerolle, Doursther, *Dictionnaire universel*; Francœur et al., *Dictionnaire technologique*; Savary Des Brulons, *Dictionnaire universel*; Witthöft and Göbel, *Deutsche Masse und Gewichte*; Darcy-Bertuletti, "Tableau Des Mesures".

4 Two Sources, One Story?

The adaptations made to the raw data now made it possible to compare the trade flows between France and the Baltic as reported by FBT and STRO. However, crucial differences remained. Firstly, despite the fact that the ports mentioned in STRO were aggregated, the geographical areas registered in both sources did not match perfectly. Secondly and even more problematically, the flows extracted from each source were measured in different ways: values were predominant in FBT, (mostly) volumes in STRO (see above). Although it is certainly not intended to underestimate the methodological issues at stake here, it remains a useful exercise to check what knowledge can be gained from the comparison of two sets of data, which *ceteris paribus* should both provide a similar evaluation of trade between France and the Baltic.

Three approaches were developed to build a useful comparison between the two sources. Firstly, the absolute volume of trade was compared, using values for FBT and either number of cargoes, kilograms or collected taxes for STRO. Secondly, the analysis was refined by decomposing total trade into sectors for a given year or period. Finally, some reflections on trends were provided by looking at the longitudinal evolution of trade throughout the observed period.

4.1 *Comparing the Absolute Volume of Trade*

In Table 7.3, the absolute volume of trade in terms of kilograms, number of pieces, etc. as given in STRO and FBT are compared. Some differences are expected, as the collectors of the Sound dues and the French employees did not use the same units of measurement and the geographical coverage of both sources is not the same. Most of the time, the reported flows are quite different. In some instances, there is an important, often massive gap. However, it must be stressed that some of these gaps make a lot of sense. First, as expected, both French exports to and imports from Denmark are hugely undervalued in STRO. Here we have a combination of trade flows that went to Norway directly, bypassing the Sound, and the fact that most of the Danish trade was free from taxes and therefore loosely measured by the fiscal administration in the Sound. Another source of discrepancy is the variation in measuring: items that are measured by the piece in FBT may be measured by weight or *ad valorem* in STRO, and inversely. This suggestion might be tested by looking how individual goods, or types of goods, such as planks or poles are covered in the two types of sources.

TABLE 7.3 Absolute volume of trade as registered in STRO and FBT

		Denmark		Russia		Sweden	
		FBT	STRO	FBT	STRO	FBT	STRO
Exports from France	Bundles	208		50		3,613	
	Kg	70,092,128	23,113,600	68,041,336	81,677,504	123,220,336	62,321,928
	Litres	68,656,016		11,898,402		16,880,192	
	Meters	2,073		29,261		6,279	
	Pieces	6,232,975	16,600,235	1,322,931	11,714,780	4,925,995	12,808,564
	Silver kg	37,562	401,393	39,623	57,459	16,574	40,736
Imports to France	Bundles	1,964				220	
	Kg	259,623,472	1,270,031	69,724,144	115,677,840	289,704,160	112,079,064
	Litres	4,038,574		273,907		2,551,001	
	Meters	7,285,050		273,907		17,345,048	11.15
	Pieces	9,239,616	700,267	1,371,481	3,653,125	9,445,241	2,803,068
	Silver kg	20,069	50	32,793	96,187	36,192	1,283

NOTES: Years covered are 1750, 1771–1777, 1779, 1780, 1782, 1787 and 1789. Silver kg is the converted volume of goods not covered in the other categories (when available).

Looking at individual categories of commodities,[29] we see that the discrepancy between FBT and STRO for the French imports from Denmark are concentrated in sector 2 "Raw materials", which includes timber products (coming from Norway). All in all, though, there is not much there than can dramatically increase our trust in the pertinence of the comparison.

4.2 *Comparing the Sectoral Composition of Trade*

Another way to compare the sources is to check the sectoral composition of trade. Insofar as FBT was concerned, we compute the shares of each sector in total trade by using the values indicated in the French source. For STRO, the picture was more complex. As it was impossible to add together kilograms, pieces and rigsdalers, three types of indicators were selected: kilograms (Table 7.4 shows that this is the dominant measure), cargo taxes (although they are missing for 45% of the cargo registrations; being omitted in particular for trade with Denmark) and number of cargoes.

29 The excel tables for each industrial sector are available on the website http://toflit18.hypotheses.org/241.

TABLE 7.4 Correlation of the sectoral composition of trade in FBT and STRO (Standard International Trade Classification)

	Unit in 'converted' STRO	Denmark	Russia	Sweden
Exports from France	Kilograms	0.64	−0.01	0.07
	Number of cargoes	0.41	0.24	0.19
	Taxes	0.64	0.58	0.62
Imports to France	Kilograms	−0.12	0.67	0.02
	Number of cargoes	0.19	0.83	0.08
	Taxes	−0.06	0.89	0.04

NOTES: Years covered are 1750, 1752, 1754, 1756, 1757, 1758, 1759, 1760, 1761, 1767, 1768, 1769, 1770, 1771–1777, 1779, 1780, 1782, 1787–1789. The unit in the French source is always the value of trade.

Like Table 7.3, Table 7.4 shows that FBT and STRO do not measure the same French imports from Denmark. Again, trade with Norway is probably part of the explanation. French imports from Sweden also seem very different. In all the other cases (French imports from Russia, and French exports), the data are more alike. For all French exports, the Sound taxes indicator provides the best fit with the French sources. They are positively correlated for all three countries in the case of French exports. Moreover, they do a good job for French imports from Russia. This finding suggests that the taxes in STRO might be a reasonable indicator of the sectoral composition of trade.

Table 7.5 and Table 7.6 provide a closer look at the composition of French imports and exports. The main French exports are colonial foodstuffs (0b) and drinks (1, mainly wine and spirits) and, to a lesser extent, European foodstuffs (0a, including vinegar and Mediterranean products (prunes, etc.) and raw materials (2, mainly indigo and salt – this last one being very important for French-Russian trade). If we concentrate on colonial foodstuffs and drinks (by far the two most important categories according to the French sources) two points needs to be underlined. Firstly, colonial foodstuffs as expected are usually more important in values and taxes than in kilograms and cargoes, as they are high value-to-weight goods. Secondly, the gap between the French source and the indicator of Sound taxes are of the same magnitude for the three countries. The category 0b weights slightly more in the French source (between 40 and 50%) than in the Sound, while category 1 weights slightly more according

TABLE 7.5 Sectoral composition of French exports, 1750–1789[a] (Standard International Trade Classification)

SITC	Russia				Denmark				Sweden			
	FBT	STRO			FBT	STRO			FBT	STRO		
	Values	Taxes	Kg	Cargoes	Values	Taxes	Kg	Cargoes	Values	Taxes	Kg	Cargoes
0		0%		0%						0%		0%
0a	1%	4%	5%	19%	3%	3%	7%	22%	3%	8%	13%	20%
0b	50%	35%	8%	9%	40%	38%	14%	5%	58%	44%	68%	11%
1	26%	36%	8%	32%	41%	49%	48%	32%	20%	33%	8%	27%
2	11%	13%	76%	16%	10%	3%	26%	7%	13%	3%	8%	8%
3									0%			
4	0%		0%	0%	1%		0%	0%	1%	0%	0%	0%
5	1%	0%	0%	3%	1%	1%	2%	9%	1%	1%	0%	7%
6	4%	1%	0%	4%	1%	1%	0%	7%	1%	1%	1%	9%
6a	1%	0%		0%	0%	0%	0%	0%	0%	0%	0%	0%
6b	1%	0%	0%	0%	0%	0%	0%	0%	0%	1%	0%	1%
6c	2%	0%	0%	0%	1%				1%			0%
6d	0%				0%	0%	0%	0%	0%			
7	0%			0%	0%			0%	0%			
8	2%	0%	0%	0%	1%	0%	0%	0%	1%	0%		0%
9	0%			0%	0%				0%			
???	0%	2%	1%	6%	0%	2%	2%	6%	0%	4%	2%	7%
Mixed	2%	9%	2%	10%	1%	4%	0%	10%	1%	4%	2%	9%

a This stage allowed us to correct a mistake in the conversion of the *lispund* that made the "???" category represent 94% of French exports to Sweden in kg.

NOTES: Years covered are 1750, 1752, 1754, 1756, 1757, 1758, 1759, 1760, 1761, 1767, 1768, 1769, 1770, 1771–1777, 1779, 1780, 1782, 1787–1789. When no number is mentioned, no trade in that category is recorded.

to the Sound tax registers (between 33 and 46 %) than in the French source. This suggests that the Sound administration goods from category 0b are taxed heavier in proportion to their values at departure (France) than goods from category 1. If such a result were confirmed, it would clearly show that the two sources provide the same kind of information on the composition of French-Baltic trade, a fresh and unexpected result.

The main French imports are made of European foodstuffs (0a, especially grain), raw materials (2, including wood) and manufactured products (6, including iron). Each country had its own specialty: raw materials for Russia and Denmark, manufactured products (mainly iron and its derivatives) for Sweden. There are several odd features of our statistics that are interesting to reflect upon. First, according to the Sound registers a significant share of Danish exports to France was made of colonial goods and drinks: that seems odd. There are three plausible explanations. The simplest is that it is an error in STRO – a large cargo of coffee wrongly registered might be enough to explain a large part of this difference. It is not rare in STRO to see errors in the direction of trade. Another explanation is that the cargo(es) did not go to France, but to other country(ies). Finally, it might be a case of falsification of the registers to carry goods from France at a better tax rate. Similarly, STRO registers a significant proportion of linen in the Swedish exports to France. Here, it might be a more obvious case of falsification since we know linen goods were coming from German states (the only significant exporter of these goods in the Baltic area), but maybe the tax rate was significantly lower for Sweden exports. Re-exports from Swedish Pomerania are another possibility. Finally, the discrepancy between the proportion of Swedish exports in iron and iron wares measured by the French balance of trade, might be explained by the fact that some of this trade was coming from Göteborg rather than Swedish Baltic ports.

4.3 *Comparing the Chronological Evolution of Trade*

The last approach to compare the data provided by the two sources is to examine the evolution of trade throughout the period, i.e. the trend. Table 7.7 confirms that French exports are easier to reconcile in the two sources than French imports, except French imports from Russia. Besides, the indicator of the Sound taxes tracks the value from French sources much better than weight or number of cargoes, which is a confirmation of the result we obtained in the last two sections. We have selected two series for illustration. Graph 7.1 gives the best fitting series (French imports from Russia, using tax data from STRO) and Graph 7.2 gives a not-so-good fitting series (French exports to Sweden, using tax data from STRO).

Both the tables and the graphs offer interesting information on our sources. First, we can see that the low correlation of French statistics to Sound taxes is not due to the presence of extreme values – it is visually evident in graph 7.2. Moreover, correcting for those by removing the highest and lowest 5 percent observations does not improve the fit by much for the other series either. There seem to be fundamental differences in the series, except French

TABLE 7.6 Sectoral composition of French imports, 1750–1789 (Standard International Trade Classification)

SITC	Russia				Denmark				Sweden			
	FBT	STRO			FBT	STRO			FBT	STRO		
	Values	Taxes	Kg	Cargoes	Values	Taxes	Kg	Cargoes	Values	Taxes	Kg	Cargoes
0a	4%	2%	13%	6%	22%	7%	39%	12%	2%	3%	8%	4%
0b	0%	0%	0%	0%	0%	29%	7%	3%	0%	2%	0%	0%
1	1%	8%	1%	1%	0%	35%	10%	7%	0%	2%	0%	1%
2	62%	70%	65%	50%	53%	10%	8%	24%	4%	8%	28%	25%
3	0%	0%	0%	0%	1%	1%	9%	2%	1%	5%	15%	7%
4	14%	6%	5%	5%	1%				0%	0%	0%	0%
5	2%	1%	0%	1%	3%	0%	1%	2%	2%	2%	1%	5%
6	10%	7%	15%	20%	13%	12%	11%	19%	90%	56%	41%	47%
6a	2%	2%	0%	3%	0%			0%	0%	19%	4%	5%
6b		0%	0%	0%	0%					0%	0%	0%
6c	0%				0%				0%			0%
6d	0%				4%	1%		0%	0%	0%		0%
7	3%	0%	0%	5%	2%	0%	0%	1%	0%	0%	0%	1%
8	0%	0%	0%	0%	0%			0%	0%	0%	0%	0%
9		1%		4%	0%			0%	0%	1%	1%	1%
9a					0%				0%			
???	0%	1%	0%	3%	0%	5%	15%	25%	0%	2%	1%	3%
Mixed	1%	2%	0%	2%	1%	2%		4%	0%	0%	0%	1%

NOTES: Years covered are 1750, 1752, 1754, 1756, 1757, 1758, 1759, 1760, 1761, 1767, 1768, 1769, 1770, 1771–1777, 1779, 1780, 1782, 1787–1789. When no number is mentioned, no trade in that category is recorded.

exports to Denmark and French imports from Russia. In the case of French trade with Sweden and French imports from Denmark, the most likely explanation is that a large part of the trade escaped the statistics based on STRO: a large part of Danish exports to France consisted in Norway's timber and a significant share of Swedish trade to and from France went through Göteborg. Conversely, the good correlation of both sets of data for French exports to Denmark and Russian trade corresponded to routes that essentially went through the Sound: While France imported wood from the relatively scarcely populated and poor Norway, its colonial goods and drinks went to denser and richer areas in Copenhagen and its surroundings.

TABLE 7.7 Correlation of the evolution of French trade in FBT and STRO, 1750–1789 (Standard International Trade Classification)

	Sector	Denmark			Russia			Sweden		
		Kg	Nr	Taxes	Kg	Nr	Taxes	Kg	Nr	Taxes
Exports	0a	.69	.84	.85	.40	.73	.79	–.17	.27	.17
	0b	.41	.49	.44	.27	.38	.29	–.20	.45	.48
	1	.85	.84	.80	.54	.47	.53	–.05		.08
	2	.14	.80	–.20	–.33	–.26	–.20	–.23	–.01	–.06
	6	.59	.68	.42	.36	.62	.36	–.09	.10	
	8	–.36	–.09	–.75		–.38	.82		–.38	–.43
	Total	**.48**	**.64**	**.70**	**–.27**	**.47**	**.46**	**–.21**	**.27**	**.31**
Imports	0a	–.33	.08	–.25	.28	.31	.19	–.02	–.18	–.23
	0b							–.58		–.88
	1				.53	–.44	.20			
	2	–.61	–.14	.45	.50	.78	.85	.16	.54	.57
	4				.88	.77	.85	–.13	–.09	.05
	6	–.13	.13	.11	.89	.80	.59	–.11	–.10	–.11
	6a				.52	.72	.73	.09	.76	.22
	Total	**.11**	**.13**	**.27**	**.62**	**.81**	**.84**	**–.12**	**–.07**	**–.09**

NOTES: Years covered are 1750, 1752, 1754, 1756, 1757, 1758, 1759, 1760, 1761, 1767, 1768, 1769, 1770, 1771–1777, 1779, 1780, 1782, 1787–1789. The units in the French source is always the value of trade.

5 Conclusion

In this chapter, two sources of French-Baltic trade flows in the second part of the eighteenth century were presented: the French balance of trade (FBT) and the Sound Toll Registers Online (STRO). Despite obvious differences, a comparison was executed between these two sets of data based on these sources. Although many methodological issues that were uncovered during the process could not be cleared at this stage of the research, it is significant to note that some fresh and interesting results were found.

A first and important conclusion is that in the context of the French-Baltic trade physical quantities are not a good proxy for economic values. The comparison of the flows registered in STRO in physical quantities (and converted to volumes) and the French data registered in values is disappointing. The two

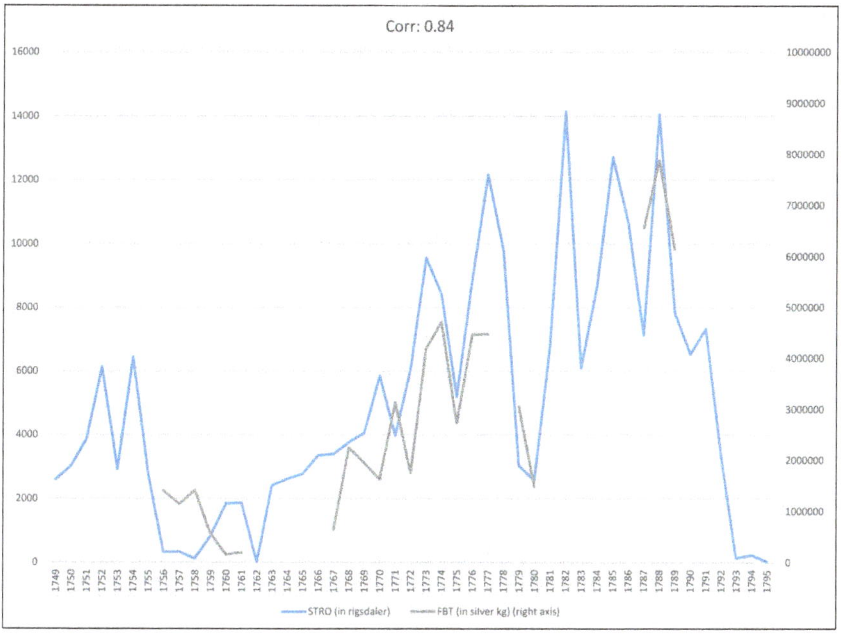

GRAPH 7.1 Total French imports from Russia, 1750–1795

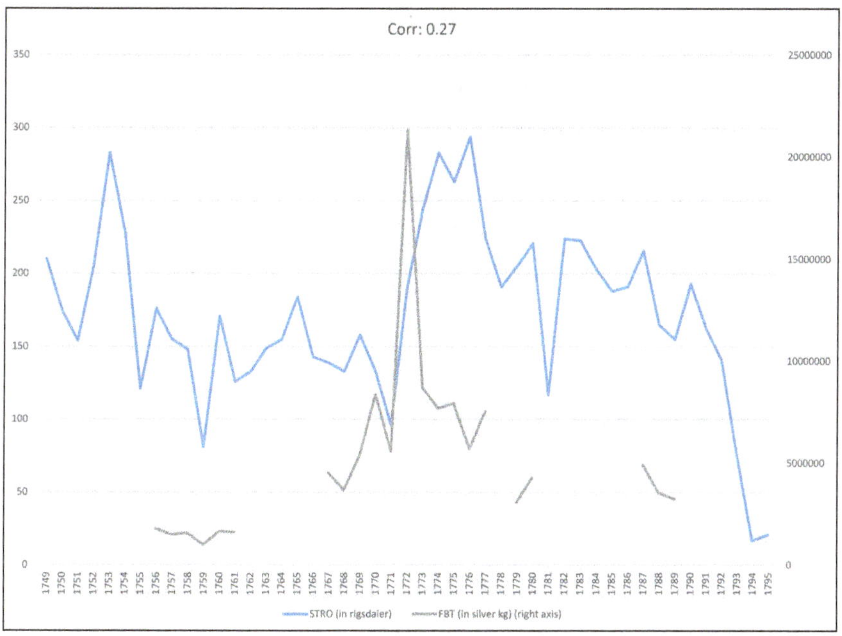

GRAPH 7.2 Total French exports to Sweden, 1750–1795

series do not match, whatever approach we used, and we have not been able to extract valuable economic information from the comparison. The same is also true for the number of cargoes: even if the match is slightly better than with kilograms, it does not make a lot of sense. Conversely, the tax indicator in STRO is a reasonable proxy for the values measured by the French bureau and registered in FBT. Interestingly, that is true whether we test the comparison for the total volume of trade for each country, for the sectoral composition of trade or for the dynamics of trade. By looking at the sectors of trade, it was possible to trace some issues with STRO. It seems that the tax collectors in the Sound (or the transcribers) made significant mistakes when writing the ledgers. Consequently, STRO should be used with caution when working with relatively small data samples – such as French trade with one of the Baltic countries. Overall, the French data seems more consistent, or at least it was not possible to spot significant bias in the information it contains.

Although the present article is mostly concerned with methodological issues, it should be underlined that it has also produced some positive results: Norway accounts for a significant part of French imports from Denmark, but it is not the case for French exports to the same country. It is also clear that, while French exports to each of the Baltic countries share a similar structure and are dominated, in terms of value, by wine and colonial goods, there is a strong differentiation of French imports from these countries. Swedish exports are made almost exclusively of iron and its derivatives, Danish exports are made mostly of wood coming from Norway and to a lesser extent of European foodstuff from Denmark, and Russian exports are dominated by raw materials.

A way to deepen the analysis would be to use more local data from ports rather than countries. This has not been possible within the scope of the present article, which primarily serves as an example for more the detailed analyses that will become possible in the near future, as more and more French data become available.

CHAPTER 8

Trade between Sweden and Portugal in the Eighteenth Century: Assessing the Reliability of STRO Compared to Swedish and Portuguese Sources[1]

Jari Ojala, Lauri Karvonen, Maria Cristina Moreira and Jari Eloranta

1 Introduction

The scarcity and unreliability of information, but also the weights and measures prior to the metric system have meant a daunting workload for any economic historian wishing to analyze trade flows in the early modern period.[2] The recent digitization of the Danish Sound toll registers (STRO) has made a uniform and continuous dataset easily available to researchers interested in studying the commercial shipping and commodity flow patterns of early modern Europe in aggregate and in detail.[3] Because all vessels passing through the Sound have been registered (except in time of war or when certain privileges applied), these registers reveal a lot of information about the micro and macro developments in shipping and trade with the Baltic.[4] However, STRO's value as a historical source must be considered carefully. There are several source-critical analyses focusing on the use of the Sound Toll Registers[5] – some of

1 Funding for this project was provided by the Fundação para a Ciência e Tecnologia, FEDER, PTDC 2010 project PTDC/HIS-HIS/118984/2010: *Trade Networks of Small and Neutral States before, during, and after the Revolutionary and Napoleonic Conflicts (1750–1850)* and by the Academy of Finland's Center of Excellence "History of Society" and project no. 269654.

2 E.g. Scheltjens, "The Volume," 74–75.

3 On the Sound Toll Registers see, for example, Gøbel and Flaskager Hansen, "Denmark."

4 Ahonen found only few cases in the Sound toll registers of vessels, which entered the Baltic but never returned. The potential reasons include the possibility that the ship was sold or that the ship's name was changed. There also may have been a shipwreck, the vessel may have returned via the Great Belt, or for some reason it may have stayed in the Baltic for a longer period. The use of alternative shipping lanes, especially via Hamburg in the nineteenth century, also increased during crises. See Ahonen, *From Sugar Triangle*, 23–24 and 26. Arup has claimed that ships passed Kronborg under the cover of the night or fog, as mentioned in Zins, *England and the Baltic*, 156.

5 See e.g. the list in Devine, *Exploring the Scottish Past*, 16 and Scheltjens, *De invloed.*

 | DOI:10.1163/9789004371781_010

the older ones include Eli F. Heckscher (1942),[6] J. Dow (1964),[7] T.M. Devine and S.G.E. Lythe (1971),[8] and Sven-Erik Åström (1965 and 1988),[9] just to mention a few that have attempted to assess their reliability as a source for historical research. The Sound toll data have been compared with, for example, the Rostock toll registers,[10] English port books,[11] Dutch notarial archives, the archives of Claes Adriaensz van Adrichem[12] and the Stockholm maritime customs accounts.[13] These earlier source-critical examinations have focused either on a few individual products or ships, featured a short time period, or have concentrated mostly on the so-called *hjemstedt*-problem. The overall conclusion arising from these previous studies is that the Sound toll registers are reliable to a certain extent, even though serious challenges remain.

This article continues this tradition of source-critical surveys, but addresses the *online* version of the original tax registers. The aim of this paper is to evaluate the reliability of the cargo and shipping data in STRO during the period 1738–1800, by comparing it with customs accounts from Sweden and Portugal. By analyzing the number of ships and major commodities in this trade, and by testing statistically the information from different datasets it is possible to draw conclusions about the accuracy of STRO as a source for the study of trade and shipping in general. This study adds to the previous debates by including two separate sources to evaluate statistically the reliability of the Sound toll registers. The aim of this research, however, is to neither disparage nor discourage the use of any of these records, but to offer some prudent advice on how usable, complementary, and comparable these different historical sources are. Thus, this article is primarily a source-critical survey, although it also offers some insights on the bilateral trade between the northern and southern peripheries of Europe during the eighteenth century.

Even though the availability of a large amount of micro- and macro-level data is an obvious strength of the Sound toll registers, few studies have focused on the reliability of the *entire* dataset or employed statistical methods to analyze the accuracy of the data. Because trade in the early modern period mainly involved bulk cargoes, STRO provides a great source to analyze this type of trade. Our focus lies on the comparison of all bulk trade between Sweden

6 Heckscher, "Öresundstullräkenskaperna."
7 Dow, "A Comparative Note."
8 Devine and Lythe, "The economy of Scotland."
9 Åström, *From Cloth to Iron*, vol 2. Åström, *From Tar to Timber*.
10 Huhnhäuser, *Rostocks Seehandel*.
11 Åström, *From Cloth to Iron*, vol 2.
12 Christensen and Haislund, *Dutch trade to the Baltic*.
13 Åström, *From Cloth to Iron*, vol 2.

and Portugal from 1738 to 1800 carried by Swedish ships. Due to the Swedish Navigation Act valid at the time, it was practically impossible – or profitable – for foreign ships to carry cargoes to and from Sweden. Almost 90 per cent of the goods traded between Portugal and Sweden were carried by Swedish ships (Table 8.1). As the data from STRO are compared with two other datasets, namely the Swedish Board of Trade Statistics (SBT) and the Portuguese General Balance of Trade (PBT), the similarity of the Swedish and Portuguese customs records can be reassessed as well. It will be argued that the information provided by STRO and the documentation compiled by the Swedish and Portuguese authorities on the trade volumes match quite well and that, therefore, all three sources are fairly accurate.

First, the overall patterns and importance of trade and shipping between Portugal and Sweden are analyzed briefly. Then, STRO is compared with the Swedish and Portuguese datasets. Finally, some general conclusions are drawn.

2 Swedish-Portuguese Trade

In the eighteenth century, economic relations between Sweden and Portugal were extensive. In Southern Europe and the Mediterranean Portugal was the most important trading partner for Sweden; the oldest Swedish consulate (founded in 1641) was located in Lisbon.[14] During the eighteenth century, Portugal was the most important salt exporter to Sweden.[15] In the mid-1750s, for example, a quarter of Setubal's salt went directly to Sweden. For Sweden, it was the salt, and for Portugal, it was the iron imported from Sweden, which were considered as strategic products. In this bilateral trade, some other products were also important in certain periods. In the 1720s, for example, over 50 per cent of the Swedish export of boards went to Portugal. During the seventeenth century, the Dutch shipmasters had carried the salt imports of Sweden, yet because the key aim in Swedish mercantilist policy was to reduce foreign shipping, Sweden managed to expand its own salt shipping from Portugal after the passing of the Navigation Act in 1724. The Dutch were practically pushed out of this trade between Sweden and Portugal. Throughout the eighteenth century, Sweden also managed to secure its shipping interests in the Mediterranean by making treaties, paying tributes, and maintaining political connections with the Corsair States of Northern Africa.

14 On Swedish-Portuguese trade, see especially Müller, *Consuls*. See also Müller, "Swedish-Portuguese trade"; Lindberg "An 18th Century Swedish Perspective".

15 On the Swedish salt trade, see especially Carlén, *Staten*.

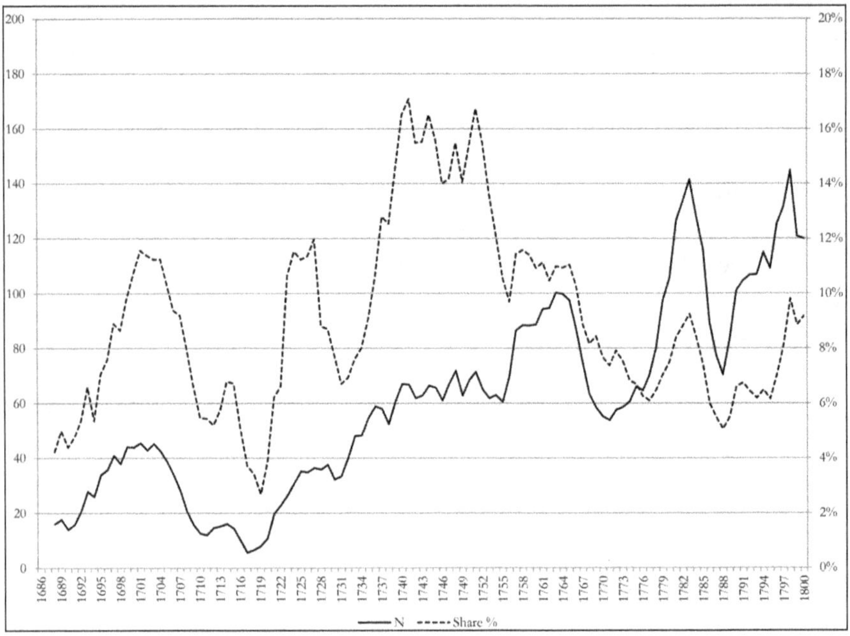

GRAPH 8.1 Number of Swedish ships sailing to and from Portugal, 1686–1815 (left axis), and percentage share of this shipping in total Swedish shipping through the Danish Sound (right axis), Five-year moving averages.
NOTE: The figure includes all ship traffic from Sweden proper to Portugal. It does not include the shipping to and from ports of Sweden's Baltic dominions (e.g. Stralsund, Riga and Narva).
SOURCE: STRO

The number of Swedish ships calling at Portuguese ports continued to grow during the eighteenth century. Their trade, however, was disrupted by the Great Northern War (1700–1721), especially when Danish privateers threatened the Swedish vessels. The Swedish consuls reported that in the late seventeenth century some 20 Swedish ships visited Portuguese ports annually.[16] A century later, the Swedish consuls in Setubal reported large numbers of Swedish ships entering and leaving the town: 133 ships in 1800, 91 ships in 1801, and altogether 94 Swedish ships in 1803.[17] The information provided by the consular reports confirms the information from STRO on the overall growth trend in shipping between these two countries. However, the number of Swedish ships calling at Portuguese ports was clearly higher in the consular reports than what was

16 Ekegård, *Studier*, 70–71.

17 Swedish National Archives, Board of Trade, Consular reports, Setubal 1800, 1801, and 1803, fol. 422, 426.

reported at the Danish Sound. This is explained by the fact that Swedish ships were used to carry cargoes between Western and Southern European ports. This practice grew in importance during the French Revolutionary and Napoleonic wars as the Swedes were able to benefit from their neutrality. Carlson argues that as much as half of the Swedish tonnage in the Mediterranean area during the eighteenth century was used in this type of tramp shipping. Moreover, a sizable number of Swedish ships arrived in Portuguese ports from various other European ports in ballast to load a cargo of salt before returning to the Baltic.[18]

The records of the Danish Sound toll registers illustrate the Swedish-Portuguese trade patterns quite clearly. First, the ships that carried the commodities between these two countries were mainly Swedish (including those from Finland and the Swedish dominions), with a share of about 90 per cent. Portuguese ships and other nationalities played only a minor part in carrying the total commodity trade between these countries (see Table 8.1). Second, the holds were almost entirely filled, in terms of both volume and value, with only a few bulk commodities: iron from Sweden and salt from Portugal. Circa two-thirds of the volume of Swedish exports consisted of iron. The Portuguese exports were even more concentrated; in STRO, salt accounted for 99.1 per cent of the tonnage. The remaining 0.9 per cent consisted of wine, fruits, sugar, and various luxury items (Table 8.2).[19]

3 Comparability of the Data

In order to evaluate the quality of STRO, we have compared it to similar datasets. Our focus is on the bulk cargoes. The amounts of the most important product groups are easy to compare. Data aggregation makes it possible to evaluate the differences in volumes found in different sources and to assess whether these differences were systematic or not. The Swedish Board of Trade data (SBT) and the Portuguese General Balance of Trade (PBT) were based on information from customs houses located in different ports. The Swedish data was originally organized and grouped according to product category and then summarized in tables that can be found in the annual reports from the Swedish

18 Carlson, "Sveriges handel och sjöfart," 14–15 and 20. See also Ojala, *Tehokasta*, 144–156.

19 In the Swedish Board of Trade tables (Swedish National Archives (Stockholm), Annual reports of foreign trade and shipping), published since 1738, the cargoes from Portugal to Sweden appear to be more diverse. However, the share of salt in the entire cargo volume was substantial.

TABLE 8.1 Nationality of the ships sailing from Sweden to Portugal via the Danish sound, 1700–1800

Shipmaster's home country	N	%
Sweden (incl. Finland)	2,891	89
Dominions of Sweden	86	3
England	67	2
Netherlands	62	2
Prussia/Mecklenburg	62	2
Denmark	30	1
Norway	13	0.4
Portugal	9	0.3
France	3	0.1
Russia	3	0.1
Italy	2	0.1
Spain	2	0.1
United States	2	0.1
Total	3,232	100

SOURCE: STRO

TABLE 8.2 Trade composition measured from tonnage (percentages of total volume), 1738–1800

Swedish exports to Portugal	%	Portuguese exports to Sweden	%
Iron	74.4	Salt	99.1
Steel	4.0	Wine	0.21
Timber	5.0	Sugar	0.08
Tar and Pitch	8.4	Fruits	0.003
Copper	0.3	..	..
Miscellaneous	7.9	Miscellaneous	0.61
Avg. Export Tonnage per Year	8,508 t.		14,171 t.

SOURCE: STRO

National Archives.[20] The Portuguese source used in this study is Portugal's General Balance of Trade with Foreign Nations and Portuguese Colonies.[21]

In order to analyze the reliability of STRO, a database covering the years 1738–1800 was compiled. This STRO-based database included 16,450 product observations, while the database based on the Swedish data (SBT) included 4,911 observations. The Portuguese data (PBT) covered the last decades of the research period and contained 325 product entries. The first step in the comparison of the data samples was to collect, organize, sort, aggregate, and group all the import and export data. The STRO export products from Sweden to Portugal were divided into six groups (iron, steel, copper, timber, tar and pitch, and miscellaneous), and the exports from Portugal to Sweden were sorted into five product groups (salt, wine, sugar, fruits, and miscellaneous).

The main grouping principle for cargoes was that the datasets should be as equal and, hence, as comparable as possible. Luckily, both STRO and SBT records remained unchanged during the research period. The Portuguese foreign trade datasets were published since 1776[22] with several years missing before 1796, so that a comprehensive comparison was feasible only for the last ten years of the eighteenth century.

The main concern in the comparisons involves the measures used in the original sources. In STRO, the measures (barrels, lasts etc.) and customs duties were given for every single product throughout the eighteenth century. Only

20 Riksarkivet, Stockholm, Kommerskollegiums arkiv, Berättelser om utrikeshandel och sjöfart 1738–1805. Serie 1, 2 and 5. See also Vallerö, *Svensk handels- och sjöfartsstatistik* and *Historisk statistik för Sverige*.

21 The balances of trade for each year are in different archives: Biblioteca e Arquivo Histórico de Obras Públicas (Lisbon, Portugal), *Balança Geral do Comércio do Reino de Portugal com os seus Domínios e Nações Estrangeiras* [Portugal's General Balance of Trade with Portuguese Colonies and Foreign Nations], for the years 1776 and 1777; *Alfabeto Das Importaçoens e exportaçoens do Reyno de Portugal com as Naçoens Estrangeiras* [Alphabetical list of Portuguese Imports and Exports with Foreign Nations], 1789; Fundação Biblioteca Nacional (Rio de Janeiro, Brasil), *Balança Geral do Commercio do Reyno de Portugal com as Naçoens Estrangeiras* [Portugal's General Balance of Trade with Foreign Nations], for the years 1783, 1787 and 1798; Instituto Nacional de Estatística (Lisbon, Portugal), *Balança Geral do Commercio do Reyno de Portugal com as Nações Estrangeiras* [Portugal's General Balance of Trade with Foreign Nations], 1796–1797 and 1799–1800.

22 The balances of trade for the years 1775, 1780, and 1790 were compiled, as is stated by Adrien Balbi (1822: 401), *Essai statistique sur le Royaume de Portugal et d'Algarve, comparé aux autres états de l'Europe, et suivi d'un coup d'oeil sur l'état actuel des sciences, des lettres et des beaux-arts parmi les portugais des deux hemispheres*: "Ayant entre les mains (…) les bilans du commerce du Portugal des annés 1775, 1780, 1790 et ceux de 1796 a 1820 si savamment rédigés par M. le chevalier Mauricio José Teixeira de Moraes (…)". However, they do not currently exist in the archives.

in less than one per cent of the cases, the value of the cargo was reported as well. In the Swedish Board of Trade records, the amounts of all major products were reported using volume measures, while the values were also included. Sometimes, especially in the case of less frequently traded commodities and luxury products, only the value of the commodity was reported.

The Sound dues involved specific rates for each commodity. These rates did not change during the period observed. In this study, they were used as a starting point for the comparison of STRO with the Portuguese data. However, when using the Sound dues as estimates for the value and even the volume of trade one has to be especially careful as there was a plethora of rules and regulations for any given period to determine how these duties were collected. It is important to notice, for example, that ships might have been from *privileged* or *non-privileged* countries. Vessels belonging to the latter group had to pay somewhat higher duties than others did for certain goods.[23] Even though the differences in paid customs duties were not extensive between various countries and do not, for instance, seem to have affected the sample in this research, this has to be recognized when working with STRO.

Portugal's General Balance of Trade data that was used as a source in this study does not provide commodity volumes but commodity values. Imports were registered as c.i.f. (cost, insurance and freight) and exports as f.o.b. (free on board). The major concern involves the average prices as noted in the Balance of Trade documents in 1796:

> The knowledge about the quantity and quality of the genres by Entrance or Exit was extracted from the Book of Shipments, Relations of customs all around the kingdom and fiscal documentation of this city. For the construction of the balance the prices of the first cost from the port of origin were examined, to the exports will be added the commissions and rights of export: to know these prices some traders of the market, in conference with them, and other well thought speculations, the medium prices have been extracted.[24]

These values, though problematic, make it possible to perform statistical comparisons on the annual trade between Portugal and Sweden. The comparative

23 Ahonen, *From Sugar Triangle*, 25.

24 Translated from: Instituto Nacional de Estatística (Lisbon, Portugal), *Balança Geral do Comércio do Reyno de Portugal com os seus Domínios* [Portugal's General Balance of Trade with Portuguese Colonies] (1796).

analysis of STRO and the Portuguese data was conducted by comparing the shares of different products in total imports and exports. It was not possible to carry out this analysis for the entire period due to the sporadic nature of the annual data; we therefore opted to provide only some descriptive quantitative measures to compare the different datasets.

For the comparison between STRO and SBT, some simple statistical tools were used, such as a paired *t*-test, which can tell us whether the average export or import shares of certain products in these two sources differed from each other statistically and if differences can be explained by a sample error. Because these two datasets are clearly interdependent (the same ships declared their cargoes in two different places, and the declaration was based on the same sources, namely cargo manifestos) a dependent t-test, which takes into account the linked nature of the datasets, was also conducted. The second method was based on a linear regression analysis, where the Swedish Board of Trade data was chosen as the dependent variable (the variable to be explained) and STRO as the independent variable (explanatory). While this is an imperfect method to explore the question exhaustively, due to the missing variable bias and other concerns including the interdependence of the data, at least it gives us an indication of the correlation. Before that, the datasets were converted into a logarithmic scale, which describes the percentage changes in the trade. The basic assumption in these tests was that the STRO and SBT datasets were equal. This assumption was made even though volumes in STRO should be about 20–30 per cent smaller than the SBT volumes as some shipments from Sweden were exported via Gothenburg and other North Sea ports. The importance of the Swedish west coast for Swedish shipping and trade grew during the period, and ships departing from here to Southern Europe did not have to go through the Sound at all. On the other hand, the general trends in the trade should be the same. Other variables were assumed constant. Moreover, Vallerö has noted that the Swedish ships that were loaded or unloaded in more than one Swedish port were possibly recorded at every customhouse where some form of clearance took place.[25] Thus, the SBT information may overestimate the import volumes – although in most cases the cargoes were, in fact, unloaded at only one place.

25 Vallerö, *Svensk handels- och sjöfartsstatistik*, 137.

4 STRO and the SBT Records

Comparison between the SBT and STRO reveals that the data on bulk products in these two datasets match satisfactorily. Both sources show similar levels and trend developments for all product groups. Interestingly enough, we can find no systematic errors implying that one source would give systematically higher or lower values than the other source for certain bulk products, either. For some individual years, we can trace substantial differences of several hundred percent between the two sources. However, it is hard to tell what caused these gaps.

Tar exports from Sweden were a good case to study, because all tar exports were shipped through the Sound. This is because tar was produced either in Finland or in the northern parts of Sweden and exported either via Stockholm or directly from these areas to the European markets; thus the above-mentioned challenge of exports being transported via Gothenburg does not concern the tar exports. Graph 8.2 shows a clear correlation between the SBT data and STRO. The annual tar trade was on average about 3,000 barrels, and the median difference between the datasets was only 59 barrels, implying that both datasets were painting the same picture and are, thus, quite reliable.

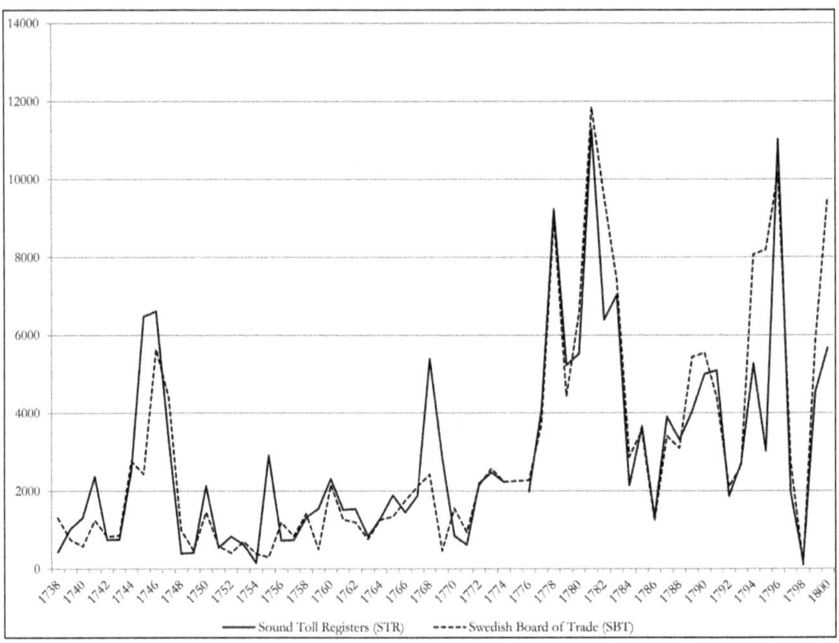

GRAPH 8.2 Volume (in barrels) of tar export from Sweden to Portugal, 1738–1800
SOURCES: STRO, SBT

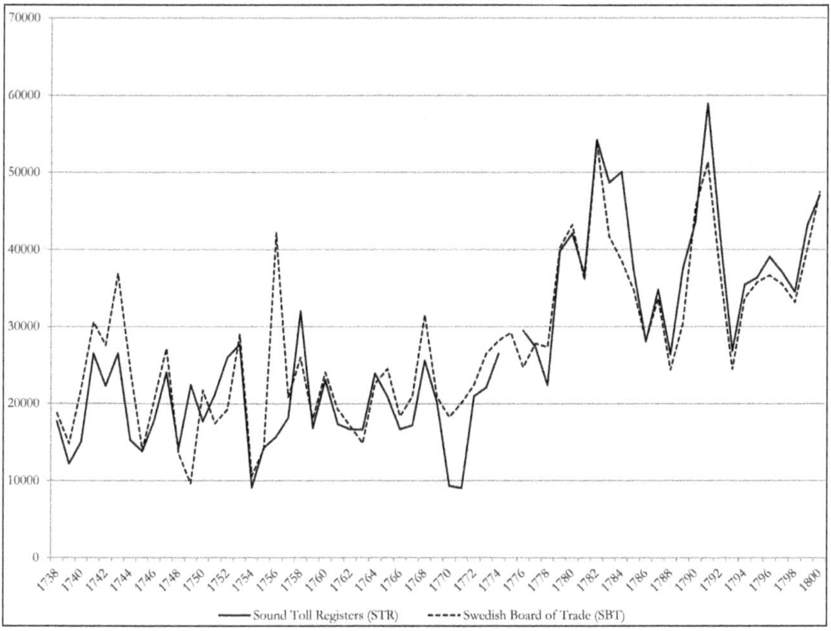

GRAPH 8.3 Volume (in shippounds) of all metal exports (iron, steel, and copper) from Sweden to Portugal, 1738–1800
SOURCES: STRO, SBT

Bar iron and iron sheets dominated Swedish exports in terms of both volume and value.[26] As Graph 8.3 shows, the two datasets corresponded also in the case of Swedish iron and other metals export, in a similar vein as the tar exports in Graph 8.2. There were also less important, manufactured metal products like nails, cannons, anchors, bolts, and household goods among the exports. The value per ton of these manufactured products was, of course, higher than that of bar iron. Some of these metal goods, like nails, were reported with their values in the SBT, and therefore, were grouped under miscellaneous products in this study.

The t-test, showing if the means of the product shares were similar or not, clearly confirmed the same phenomenon as the figures above (see Table 8.3): there was no substantial difference in the bulk cargo export volumes from Sweden to Portugal between the STRO and SBT datasets (especially columns T-test and probability). In each cargo group, the STRO values were consistently slightly smaller than in the Swedish data. We contend that the STRO statistics are precise enough when it comes to measuring Swedish bulk export cargoes,

26 Karonen, *Pohjoinen suurvalta*, 145–148 and 179–182.

TABLE 8.3 Comparison of Swedish exports to Portugal: a statistical test based on the STRO and SBT datasets, 1738–1800

Product name	Source	Mean	Std. Dev.	No. of observations	df	T-test value	Probabilit
Iron	STRO	25,534.62	11,299.87	62	123	0.31	0.76
	SBT	26,121.62	9,698.69	63			
Steel	STRO	1,389.24	622.30	62	123	0.30	0.76
	SBT	1,422.14	593.39	63			
Copper	STRO	102.43	209.77	63	120	0.34	0.74
	SBT	114.73	195.39	59			
Timber	STRO	178,403.10	69,384.89	62	123	2.84	0.01
	SBT	214,508.70	72,581.59	63			
Tar & Pitch	STRO	2,946.08	2,531.12	62	123	0.15	0.88
	SBT	3,020.34	2,858.49	63			

SOURCES: STRO, SBT

presuming that the Swedish manner of filling in freight letters and customs inspections was correct and precise.

Judging from the Swedish exports to Portugal it is likely that the tar figures can be evaluated as the most reliable in STRO and SBT. The volumes of iron, steel, and copper exports, too, seem to have been reported rather similarly in Elsinore and in the Swedish ports. According to this analysis, however, the figures for the timber trade differed substantially between STRO and SBT. This difference may have resulted from the diversity of this product group, and in a related manner, from the rather challenging measurement of timber cargoes. Numerous timber qualities and products were included in this group and we may assume that the variety of product names in the product group reflects the dissimilarity of the records, for example reporting in terms of numbers of items, tonnage etc. Moreover, the use of a simple linear regression (Ordinary Least Squares, see Appendix 1) reveals that the two sources tracked changes in the iron and tar trade fairly similarly (R^2).

When analyzing the Portuguese exports to Sweden, the different units used in STRO and the SBT and the ambiguity and diversity of the units mean that the comparison was not as simple to carry out as with the Swedish export products (see Graph 8.4). We converted all salt shipment volumes to lasts, even though

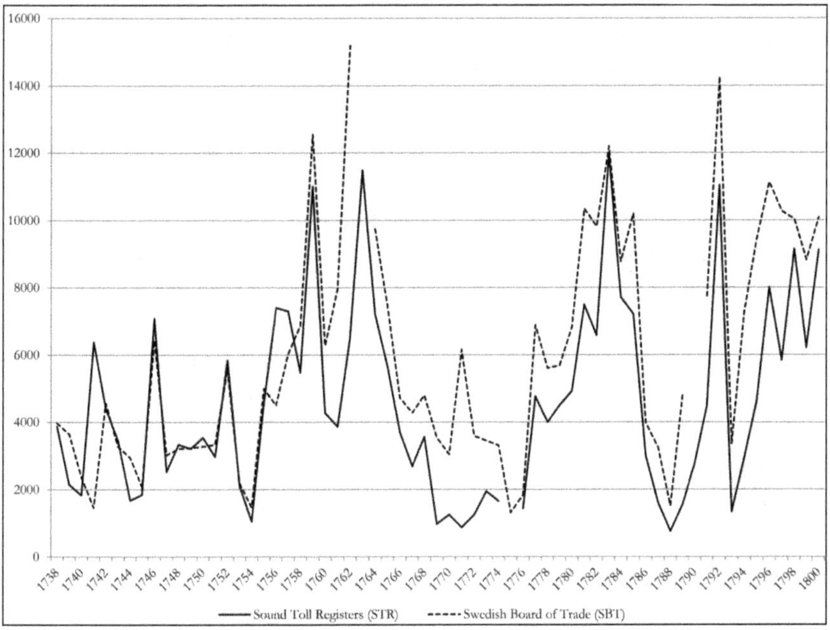

GRAPH 8.4 Volume (in lasts) of salt imports from Portugal to Sweden, 1738–1800
SOURCES: STRO, SBT

barrels were also used in the Swedish data.[27] There was a clear correlation between STRO and SBT data on salt imports from Portugal, even though some of the salt was imported via Gothenburg and, thus, did not show up in STRO. This may explain why the trends were similar, yet the SBT data suggest higher salt import volumes than STRO for most of the period.

When it comes to wine and fruit imports, a clear systematic difference was apparent. The Portuguese wine industry developed significantly during the eighteenth century, and both the STRO and the Swedish authors have recorded similar types of wine, but the SBT listed wine qualities a bit more precisely and listed a few French wines as also being imported from Portugal. Because of this, it was chosen to examine only three wines from the SBT: Portuguese, Malaga, and Muscat wines, all of which can be found in STRO. In practice, the majority

27 Note that for single years the SBT data implied that, in addition to 'Portuguese salt', also *Luneburger Salt, Collberger Salt, Franskt Salt,* and *Medelländskt Salt* was imported from Portugal. In this comparison only the 'Portugiskt och spanskt salt' imported from Portugal was included.

of the imports from Portugal constituted "normal" Portuguese wine, supplemented with some more expensive wines. Thus, the general trends and import amounts can be distinguished by comparing the datasets. The various types of wine posed some challenges for the analysis, as we had to convert the amounts into liters. The most significant challenge was the conversion of *oxehoved* (in STRO). As we could not find a precise converter for *oxehoved*, and only an inaccurate measure of 183–325 liters was available, we used the approximation of 206 liters as a converter. For the Swedish unit *åmar*, there was a more precise converter of 155 liters, which was used in our study.[28] As fruit was a continuous part of the imports from Portugal, it is interesting that the Danish and Swedish officials used different units of measurement. In STRO, the measure for fruits was *kiste*, meaning a case, while in Sweden the fruit trade was documented in barrels, as well as in terms of value. As we could not know whether the Swedish barrel and *kiste* in STRO were equivalent or not, an index was used as a basis for the comparison. All in all, STRO and SBT data do not track well with each other in the case of wine and fruit. Thus, with these commodities one should be cautious when using STRO.

TABLE 8.4 Comparison of Portuguese exports to Sweden: a statistical test of the STRO and SBT datasets, 1738–1800

Product name	Source	Mean	Std. Dev.	No. of observations	df	T-test value	Probability
Salt	STRO	4,562.65	2,874.76	62	121	2.36	0.02
	SBT	5,898.96	3,394.79	61			
Wine	STRO	29,847.98	33,539.44	63	124	3.89	0.00
	SBT	536,818.24	35,010.66	63			
Sugar	STRO	39,894.32	50,556.50	38	99	0.32	0.75
	SBT	63,790.32	73,241.00	63			
Fruits	STRO	483.50	310.23	62	123	−6.69	0.00
	SBT	208.37	101.31	63			

SOURCES: STRO, SBT

28 See, for example, Morell, *Om mått- och viktsystemens utveckling*.

As the probability values seen in Table 8.4 show, there were obvious differences in the means of STRO and SBT data concerning the Portuguese exports to Sweden. The volumes were consistently and significantly larger in the SBT data than in STRO. When it comes to the most important commodity, salt, the difference in the mean volume in STRO was 77 per cent of the SBT. This is in line with the assumption that the North Sea coast accounted for some 20–30 per cent of Swedish foreign trade. Along the same lines, the wine and sugar trade showed notably lower volumes in STRO than in the SBT.

There were also substantial differences in the fluctuations of the series, not just in the levels. The linear regression model (OLS, see Appendix 2) shows that the coefficients of all the Portuguese export products were smaller than those of the Swedish exports of metals and tar. Nevertheless, even here the R^2 values for the salt (0.57), sugar (0.57), and wine (0.42) series were high enough to suggest that the trends in the two sources were indeed rather similar.

STRO and SBT records on the Swedish-Portuguese trade were unanimous when it came to most of the trade in bulk products. However, more differences emerged from the analysis of the less frequently traded products, namely sugar and copper. The fact that there were several years in STRO without any mention of sugar or copper, while the SBT data indicated that such trade took place during the missing years as well, implies a shortcoming in the information in STRO. The discrepancy in the information on timber, wine, and fruit trade could be related to the large number of different product names and units in these product categories. It also supports our assumption that the large product groups were more accurately recorded than the smaller ones. The Swedish exports were reported more consistently in the two datasets than the Portuguese exports; this may indicate that the cargo manifestos were completed out more precisely in Sweden than in Portugal.

5 STRO and PBT Records

When examining STRO and PBT records, both notable differences and clear similarities emerge. Some of the differences can be explained by different bookkeeping methods. The method and rationality of this comparison of course can be questioned as the Portuguese records were based on the value of the trade measured in the Portuguese monetary unit, the *réis*, while the STRO shares, measured from customs payments, indicate the trade value only in a very rough manner, since the STRO documentation is based on cargo quantities. Therefore, the possible differences between the Portuguese and Danish datasets may be explained by the different ways the customs valued the products. As the exact values cannot be found in STRO, the rate of the Sound dues constituted the basis of our analysis. The Sound dues were, roughly, about two per cent of the cargo value, so there should have been an approximate correlation between the value of the goods and the customs duties paid at the Sound. In addition, the comparison with the values in the consular reports indicates that the Sound dues were a fairly good, albeit rough, estimate of the cargo values.[29] In general, similar export and import products can be found in the Portuguese custom records and STRO.

When comparing the Portuguese and STRO datasets, the national differences in the compilation of these trade records are notable. In Sweden and the Sound, the foreign trade of the Dominions of Sweden was always recorded separately from that of Sweden proper. For example, the trade between Swedish Pomerania and Sweden was considered to be foreign, whereas in the Portuguese statistics the trade with Sweden included both Swedish and Pomeranian goods. Because of this, we have included the trade flows from Swedish Pomerania (the ports of Barth, Greifswald, Wolgast and Stralsund) in the analysis of STRO. When comparing STRO and SBT these areas were not included in the analysis.

Tables 8.5 and 8.6 display a clear difference in the shares of the most important products in the Swedish-Portuguese trade in the Sound Toll Registers, on the one hand, and in the Portuguese customs records, on the other. In STRO, the iron and steel cargoes made up most of the value of the commodities carried on the Swedish ships (Table 8.6). This information is clearly in line with the overall picture of the Swedish export trade at the time.[30] Likewise, Tables 8.7 and 8.8 indicate that salt was the main product imported in Sweden arriving from Portugal. However, the shares of Portuguese exports to Sweden differ notably in both sources. Salt, for example, played a more pronounced role in STRO, whereas in the PBT wines and sugar were more significant trade items than in STRO.

Nevertheless, the same products can be found in both data sets and, also, closer examination and analysis of the changes in the trade reveal similarities. For example, in both sets of records, the timber trade seems to have been at a high level in 1787–89 and 1796, and clearly, both statistics reveal a significant grain trade in 1798.

---

29 There were differences in the cargo valuation at the Sound and in Portugal. The consular reports indicate that the value of timber was higher in Portugal than at the Sound (relative to other commodities inspected here). For instance, a 1729 consular report of the product values in Portugal gives the following shares: 87 per cent iron and steel; 13 per cent timber; 0.34 per cent tar. At the same time, the STRO shares (measured from customs duties) are: 91 per cent iron and steel; 8 per cent timber; 0.6 per cent tar. Müller, *Consuls*, 98.

30 Heckscher, *Sveriges ekonomiska historia*. See also Åström, *From Tar to Timber*.

TABLE 8.5 Swedish exports to Portugal according to the PBT dataset, percentages of values, 1776–1800

	Iron	Steel	Timber	Grain	Tar & Pitch	Copper	Metals	Others	Total
1776	55.0	4.9	33.0		2.8	3.8		0.5	100
1777	59.1	4.1	31.1		5.0			0.7	100
1783	67.3	3.4	20.3	1.5	7.3	0.1		0.1	100
1787	54.2	8.3	30.9		5.8			0.8	100
1789[a]	52.6	9.2	29.3		5.4	0.3		3.3	100
1796	51.4	24.9	15.7		6.2	1.1		0.7	100
1797	50.6	10.8	11.6	14.8	4.3	1.3		6.6	100
1798	31.3	3.0	17.4	41.0	3.1		3.5	0.7	100
1799	64.9	5.8	9.4	11.2	4.2		3.2	1.3	100
1800	67.3	4.0	10.4	5.6	2.8	3.8	5.3	0.9	100

a The Balance of Trade for this year does not provide total values for each product and market. Only the overall total of each product and its quantities are available. Therefore, these values reflect mere approximations, as they were calculated with average prices.

NOTE: STRO and SBT data do not track well in the case of wine. One should therefore be cautious when using STRO for this commodity.

SOURCE: PBT

TABLE 8.6 Swedish exports to Portugal according to STRO, percentages of volumes, 1776–1800

	Iron	Steel	Timber	Grain	Tar & Pitch	Copper	Others	Total
1776	80.9	10.5	6.1		2.1		0.4	100
1777	76.6	10.9	4.3		4.2	1.8	2.3	100
1783	80.1	8.8	4.4		4.8	0.1	1.8	100
1787	75.1	14.3	6.9		3.1	0.0	0.6	100
1789	72.2	13.3	7.2		3.0	1.1	3.3	100
1796	62.0	17.1	5.6	2.1	6.9	1.7	4.6	100
1797	64.0	17.5	2.8	9.5	1.8	1.2	3.1	100
1798	68.1	9.1	2.5	17.1	0.2	0.1	3.0	100
1799	72.5	6.8	3.0	7.4	2.9	5.3	2.1	100
1800	70.1	15.0	3.3	4.5	3.1	2.4	1.7	100

SOURCE: STRO

We suggest three possible reasons why the Portuguese data systematically indicate larger shares of timber and grain, and smaller shares of iron and steel. The first involves different customs practices. In the Portuguese data, the shares are value-based in local prices, while in STRO the shares are related to the trade volumes. The differences could indicate that the Sound dues are not an optimal measure to analyze product values. The second possibility is that, unless otherwise stated in STRO, a large share of the steel and iron cargoes in most cases would have gone to the Netherlands or Britain, while timber cargoes would have reached Portugal as registered in STRO. Because there is no evidence of this in the existing literature, this explanation seems tenuous at best. The third option is that in the Portuguese data only Swedish vessels would have been registered, and not the foreign vessels also participating in this bilateral trade. This is not likely, because almost all ships sailing from Sweden to Portugal were Swedish, even though the Swedish Navigation Act was not as firm for Swedish export trade as it was for import trade. The same reasons might also explain the differences in the share of salt, wine, and sugar imports from Portugal to Sweden.

TABLE 8.7 Portuguese exports to Sweden, according to PBT, percentages of values, 1776–1800

	Salt	Wine	Sugar	Fruits	Beverages	Tissues	Hides	Tobacco	Cotton	Others	Total
1776	69.4	22.3	0.4	4.1	2.1					0.4	100
1777	84.4	7.8		2.2	4.2					2.3	100
1783	75.7	13.9	2.4	2.6	0.2				0.1	1.8	100
1787	87.7	3.2	0.6	3.5	0.1		1.1			0.6	100
1789[a]	52.4	25.9		8.8	0.3	8.1	2.4			3.3	100
1796	71.1	3.6	18.1	3.6	1.2		0.1		0.2	4.6	100
1797	69.7	4.3	14.8	6.5	1.6		0.8			3.1	100
1798	68.2	12.0	3.3	3.3	0.2		1.4	6.3	3.4	3.0	100
1799	58.7	20.3	9.7	8.2	0.2		1.1		0.2	2.1	100
1800	57.7	11.9	3.3	14.7	0.4	0.4			1.3	1.7	100

a Please see explanatory note under Table 8.5.

SOURCE: PBT

TABLE 8.8 Portuguese exports to Sweden according to STRO, percentages of volume, 1776–1800

	Salt	Wine	Sugar	Fruits	Others	Total
1776	85.9	11.5		2.6		100
1777	99.2	0.1		0.7	0.0	100
1783	98.6	0.7		0.2	0.5	100
1787	95.3	0.6		4.0	0.0	100
1789	82.0	14.0	1.2	0.7	2.1	100
1796	91.9	0.0	4.7	0.3	3.0	100
1797	85.8	2.9	8.7	0.7	1.9	100
1798	98.5	0.2		0.3	1.0	100
1799	91.4	1.5	4.9	1.7	0.5	100
1800	99.7	0.1		0.2	0.0	100

SOURCE: STRO

6 Conclusion

The Sound toll registers are often described as a unique source with obvious potential for researchers to study the maritime history and trade between the Baltic and Western Europe.[31] Our comparison firmly supports the argument by Ahonen that the Sound toll registers are an effective barometer of transactions in Northern European East-West trade.[32] The registers can also be used to study early modern trade in detail, at the level of an individual vessel, although this approach calls for a measure of caution. When it comes to less frequently traded goods, our research indicates that there is an asymmetry in the STRO data, as the custom registers did not tell the whole story at the level of minute details. In micro-level research, regarding individual ships or specific products, the cargoes registered in STRO have to be viewed with caution, and it is strongly recommended to use complementary shipping documents as well.[33]

31 See for example Gøbel, "The Sound Toll Registers Online Project," 305 and Rich and Wilson, *Economic Organization*, 226.

32 Ahonen, *From Sugar Triangle*, 23–24.

33 E.g. Gøbel, "The Sound Toll Registers Online Project."

Our analysis suggests that harsh criticism of STRO should be disregarded; the registers do provide quite accurate information on trade.[34] Although STRO provides us with a good overall picture of the trade between Baltic and the rest of Europe – and even to a certain extent with the rest of the world – the picture is not complete. The Danish Sound was just one spot in the complicated and emerging networks of global shipping and trade. Furthermore, the records reveal only those aspects of trade that were compiled in them in the first place. As Gøbel has emphasized, the registers are correct but not complete.[35] The value of trade is a complicated issue during the early modern period. The market prices were highly volatile, fluctuating often and widely. This problem cannot be resolved using the customs books.[36] Moreover, the problem of product values and thus trade balance, not to mention the constantly changing exchange rates, must be recognized.[37] Our analysis suggests, however, that by means of the combination of the volumes of trade registered in STRO with national commodity price datasets, the challenges of total trade values can at least partly be resolved. Therefore, it is suggested to use STRO together with national trade and shipping records.

Appendix 1: Linear Regression Analysis (Ordinary Least Squares, OLS) of the SBT (Swedish National Archives, Annual Reports of Foreign Trade and Shipping) and STRO Datasets for Swedish Exports to Portugal, 1738–1800

The datasets used here were transformed into a logarithmic scale. The STRO data was chosen as the dependent variable and the SBT as the independent variable.

34 For instance Schreiner claimed that "the figures on goods passing the Sound had little to do with the facts" – Schreiner, *Nederland og Norge*, 9.

35 Gøbel, "The Sound Toll Registers Online Project," 321.

36 Ahonen, *From Sugar Triangle*, 23–24.

37 Denzel, *Handbook*.

Iron

	Coefficient	Std. Error	t	Prob.
C	3.07	0.65	4.74	0.00
Beta	0.70	0.06	10.86	0.00
R^2	0.66			
F-statistics	117.94			
Prob(F-statistics)	0.00			

Steel

	Coefficient	Std. Error	t	Prob.
C	1.34	0.45	2.96	0.004
Beta	0.82	0.06	12.93	0.00
R^2	0.74			
	167.19			
Prob(F-statistics)	0.00			

Copper

	Coefficient	Std. Error	t	Prob.
C	−0.21	0.45	−0.47	0.64
Beta	1.04	0.11	9.81	0.00
R^2	0.74			
F-statistics	96.32			
Prob(F-statistics)	0.00			

Timber				
	Coefficient	Std. Error	t	Prob.
C	6.74	1.09	6.18	0.00
Beta	0.46	0.09	5.03	0.00
R^2	0.30			
F-statistics	25.29			
Prob(F-statistics)	0.00			

Tar & Pitch				
	Coefficient	Std. Error	t	Prob.
C	0.81	0.58	1.40	0.17
Beta	0.89	0.076	11.73	0.00
R^2	0.70			
F-statistics	137.52			
Prob(F-statistics)	0.00			

Appendix 2: Linear Regression Analysis (Ordinary Least Squares, OLS) of the SBT (Swedish National Archives, Annual Reports of Foreign Trade and Shipping) and STRO Datasets for Portuguese Exports to Sweden, 1738–1800

Salt				
	Coefficient	Std. Error	t	Prob.
C	0.59	0.88	0.67	0.51
Beta	0.89	0.10	8.69	0.00
R^2	0.57			
F-statistics	75.57			
Prob(F-statistics)	0.00			

Wine

	Coefficient	Std. Error	t	Prob.
C	0.65	1.36	0.48	0.63
Beta	0.85	0.13	6.62	0.00
R^2	0.42			
	43.87			
Prob(F-statistics)	0.00			

Sugar

	Coefficient	Std. Error	t	Prob.
C	−1.45	1.53	−0.94	0.35
Beta	1.03	0.15	6.92	0.00
R^2	0.57			
F-statistics	47.90			
Prob(F-statistics)	0.00			

Fruits

	Coefficient	Std. Error	t	Prob.
C	1.10	0.79	1.39	0.17
Beta	0.92	0.15	6.09	0.00
R^2	0.38			
F-statistics	37.04			
Prob(F-statistics)	0.00			

PART 4

Name Data Analyses

the shipmaster (or the whole ship?) simply never passed the Sound ever again. It seems more plausible that this is a problem with the source material. Two obvious reasons come to mind: spelling variation and/or toll evasion.[11]

Computer-matching of historical records is fraught with problems.[12] The names of the shipmasters are not spelled consistently, either when the material has been digitized, or more probably in the original source. At a glance, it is easy to find many examples of individual shipmasters with names that sound completely or almost alike, coming from the same port. One reason might be that how the writers at Elsinore transcribed names, both Danish and non-Danish, might have shifted over time. There is also a problem of multilingualism: the writers at Elsinore had to work with names of shipmasters from several different European countries. For example, it is possible that they spelled more 'familiar' names (most importantly Danish names) more consistently than foreign names, which presumably might have been more unfamiliar to them. In the paper, I have used four different ways of matching entries, in order to see if the routine for matching records has any impact upon the results: along one dimension, records are matched requiring only matching the name of the shipmaster, or matching both the name and homeport of the shipmaster, in two different entries. Along another dimension records are matched either using identical name matching (including both first name and surname) of the shipmaster or using 'fuzzy matching' of the names (using a routine called Soundex).[13] Concerning 'fuzzy matching', the problem of multilingualism becomes a special problem since the particular routine used in this case, Soundex, was initially developed for English-language standardization of records. This might give rise to a bias in the matching, with more successful matches of shipmasters with English-sounding names. This must be kept in mind when comparing results between the different matching routines.

Requiring identical spelling of names, as well as matching homeports, does of course give rise to the smallest sample of matched data, whereas fuzzy matching only using names (i.e. without homeport) gives rise to the largest sample. Table 9.1, panel A, shows the total size of the whole sample of the four ways of matching the data.

---

11 These issues are treated more extensively in the Introduction to this volume.

12 For a discussion of some central issues, see Bloothooft, "Assessment of Systems," 39–56.

13 The 'fuzzy matching' uses a routine called Soundex. All names in the sample are assigned a code of a letter and three digits, based on the initial letter of the name and the three following consonants in the name. The consonants are assigned digits according to the following scheme: [bfpv]=1, [cgjkqsxz]=2, [dt]=3, [l]=4, [mn]=5 and [r]=6. For example, Linckleller and Linkletter are both assigned the code L524. The Soundex-code is then used for matching shipmasters in STRO.

TABLE 9.1 Descriptive statistics of matches based on STRO, 1699–1819

	Obs.	$TBSP_x$ (days)		
		Mean	Median	Max
Panel A. Full sample				
1. Name and domicile, identical name	105,194	400	71	38,365
2. Name only, identical	120,774	356	67	41,249
3. Name and domicile, fuzzy match of name	168,886	344	65	41,309
4. Name only, fuzzy match	183,814	260	61	41,318
Panel B. Reduced sample (first and tenth decile removed)				
1. Name and domicile, identical name	83,392	159	72	825
2. Name only, identical	95,763	138	68	698
3. Name and domicile, fuzzy match of name	134,939	115	65	544
4. Name only, fuzzy match	145,887	99	61	353

SOURCE: OWN CALCULATIONS BASED ON STRO [ACCESSED JANUARY 2013]

There might also be a problem with toll evasion, just as when any customs-related source material is used as a source of data. If a shipmaster manages to bypass the Sound without officially paying the toll on one single leg of the journey, this will show up as a one-way trip in STRO. This could perhaps be used in itself as a measure of tax evasion, but in this study, it only reduces the number of successful matches (i.e. reducing the sample size). If toll evasion was more widespread, however, it could pose a problem for the analysis in this study. Assume a situation where we have a shipmaster going for two round-trips to the Baltic. Assume furthermore that the second and third of the four passages of the Sound (one eastward, one westward) are not entered in STRO, perhaps because the shipmaster manages to slip through the Sound undetected, through bribes, or for some other reasons. In the database of matched entries, this would overestimate $TBSP_X$. This can potentially explain some outliers in the dataset. This is dealt with here by using data on median (rather than significantly more unreliable mean) times between passages for the analysis, as well as by not including the lowest and highest decile from the samples in the analysis: any outliers (i.e. abnormally 'fast' or 'slow' journeys) will thereby be removed from the estimates. Descriptive statistics of the reduced samples are shown in table 9.1, panel B.

A third problem is that a single shipmaster might have been involved in tramp shipping, thus visiting many ports before returning through the Sound. In most cases the data in the STR only state the last port visited before arriving at Elsinore, therefore we cannot know if/when this is happening. In order to reduce the problem of biases from shipmasters involved in tramp shipping, I have only included the trips *where the port of destination in a first entry is identical to the port of origin in the following entry related to the same shipmaster*. This can still give rise to a number of errors due to what we might call 'undetected' tramp shipping: there is still the possibility that the shipmaster has gone from the Sound to a first destination, then heading on to a second destination, only to return to the first destination before returning through the Sound. In the STR database alone, such trips will not be possible to trace, but will give rise to errors in the estimated results. To some extent, this problem might be reduced by excluding the first and tenth decile from the sample. This must however be kept in mind when discussing any results.

A fourth potential problem is the fact that many shipmasters might stay at the port longer than necessary from the point of maximizing the use of the capital invested in the ship. This might be a problem particularly when shipmasters arrive in their homeport. Assuming that most agents involved are profit maximizing when working, however, this is perhaps not that big a problem when the ship is in a foreign port. When the shipmasters arrive in their homeport, there might however be a different story of shipmasters not only visiting their family while the ship is unloaded and reloaded, but staying for a prolonged period of time (taking a 'vacation', if nothing else). This problem is dealt with here by requiring that the port of destination is on the 'other side' of the Sound than the homeport of the shipmaster, i.e. to the east of the Sound if the homeport of the shipmaster is to the west of it, and vice versa. For example, if a shipmaster were from Amsterdam, only his voyages in the Baltic Sea would be included in any estimates, whereas all other matched voyages are excluded from the sample used. Vice versa, if a shipmaster came for example from Stockholm, only his voyages in the Atlantic would be included in the estimates, leaving out any voyages in the Baltic Sea. This reduces the problem of the shipmaster staying longer in his homeport than usual, and can perhaps contribute to reducing the problem of tramp shipping.

The data shown in the graphs and the table below are all based on matching routine 1, requiring identical names as well as matching domicile of the shipmaster. Using any of the other matching routines does not change the results in any significant way (i.e. the median times shift slightly, but both the geographical patterns and the patterns of change over time remain the same). This provides some confidence that, to the extent that there is a bias problem from using the Soundex-routine, discussed above, it is not very large.

5 Data

Graph 9.1 shows data on the median time between Sound passages for a number of the largest ports in the Baltic in relation to the geographical distance from Elsinore[14] to the port in question. Since it only shows a limited number of ports within the Baltic, and since only ships with shipmasters from outside the Baltic Sea region are included, the sample size underlying the graph is only a fraction of the whole sample.

The data in graph 9.1 show, as would be expected, that the time it took to travel from Elsinore, to a specific port in the Baltic and then back again, was determined largely by the distance to the port of destination. The median time between Sound passages for ships going to Copenhagen was for example only around 20 days, whereas the median time necessary to go to St. Petersburg and back was 67 days. The relationship seems to be linear. We can thereby estimate that the average time spent in a Baltic port was around a month.[15] Shipping does however seem to have been comparatively faster than the average on three routes in particular: København, Klaipeda and Vyborg. Why this was so might be the topic of future research.

Graph 9.2 shows data on the median time between passages per port, divided into two separate samples based on the year of the passage, so that it becomes possible to see if there is any change over time.

Graph 9.2 shows how the median time between Sound passages changed over the years, by dividing the sample into two: ships passing through the Sound prior to and after the middle of the eighteenth century, respectively. As can be seen in the graph, the time spent between Sound passages seems to have decreased on all routes except one (to/from Szczecin). The decrease is furthermore quite substantial, ranging from 10 to 35 per cent between the first and second half of the eighteenth century. If Szczecin really is an exception to this pattern (and if so, why) might also be a topic for future research.

14 The shortest distance by sea has been estimated using the shipping distance calculator available at Searates.com: [http://www.searates.com/reference/portdistance/].

15 The exact estimate will depend on how the model is specified. Estimating a linear relationship in the sample of ships going to the major ports in the Baltic, removing outliers in the form of any journey that took longer than one year from the estimate, for example yields a constant (i.e. an estimate of the time spent in port) of 36 days.

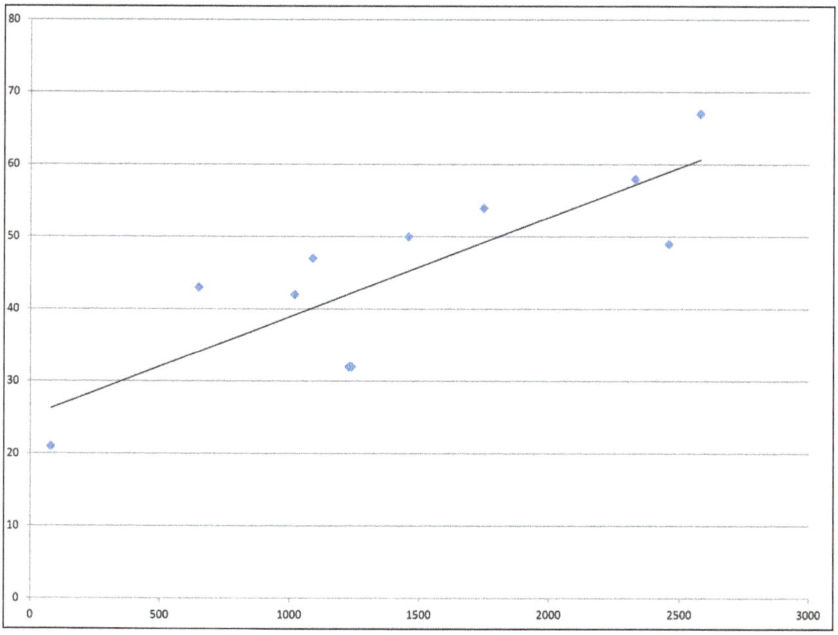

GRAPH 9.1 Median Time between Sound Passages (days) by port of destination, in relation to travelled distance (km), for eleven large ports in the Baltic, 1699–1819.
NOTE: Domicile of shipmasters are *not* in the Baltic. N=26,492. Ports shown in the graph are Gdańsk, Kaliningrad, Klaipeda, København, Liepaja, Narva, Riga, St. Petersburg, Stockholm, Szczecin and Vyborg.
SOURCE: OWN CALCULATIONS BASED ON STRO [ACCESSED JANUARY 2013]

Table 9.2 is similar to graph 9.2 in that it shows the change over time, but in this case, the data represents an estimated *minimum* time necessary for the journey from Elsinore, to a specific port, and back again.

The minimum time necessary between passages did most certainly experience important seasonal fluctuations, not the least since turnover time in port might have been impacted by several seasonal factors (e.g. waiting time for cargo, ports that freeze over in wintertime etc.). By comparing the samples in the aggregate between the time different time-periods, however, it does seem as if the minimum time also decreased between the periods.

6 Discussion and Future Research

The preliminary data shown above indicates that the speed of shipping in the Baltic trade might have increased over time. As was discussed in the section on methodology, the method used does not enable us to analyze in

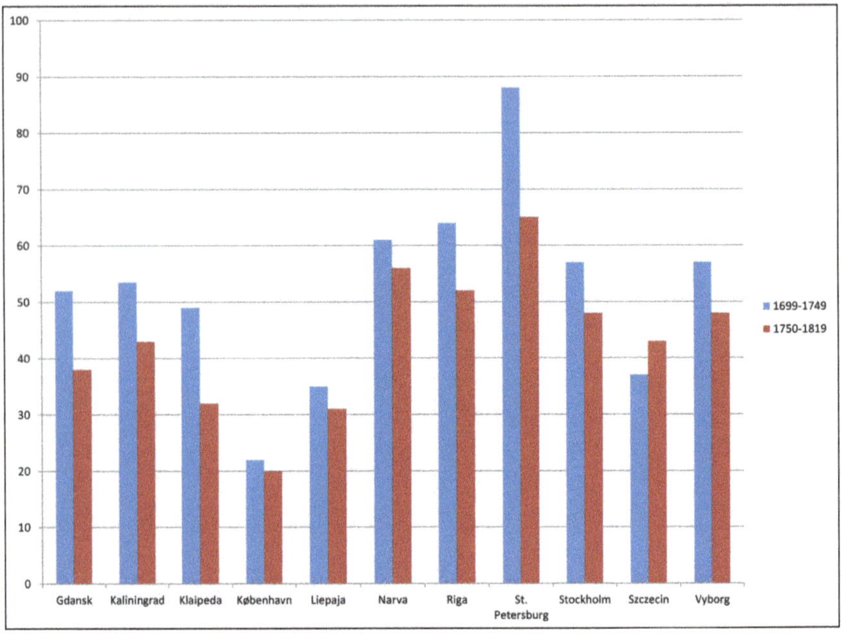

GRAPH 9.2 Change in Median Time between Sound Passages (days) over time for eleven large ports of destination in the Baltic, 1699–1819.
NOTE: domiciles (homeports) of shipmasters are *not* in the Baltic. N=26,492.
SOURCE: OWN CALCULATIONS BASED ON STRO [ACCESSED JANUARY 2013].

detail whether this increase in speed was due to shorter time in ports (for example due to a growth in the volume of goods traded decreasing waiting time, improved loading of goods, or some other factor), or faster speed while at sea. The results do however suggest that there might have been important gains in shipping speed already prior to the nineteenth century transport revolution.

Much research remains to be done on the topic. Most importantly, there is a need to analyze if there is a change in speed over time, when at the same time controlling for other factors that might influence the results, so that the changes in time between Sound passages shown in the section on data above are just not because of any confounding factor. The dataset unfortunately limits the number of factors we might control for in a regression analysis, but some important variables are possible to include in the future analysis. In the graph above, the sample has just been divided into two very rough groups – before and after 1750. Does the change in speed that this graph indicates occur slowly over a longer period, or are there sudden bursts of increasing speed? Is there any relationship between the change and external factors, such as wars in the region? Is there a shifting seasonal pattern to the shipping, that might

TABLE 9.2 Minimum time between sound passages (days) over time for eleven large ports of destination in the Baltic

	1699–1749	1750–1819
Gdansk	27	25
Kaliningrad	30	26
Klaipeda	31	22
København	12	11
Liepaja	21	20
Narva	40	38
Riga	41	36
St. Petersburg	59	45
Stockholm	36	34
Szczecin	18	27
Vyborg	42	34

NOTE: 'minimum' time between Sound passages is defined here as the time between passages of the tenth percentile in the sample. Domicile of shipmasters are *not* in the Baltic. N=26,492.
SOURCE: OWN CALCULATIONS BASED ON THE SOUNDTOLL ONLINE DATABASE [ACCESSED JANUARY 2013].

contribute to explaining the results, for example a relative increase of shipping in summer-time when there is no risk of getting stuck for long periods of time because of ice? Does the tonnage of the ships matter, so that for example there is a shift towards faster but smaller ships? Future research will try to answer these questions.

CHAPTER 10

Shipmasters from the West Frisian Islands in Baltic Shipping, 1737–1800

Maarten Draper and Jerem van Duijl

1 Introduction

The people of the West Frisian Islands, also known as the Dutch Wadden Islands, have a long and rich maritime past. Since their settlement on the islands, the inhabitants of Texel, Vlieland, Terschelling, Ameland and Schiermonnikoog have turned to the sea for a living. In local historiography, it is traditionally stressed that most inhabitants had a tough life working in the agricultural sector, which was plagued all too often by coastal flooding and storms.[1] Small-scale fishing was therefore an indispensable part of the local economy.[2] Many of these farmers and fishermen also found part-time employment as seamen to add to their income; others were fully employed in the maritime sector.[3] During the sixteenth century, the mariners of these islands facilitated and benefitted from the rise of Amsterdam as trade hub, and in the subsequent period, which is known as the 'Dutch Golden Age', the merchant marine of the West Frisian Islands thrived thanks to its connection to the vibrant metropolis on the banks of the Amstel.[4] The West Frisian Islands were positioned conveniently on important shipping routes connecting Amsterdam to the North Sea. The shipmasters from these islands profited from this advantage by providing important services to the Dutch whaling industry and the Dutch Baltic trade, especially in the grain trade, commonly referred to as "the mother of all trades".[5]

During the eighteenth century, the Dutch Republic lost its dominant position in international trade. Between 1737 and 1799, the total number of annual passages through the Sound increased from about 3,000 to about 9,500. Between 1,000 and 2,000 passages departed from or were destined to Amsterdam.[6] In

1 Allan, *Het eiland Ameland*, 55–57; Schoorl, *De convexe kustboog*, 888–889.
2 Van Leunen, *Terschelling en de visserij*, 54; Vermeulen, *Op zoek*, 132.
3 Schoorl, *De convexe kustboog*, 1, 794.
4 Schoorl, *De convexe kustboog*, 1, 786; Dekker, "De Amelander walvisvaart," 212.
5 Van Tielhof, *The "mother of all trades"*, 1–5.
6 Bang and Korst, *Tabeller over skibsfart 1*.

 | DOI:10.1163/9789004371781_012

general, the number of ships arriving in Dutch ports and the size of the Dutch merchant fleet remained stable between 1700 and 1780.[7] Consequently, the number of Dutch ships passing the Sound largely remained constant during the eighteenth century, whereas the share of ships from other countries increased.[8] However, this relative but not absolute decline corresponds only to the Dutch Republic as a whole. The structure of Dutch Baltic trade changed. The traditional center of the trade, Amsterdam, lost its grip on Baltic trade, whereas other ports, such as Rotterdam, expanded their commercial relations with the Baltic region.

In the eighteenth century, the Dutch Republic's maritime trade and shipping were two separate but closely related sectors of the economy. Therefore, structural changes in Dutch Baltic trade had an impact on the supply of maritime transport services. Some places faced a period of relapsing Baltic shipping, while others flourished. For example, Lemmer and Dokkum, in the Dutch province of Friesland, succeeded in getting more involved in Baltic maritime transport.[9]

Jonathan Israel suggests that an actual decrease of Dutch maritime trade was camouflaged by increased activity of small ships from Friesland and the West Frisian Islands.[10] This seems to be in contradiction with the declining number of passages of shipmasters from these islands through the Sound during the eighteenth century. In the opening decades of that century, shipmasters domiciled in Terschelling and Ameland made more than 100 passages annually. This number steadily declined, until nothing was left of their participation in Baltic maritime transport at the end of the eighteenth century.[11] In local historiography, the eighteenth century is described as a period of severe economic tribulations, mainly caused by the decline of the shipping sector.[12] For example, the number of inhabitants of Terschelling dropped from about 2,650 in 1732, to about 2,000 in 1743, to approximately 1,800 at the end of the eighteenth century.[13]

The question then arises: What caused the decline of Baltic maritime transport of shipmasters from the West Frisian Islands during the eighteenth century? This article aims to give answers to this question by relating the specialization of shipmasters from the West Frisian Islands to structural

7 De Vries and Van der Woude, *The first modern economy*, 492.
8 Bang and Korst, *Tabeller*.
9 Faber, "Friesland," 20.
10 Israel, *The Dutch Republic*, 1000.
11 Bang and Korst, *Tabeller*; Schoorl, *De convexe kustboog*, 1, 794.
12 Allan, *Het eiland Ameland*, 52–57. Vermeulen, *Op zoek*, 224.
13 Schoorl, *De convexe kustboog*, 1, 895.

changes in the Dutch maritime transport sector. To achieve this goal, an analysis of STRO is executed, using data covering the period between 1737 and 1800.[14] After a discussion of the results, a comparison is made to recent literature on changes in the spatial structure of the Dutch economy in the early modern period. We will argue that shipmasters from the West Frisian Islands specialized in trade routes that were successful at the beginning of the eighteenth century, but were abandoned during the second half of the century. Their dependency on certain trade routes made it impossible for the shipmasters from the West Frisian Islands to switch to new upcoming routes.

2 Method and Results

The data from STRO needed some preparation before they were suitable for analysis. The main problem that needed to be dealt with was the large variation in the spellings of names, places, and cargoes. As there was no standard spelling in the early modern period and the Danish clerks in Helsingør did not register foreign names with great consistency, it is necessary to bring some standardization to the spelling variations in STRO. The variation of place names could be overcome by linking Welling's database of place names to the data of STRO.[15] The variation in personal names was reduced 'manually', that is, names that the authors deemed to refer to the same person were standardized. Thereafter, it was possible to estimate the size of the population of shipmasters and their specialization in terms of numbers of passages and routes. This analysis was based on an unpublished guide created by Werner Scheltjens that is tailored to working with STRO.[16]

The method described above results in data that clearly chart the downward trend in eighteenth-century Baltic shipping (graph 10.1). Gradually, the number of passages by West Frisian shipmasters declined from 283 in 1740 to 89 in 1773, and finally to zero in 1799.[17] Logically, the number of West Frisian Islands shipmasters active in the Baltic shipping declined at an even rate over time:

14 At the start of our research, only data for this period was available.

15 The database of place names is the work of George Welling. This database has been incorporated in STRO.

16 The method for standardizing the names of the shipmasters was developed by Werner Scheltjens. We used his unpublished manual *STR online: Van ruwe data naar analyse van schipperspopulaties*.

17 As these numbers are based on a version of STRO that was almost complete at the time of writing, the numbers in some years could be a bit higher.

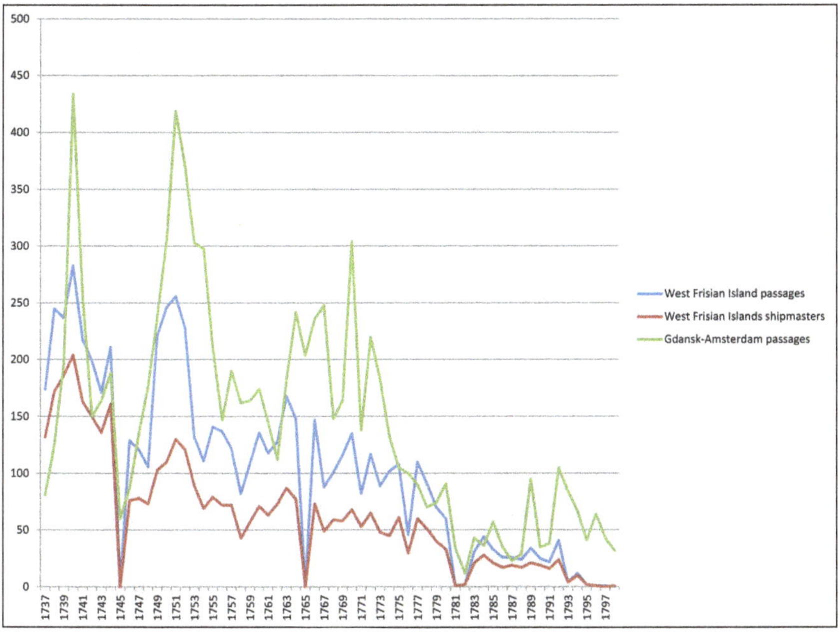

GRAPH 10.1 The number of passages of the West Frisian Islands' shipmasters, the number of West Frisian Islands shipmasters, and the number of passages on the route Danzig-Amsterdam, 1739–1800.
SOURCE: STRO

from 204 in 1740 to 48 in 1773, and to zero in 1799.[18] The low level of activity in 1781 and 1782, and afterwards, was probably related to the Fourth Anglo-Dutch War (1780–1784). West Frisian Islands Baltic shipping never recovered to pre-war level. The final blow was struck during The War of the First Coalition (1791–1795). After 1793, the West Frisian Islands were no longer active as suppliers of maritime transport services to the commercial centers of the Dutch Republic. The island of Schiermonnikoog is exceptional in this regard: shipmasters from this island were mainly active in Baltic shipping after 1815.

Starting point for the analysis were the passages by shipmasters who reported to be of the West Frisian Islands. This starting point is somewhat problematic because the data on the origin of the shipmasters is not always reliable. Shipmasters could report a false domicile, or they could have reported their domicile inconsistently. In particular, the tendency to report larger and better-known cities as their domicile hinders this research.[19] In case of

18 Incomplete data for the years 1745 and 1765 were excluded from the graph.
19 Christensen, *Dutch trade*, 60–64; Dekker, "Friese schippers," 233–240.

the shipmasters from the West Frisian Islands, it is very likely that a number of them are registered as Amsterdam shipmasters, instead of, for example, Ameland or Terschelling.

The shipmasters of the West Frisian Islands in the period 1737–1799 exclusively sailed in service of Amsterdam, which is in line with the economic orientation of the islands towards the Dutch capital. The most important destinations were Danzig, Riga and Königsberg (Table 10.1).[20] The eastern Baltic ports of Reval, Narva, and St. Petersburg were not frequently visited. The importance of the route Danzig-Amsterdam is striking: the route accounts for 38 percent of the westbound passages made by the shipmasters of the West Frisian Islands in the studied period.

Thus far, the West Frisian Islands have been discussed as one category; however, the islands differ significantly among themselves. First, Ameland (57,5%) and Terschelling (35%) together are responsible for 92,5% of all passages by shipmasters from the West Frisian Islands. The islands of Texel (1,5%), Vlieland (5%), and Schiermonnikoog (1%) were only marginally involved in Baltic shipping. Then, a rather small share of the West Frisian Islands shipmaster population was responsible for a large share of the passages. To approach this issue the populations of shipmasters were categorized according to the method of Scheltjens, which calculates the pattern density rate (PDR) of individual shipmasters.[21] PDR is calculated by dividing the period in which a shipmaster

TABLE 10.1 The most popular routes in westbound direction of shipmasters from the West Frisian Islands, 1737–1799

Route (Westbound)	Passages	Share
Gdańsk-Amsterdam	1,096	50%
Riga-Amsterdam	803	36%
Königsberg-Amsterdam	167	8%
Reval-Amsterdam	59	3%
Narva-Amsterdam	47	2%
St. Petersburg-Amsterdam	37	2%
Total	2,209	100%

20 When passing the Sound in eastward direction shipmasters often reported 'Baltic Sea' as their port of destination. For that reason the westbound passages, when the shipmasters reported a more precise port of departure, are used here.

21 Scheltjens and Dopfer, "Unified Rule Approach," 238–239.

carried out his voyages by the number of voyages. Subsequently, per island the average PDR is determined. The average is used as a benchmark to divide the populations of shipmasters into four categories: specialist, regular, sporadic, or once only. Shipmasters with the highest passages/time ratio are labeled as specialist, those with the lowest as sporadic. A shipmaster is labeled as a specialist if his PDR is lower than the average PDR divided by two. The label sporadic is attributed to the shipmasters with a PDR higher than the average PDR multiplied by 1.5. The 'regulars' form an intermediary category. For example, Fopke Cornelis from Ameland made 111 registered voyages to the Baltic in 26 years. Therefore, his PDR is 0.234 (26/111). As the benchmark of the Ameland population is 1.33 he is labeled as specialist (0.234<1.33/2). The specialists and regulars of the islands, which were more involved in Baltic shipping, Ameland and Terschelling, account for a larger share of the passages than their equals from the other islands do. The most active quarter of the shipmasters from Ameland were responsible for 85% of the islands' passages. However, the most active 30% of the shipmasters from Texel made only 60% of the total passages. The specialist's share of the total number of passages is probably higher because the shipmasters that feature in the dataset only once often actually belonged to a different port. Some shipmasters were inconsistent in the domicile they reported, a phenomenon known as the 'hjemsted problem' (see above). For the same reason some of the passages made by shipmasters who did live on the West Frisian Islands are missing. Based on these findings, we can conclude that the Baltic shipping sector of the West Frisian Islands was dominated by quite a small number of highly specialized shipmasters from Terschelling and Ameland.

3 Case Study Ameland

As specialized shipmasters had such a great influence on the development of the Baltic transport sector on the islands, it is important to know what their specialization entailed. Therefore, STRO was used to reconstruct the careers of individual shipmasters of Ameland, which was selected as a case study because it was the island with the most shipmasters and the most passages. Subsequently, the results were analyzed to find patterns that can give us insight in the way specialization took place.

During the late sixteenth century, technical innovations resulted in new types of ships in the Dutch merchant fleet. These ships were larger, making them especially suitable for the transport of bulk carriage. At the beginning of the seventeenth century, the 'fluyt' had become the typical ship of the Dutch merchant fleet, for which Baltic grain transport had become the most important activity.[22] The average tonnage of these ships lay well above 100 lasts. A reversing trend took place during the late seventeenth and eighteenth centuries. Merchant ships became smaller as wars made the northern European seas unsafe; smaller ships were able to stay closer to the coast and were more suitable for transporting mixed cargoes.[23] One could reason that the West Frisian Islands had a favorable location on the North Sea for the transport of bulk goods on the large 'flute' ships, especially in comparison to Amsterdam, which was located at the shallow Zuiderzee, and that the rising popularity of smaller ships harmed the shipping of the Islands. However, already in 1731 the majority of the ships with shipmasters from Ameland, sailing from a port in the Baltic Sea to Amsterdam, had a tonnage of less than 100 lasts. The size of the ships varied greatly between ca. 35 lasts and more than 130 lasts. The same goes for shipmasters from Terschelling.[24] In STRO, it is not immediately clear if the shipmaster specialized in certain cargoes. Many shipmasters transported a diverse range of goods. For example, in 1790 Onne Kornelis from Ameland sailed eastbound through the Sound with paper, cheese, sugar, figs, groats, wine, salt, tobacco and unspecified goods aboard. [25] On his way back, he transported wooden boards, flax, hemp and herb seeds.[26] The shipmasters from the West Frisian Islands were thus specialized neither in shipping the same types of goods, nor in using the same specific type of ship.

However, when considering the trade routes, Scheltjens argues that the West Frisian Islands belong to a group of Dutch places whose communities of shipmasters were heavily involved in shipping on traditional routes, such as the transport of grain from Danzig to Amsterdam. He points out that the "course of development of these shipping communities is not entirely clear nor univocal" and that data that can confirm the absolute decline of the shipping community of the West Frisian Islands is scattered.[27] Table 10.1 confirms the importance of Riga and especially Danzig for the shipmasters from the West Frisian Islands. With few exceptions, all of the westbound passages had Amsterdam as the destination. Moreover, individual shipmasters tended to specialize on one specific route. Based on the given port of departure when passing the Sound westbound, we can say that the shipmasters from Ameland that were labeled by us as "regulars" often went to two or three Baltic ports

22 Unger, *Shipping and economic growth 1350–1800*, 49.
23 Van Tielhof, *The "mother of all trades,"* 185–190.
24 Dekker, "Friese schippers," 243–248.
25 www.soundtoll.nl, 18644, 18-07-1790.
26 www.soundtoll.nl, 19246, 29-08-1790.
27 Scheltjens, "The changing geography," 25; 34.

during their career. Not surprisingly, Danzig was the most frequented, followed by Riga and Königsberg. Other ports were only sporadically visited by these shipmasters. Some of them were particularly active on one route, especially shipmasters that were only just categorized as regulars instead of specialists. For example, Jacob Haitsma left the Baltic Sea twenty-seven times; sixteen times he departed from Königsberg and only five times from Danzig.

This specialization on one route is even more prominent in the group of shipmasters that were categorized as specialists. The ports of departure of the westbound passages of the forty-five specialists of the population of shipmasters domiciled in Ameland can be seen in Graph 10.2. Whilst in general the specialists and the regulars were active on the same routes, specialists tended to focus more on one specific route. Most of the specialists went almost exclusively from Danzig to Amsterdam. Some shipmasters, like number 19, representing Siemen Jakobs, in Graph 10.2, specialized in shipping between Riga and Amsterdam. Number 16, called Pieter Hendriks, on the other hand, switched routes twice. Between 1751 and 1762, he passed the Sound fifteen times in a westbound direction, and Danzig was his port of departure in thirteen of these instances. In the following nine years, nine of his eleven westbound trips started at the port of Riga. Afterwards, he once again focused on Danzig: six out of seven trips from the Baltic Sea to the North Sea started in the port at the mouth of the Vistula. Only a few shipmasters that were labeled as specialists concentrated on the route Königsberg-Amsterdam. The category "other routes" consists mostly of passages with "Baltic Sea" as port of departure. These ships possibly sailed on the same route as the route in which the shipmaster was specialized. Again, the more voyages a shipmaster made, the more he was specialized on one route. Fopke Cornelis (number 28) was the shipmaster from Ameland, and of the West Frisian Islands altogether, who executed the largest number of journeys to the Baltic. Graph 10.2 shows that fifty-three of his fifty-five westbound voyages started in Danzig. We can conclude that a successful career of shipmasters from Ameland with a high number of passages through the Sound was tied to specialization on one route. Most often, this route was Danzig-Amsterdam.

4 Locked-in on Routes

During the eighteenth century, the Dutch Republic lost its dominant position in international trade. There is an ongoing debate about whether this was a period of decline or stagnation. It has been argued that mercantilist policies of European countries in the eighteenth century undermined Dutch

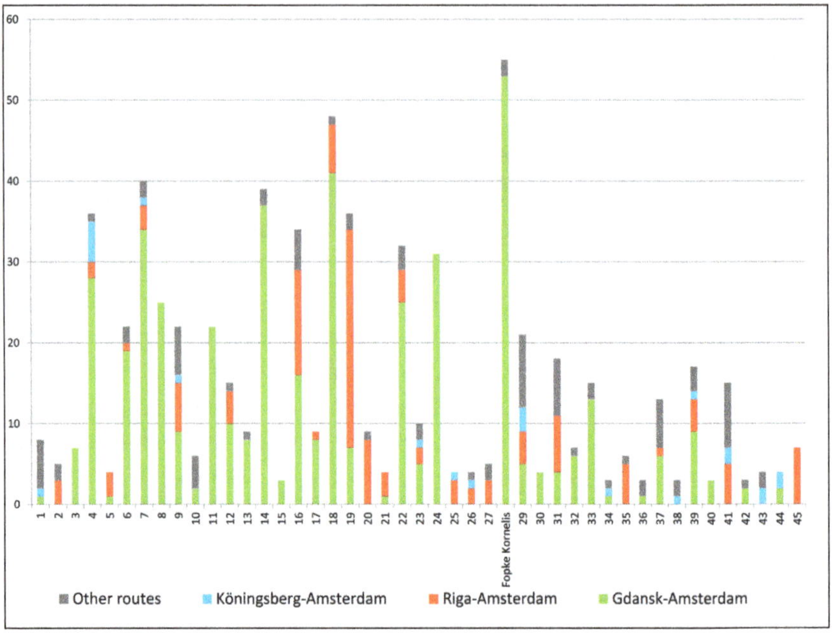

GRAPH 10.2 The routes of the 45 shipmasters from Ameland with the highest passage/time ratio through the Sound in westbound direction, 1737–1799.

trade.[28] Besides, it has been pointed out that ships increasingly sailed directly to their destination, instead of bringing their goods to the staple market of Amsterdam. In historiography, this phenomenon has been called 'voorbijlandvaart'.[29] More recently, the economic position of the Dutch Republic has been related to the availability of information. Clé Lesger has shown that the staple market of Amsterdam in the seventeenth century was, first and foremost, a center of information exchange.[30] In this line of thought, Jan Willem Veluwenkamp suggests that in the eighteenth century a 'postal revolution' made the function of Amsterdam as 'information hub' less necessary, thus damaging the city's position in international trade. Furthermore, he points towards mercantilist policies, which encouraged foreign shipmasters to sail directly to their port of destination.[31]

28 Israel, *Dutch primacy*, 383–386. See also the contribution of Magnus Ressel to this volume.

29 De Vries and Van der Woude, *Nederland 1500–1815*, 558, 578–581.

30 Lesger, *Handel in Amsterdam*, 197–201.

31 Veluwenkamp, "Het Nederlandse handelsstelsel," 73–76; Veluwenkamp, "International Business," 121–134.

Whether the eighteenth century should be regarded as a time of (absolute) decline for the Dutch economy remains a contested issue. However, it is clear that the Dutch economy underwent some profound changes. Dutch trade and shipping were no longer as dominant as in the seventeenth century; other countries, most notably Great Britain and France, expanded their commerce. The nature of Dutch trade also changed. The bulk trades on traditional routes, such as the Baltic grain trade, declined. On the other hand, trade on new routes, involving different goods increased. Most notably, the trade in overseas goods between the colonies and the German hinterland gained importance in the eighteenth century.[32] Or, as Jan de Vries and Ad van der Woude put it: Dutch maritime trade during the eighteenth century changed its focus from a north-south axis to a west-east axis.[33]

For most of the eighteenth century, however, the number of Dutch passages through the Sound remained stable, despite the reorientation of Dutch international trade. It is therefore necessary to look into the changes of the Baltic trade in order to explain the decline of the West Frisian Islands' Baltic shipping. We have noted that the shipmasters of West Frisian Islands sailed in service of Amsterdam, and were especially active on the route Danzig-Amsterdam. As Graph 10.1 suggests, the decreasing traffic on this route coincides with decline of West Frisian Islands' Baltic shipping. In his study on eighteenth century Baltic grain transport, Scheltjens addresses the changing spatial structure of the Baltic grain trade.[34] The patterns observed by Scheltjens concur with our findings. Whereas in the seventeenth century and in the first half of the eighteenth century Baltic grain trade was concentrated in Amsterdam, in the second half of the eighteenth century the trade was diverted to a large number of smaller routes, such as Libau-Schiedam. The formerly important grain routes Danzig-Amsterdam and Königsberg-Amsterdam fell into decay in the second half of eighteenth century. The declining market share of the route Danzig-Amsterdam is especially remarkable: in the period 1720–1729, the route accounted 42.78% of all grain transports through the Sound, in 1750–1759 for 34.52%, and in the period 1780–1789 for 4.48%.[35]

Scheltjens argues that changes at the supply and demand side restructured the Baltic grain trade in the second half of the eighteenth century. The most important change on the supply side is the decreased importance of Danzig. The partition of Poland in 1772 isolated Danzig from its hinterland, which damaged

32 De Vries and Van der Woude, *The first modern economy*, 681.

33 De Vries and Van der Woude, *The first modern economy*, 501.

34 Scheltjens, "The changing geography."

35 Scheltjens, "The changing geography," 14.

its position in the international grain trade.[36] The Prussian ports of Pillau, Königsberg, and Memel profited from this change. Furthermore, Russian ports on the Baltic, Riga, Pernau, Reval and St. Petersburg, also increased their grain exports.[37] On the demand side, the position of Amsterdam changed after 1760. While the city continued to be a center of the international grain trade, it lost its dominant position in the European grain market. Sweden, Norway, England and Scotland started to import more Baltic grain directly. Within the Dutch Republic Amsterdam also lost ground: other Dutch cities began to import grain directly from the Baltic region, demand especially grew in the jenever producing cities of Schiedam and Rotterdam.[38]

These changes affected the Dutch shipping market. Shipmasters from certain areas profited from the changes, while others suffered. The shipmasters active on routes linking the Baltic and Amsterdam lost their position. The shipmasters from the West Frisian Islands belonged to this category, along with their colleagues from Harlingen, Hindeloopen and Hoorn.[39] Shipmasters that were active on the emerging routes, on the other hand, managed to expand their business. They originated mainly from communities in southwestern part of Friesland, like Heereveen, Joure and Lemmer, and Pekela, located in the Province of Groningen. Finally, the most important 'winners' in the post-1760 Baltic grain market were shipmasters from the grain exporting regions western Prussia, Courland, and Mecklenburg. While the volume of grain shipped by Dutch shipmasters was stable until 1780, other nations shipped larger volumes, thus increasing their market share at the expense of the Dutch Republic.[40]

The increased importance of shipmasters from the Baltic area in the export of grain may be related to a "shift in the organization of maritime transport from the demand side of business (primarily Amsterdam) to the supply side of business (ports in the Baltic)".[41] Amsterdam merchants no longer controlled the Baltic grain trade; instead, merchants from the Baltic ports coordinated the grain trade. Shipmasters from these ports provided the required transport services. Shipmasters from the West Frisian Islands had based their shipping activities in the Baltic on demand for transport services in Amsterdam, and as demand decreased, they lost their business.

36 Van Tielhof, *The "mother of all trades,"* 61. See also the contribution of Magnus Ressel to this volume.
37 Scheltjens, "The changing geography," 11.
38 Scheltjens, "The changing geography," 9–14.
39 Scheltjens, "The changing geography," 25.
40 Scheltjens, "The changing geography," 24.
41 Scheltjens, "The changing geography," 25.

As the survey of the routes of West Frisian Islands' shipmasters indicates, they specialized in routes connecting Amsterdam with the Baltic. Their competitive advantage was their vicinity to Amsterdam, and they fully exploited this advantage. During the 'Golden Age' of Amsterdam, this brought the West Frisian Islands shipmasters great success, and their islands welcome employment. The security of this important branch of the economy of the islands was organized at the community level. For example, Terschellinger shipmasters spread their risks by investing in parts of ships of other islanders. These so-called 'partenrederijen' protected one from extreme losses in case of hazards, such as wreckage.[42] Furthermore, the seamen (and their families) of the eastern villages of the island protected themselves against the risks of life at sea through a system of mutual insurance called 'de Buul', an institution comparable to the English 'Seamen's boxes'.[43] Communities gathered knowledge on certain branches of shipping, and acquired a reputation in this branch. Thus, these communities developed a 'niche': they specialized on a certain route, cargo, or type of ship.[44] However, specialization proved to be a disadvantage when circumstances changed. In our case, the shipmasters apparently could not adapt to the new spatial structure of the Baltic grain market. They were not able to successfully change their business strategy, and find employment on the emerging routes in the Baltic. The West Frisian Islands' shipmasters were 'locked in' on shipping to and from Amsterdam.

The decline of Baltic shipping as a specific branch of the West Frisian Islands' maritime sector had a negative economic impact on the islands. The maritime sector not only provided employment to the captain, but also to a small crew, most often with the same origin as the captain.[45] The West Frisian Islander shipmaster-entrepreneur who could offer his seamanship, crew, and vessel to Amsterdam merchants in need of transport capacity for their Baltic trade ceased to exist. Some shipmasters returned to their farms, became pilots, or focused on shipping in the 'Zuiderzee area'.[46] However, it would be incorrect to state that the maritime sector completely lost its importance on the West Frisian Islands in the eighteenth century. At the end of the eighteenth and the beginning of the nineteenth century many sailors from the island of Terschelling, for example, feature in the crew lists of Dutch ships. In addition, in the second half of the nineteenth century half of the work force of

42 Zwaal, *Terschellinger historie*, 92.

43 Spanjer, "Groot-Schippersbuidel," 3–8.

44 Scheltjens, *Dutch Deltas*, 146–161.

45 Schoorl, *De convexe kustboog*, 1, 791, 796–801.

46 Zwaal, *Terschellinger historie*, 94.

Terschelling was employed in the maritime sector.[47] But the era of Baltic shipping was definitively over.

5 Conclusion

In the eighteenth century, the West Frisian Islands lost their stake in Baltic shipping. The number of islander shipmasters mentioned in STRO decreased steadily in the course of the century. During the Fourth Anglo-Dutch War, the decline accelerated, and during the War of the First Coalition, it completely ended. In general, however, traffic through the Sound increased in the eighteenth century, and Dutch Baltic shipping maintained a stable level until the 1780s. By using a new instrument for research – STRO – West Frisian Islands' Baltic shipping was studied in detail, and an explanation of the decline was proposed.

The data of STRO reveal that the West Frisian Islands' shipmasters were specialized in shipping from a small number of Baltic ports, Danzig, Riga, and Königsberg, to Amsterdam. In particular, the trade between Danzig and Amsterdam was of great importance. Positioned on the main shipping lanes of Amsterdam, the islands were perfectly located for providing shipping services to Amsterdam merchants. Specialization had brought the islander shipmasters success at the zenith of Amsterdam's position in international trade. The case study on the shipmasters of Ameland has shown that the shipmasters participating most in Baltic shipping, all specialized on a specific route. However, this specialization made the shipmasters vulnerable in the second half of eighteenth century, when Amsterdam gradually lost its importance in the European trade system. Amsterdam no longer was the staple market of Europe, and it lost ground to other cities in the Dutch Republic. Baltic trade was no longer concentrated in a few routes connecting the Baltic region to Amsterdam, but was diverted to a large number of smaller routes linking many ports east and west of the Sound. Moreover, the most frequented Baltic port for shipmasters of the West Frisian Islands, Danzig, was cut off from its hinterland by the partitions of Poland.

In the structure of Baltic trade of the second half of the eighteenth century, other shipmasters provided the shipping services. Shipmasters from the Baltic countries, England, Scotland, and Norway expanded their shipping activities in the eighteenth century. In the Dutch Republic, shipmasters from southern Friesland and the Province of Groningen became involved in Baltic shipping.

47 Van der Wal, *We vieren*, 25–30.

The shipmasters of the West Frisian Islands were not able to change their business strategy, and switch to the new shipping routes. In order to be successful in the shipping business, the West Frisian Islands' shipmasters concentrated on shipping between Danzig/Riga and Amsterdam, but when this niche became redundant in the second half of the eighteenth century, the tide turned against them. The shipmasters did not have the capacity, knowledge or contacts to change their business approach and find cargoes on other routes. After more than a hundred years of sailing in service of Amsterdam, the maritime communities were 'locked-in' on their redundant operational strategy, and saw their business decline as a consequence. Thus, this study has shown how a macro-economic development – 'the decline of the Amsterdam staple market' – affected a very specific branch of the early modern Dutch economy, West Frisian Islands' Baltic shipping.

Furthermore, it was demonstrated that the shipping market of the Dutch Republic had a dynamic of its own, which was connected, but not equal to the flow of goods. Shipmasters did not, and could not, simply go to wherever the demand was, but focused on a certain market sector. Shipping constituted an independent factor in the commercial system, which ought to be recognized and studied as such. Further research is needed to expand our knowledge on this issue. STRO has proven to be an excellent tool for this type of research, allowing focusing not only the flow of goods, or the commerce of certain ports or regions, but also on the history of transportation in a vital area of European trade.

Conclusions

Jan Willem Veluwenkamp and Werner Scheltjens

The articles in this book explore new territories and hardly could have been written without the Sound Toll Registers Online. They show that the STRO at www.soundtoll.nl is a fine instrument to search, select and analyze the information the original Sound Toll Registers contain. They also show that this information is not self-evident and that – as with all historical sources – precise source criticism, research questions and methods are needed to make the data speak and to give them meaning. Most of all, they demonstrate that STRO enables the researcher to analytically connect the major variables of trade and transport included in the STR: qualities and quantities of commodities, ports of departure and destination, shipmasters and their domiciles, toll rates and tolls paid. STRO evidently has the power to raise the study of early modern European trade and transport to new levels of coherence and understanding.

In their articles included in the first part of the book Lilja, Pourchasse and Ressel use STRO to analyze and explain the size, structure and development of trade flows between places east and west of the Sound. In doing so they contribute to the study of an old and large problem area, bringing in a measure of precision and detail which can hardly be found in the traditional historiography and has become practically only attainable with the availability of STRO. The backbone of Lilja's descriptive analysis are the number of cargoes registered in the STR and isolated through STRO. Pourchasse uses STRO in combination with other serial sources to identify the passages of individual shipmasters and assess the quantities of grain they carried, converting lasts and barrels into metric tons. Ressel, too, combines STRO with other serial sources. He counts numbers of passages on main routes by shipmasters from individual ports.

Like Pourchasse and Ressel, in the second part of the book Galani, Crespo Solana and Kikuchi employ STRO in combination with other sources. However, rather than focusing on the analysis of single commodity flows or transport routes, they study the relationship between the Baltic trade and other commercial systems. Galani analyzes the development of numbers of ship passages in the decades about 1800. Crespo Solana focuses on the main shipping connections between Cadiz and the Baltic ports. Kikuchi identifies cargoes and shipmasters' domiciles to analyze trade and transport practices of merchants and masters.

 | DOI:10.1163/9789004371781_013

A different approach to STRO is pursued in the third part of the volume. Charles and Daudin and Ojala c.s. mainly carry out source criticism of the STR and STRO and explore methods of using them for historical research. They employ STRO to compare STR with other primary sources and assess the value of the STR as a source for trade and shipping. Both surveys reflect clearly the general problem of processing serial sources for trade and transport. The authors discuss the problems of standardization and classification of geographical and commodity names and weights and measures and, in the case of Ojala c.s., the possibility of using toll rates as a gauge for the value and the volume of commodity flows. They reach deeper into the STRO's riches than the authors of the first two parts of the book – whose methods remain, perhaps quite justified, close to the surface of STRO's potential. Charles and Daudin and Ojala c.s. make evident that the reliability of early modern time series can only be assessed by means of fine-tuned methods. They indicate which direction such methods may take and suggest methods to study the STR via STRO and give meaning to the data they contain. At the same time, they make the limitations of their methods quite clear. Obviously, the development of advanced techniques remains a research *desideratum* for STRO as much as for the historical time series with which they may be compared.

Finally, in the fourth part of the book Rönnbäck and Draper and Van Duijl apply quite novel methods to STRO. As different as their analyses may be, both relevant chapters aspire to exploit the rich personal name data contained in STRO in quite ingenious and intricate ways. Rönnbäck combines in his analysis the names of shipmasters, the names of their Baltic ports of call and the dates of passage. Van Duijl and Draper combine the names of shipmasters, the names of their domiciles and the routes they sailed. They adhere strongly to the recent research of Scheltjens on STRO in general and the Dutch maritime transport sector in particular.[1]

The articles collected in this book show that the use of STRO can contribute to the study of Baltic – or, more generally, maritime – transport and trade in many ways. They discuss a wide range of relevant topics applying quite different approaches and methods. They demonstrate the richness of the information the STR contain, how this information is available through STRO, how it can be employed in historical research and what skills are needed to realize that. In pre-digital times, the use of the STR remained necessarily shallow and usually based on the STT, as there were no instruments to exploit fully the richness of the original source. It was generally limited to a single dimension such

1 Scheltjens, *Dutch Deltas*.

as the quantification of ship movements or general commodity categories. Just two examples are Israel's and De Vries and Van der Woude's discussions of the Dutch Baltic trade.[2] Combining STR's different dimensions – place, time, cargoes, and individuals – was extremely time-consuming and therefore hardly feasible.[3] Now STRO has become available and several methodological tools and instruments for making use of the data are in place. There is just one more complication: historians need the skills to handle those instruments. The contributors to this book have those skills – in various degrees. In this sense, they are of a rare kind.

Accordingly, this book may be understood as a wake-up call for the historical sciences in the digital age. STRO is not the only online historical database. A swiftly increasing number of such facilities is becoming available and quite a few of them make the information from early modern serial sources concerning trade and transport instantly accessible. Relevant Dutch facilities, 'Dutch maritime historical datasets,' are listed on the *Dutch Ships and Sailors* website at http://dutchshipsandsailors.nl/, an initiative of the Huygens Institute for the History of the Netherlands (Huygens ING) – https://www.huygens.knaw.nl. Links to databases concerning Dutch maritime history are also included in the *Maritiem Portal* at https://maritiemportal.nl/, which is hosted by Huygens ING, too. Now we need the historians who can fully exploit these databases and who are technically capable of combining the different dimensions they offer: dates, names of shipmasters, ports, commodities, weights and measures, currencies, tolls, etc. This requires a deep knowledge and understanding of basic and traditional topics as paleography, chronology, historical onomastics, historical geography and topography, historical metrology and historical product nomenclature. Most of all it requires advanced skills in the writing of queries in, for example, Microsoft Access. The full potential of STRO and many other online databases of the same nature will only unfold if many researchers have these competences – and use them. For the time being, this is just a fantasy. There are few historians with the relevant capabilities. Especially the necessary skills in database management are scarce among the present generation of established historians. Is it too rash to presume that not many of them will catch up? It is clear to us that among the emerging generations of historians of the digital age only those who have received thorough relevant training will be

2 Israel, *Dutch primacy*, 92–93, 144, 214–217, 301, 366; De Vries and Van der Woude, *Nederland 1500–1815*, 414–415, 481, 485, 488–489, 495.

3 De Buck and Lindblad endeavour to calculate volumes and values but are not very clear about their sources and methods: De Buck and Lindblad, "De scheepvaart," 536–562.

up for the task. It is time that the necessary training programs are put in place in our universities.

This book is just a beginning. We feel that we are on the threshold of a new phase of the writing of maritime history as STRO offers a closer look at the incredible mass of data, which were slumbering in the more than 700 volumes of the STR but have been kissed awake at last. Indeed, STRO does not only facilitate the study of trade and transport. It opens up new possibilities for the study of economic, social, political, cultural, linguistic, ecological and local history; and the list is not complete. Moreover, the panorama of opportunities is not limited to the Baltic Sea area, either. STRO allows with equal power the study of the many regions and places that were connected by commercial navigation with the Baltic Sea area. Finally, STRO allows the combination with other data sets – as is illustrated by several articles in this volume. To sum up, STRO is not only a helpful tool for the revision of the historiography of Baltic trade and shipping, but also, and most importantly, serves as a motor for novel historical research.

Bibliography

Archives

Archiv der Hansestadt Lübeck (Lübeck)

ASA Externa, Deutsche Territorien, Nr. 5374 (Hamburger Gesuche um Durchfuhrerlaubnis); Nr. 5386 (Behinderung des Hamburger Ostseehandels durch Lübecker Durchfuhrverbote 1606); Nr. 5397 (Hamburg an Lübeck: Bitte um Ausfuhrerlaubnis).

Zulageherren, Nr. 2–5, 22, 23, 24.

Archives Nationales (Paris) (Short: AN)

F/11/223, Report signed by J.C. Bechmann, Swedish merchant living in Bordeaux (18th november 1793).

F12/1834B, "Tableau estimatif du commerce …"

Archivio di Stato (Livorno)

Magistrato poi Dipartimento di Sanità marittima. Deliberazioni di Sanità e paperi di contumacia, f. 621–626, 696–705.

Bibliothèque municipale de Saint-Brieuc

Fonds Gournay, ms. 87, folder n°2.

Nederlandsch Economisch-Historisch Archief

Pierre Bruyard papers, files 76–77.

Rigsarkivet (Copenhagen) (Short: Rigsarkivet)

Danica, Microfilm 71, PRO F.O.22 17. Danica, microfilm (PRO, HCA, 32–194 to 32–907). Kommercekollegiet, 1817, Letter of von Hemert of 29 juin 1793. Kommercekollegiet, Journalsager 1158, Letter of the Danish consul in Genoa of 10 May 1794.

Staatsarchiv Hamburg (Hamburg)

111-1, Senat Cl. VI, Nr. 1a. Vol. 1, Fasc. 10 (Schreiben der Stadt Lübeck 1601–1717), Lübeck an Hamburg 1634.

111-1, Senat Cl. VII, Lit. Ea Pars 1 (Zollbücher); 371-2, Admiralitätskollegium; 415-2 I, Amt Bergedorf I; 621–1, Firmenarchiv; 622-1, Familienarchiv; Archiv der Hansestadt Lübeck (Lübeck), Zulageherren.

111-1, Senat Cl. VII, Lit. Ea Pars 1 (Zollbücher) Nr. 3g, Vol. 1.

111-1, Senat Cl. VII, Lit. Ec Nr. 4, Vol. 7k (Excerpta Dei Archivarii von Som, den Oresundischen Zoll betr. 1736–1742), Q1.

111-1, Senat Cl. VII, Lit. Ec Nr. 4, Vol. 7k (König. Dänisch. Norwegische, auch Schleswig-Holsteinische Zölle), Q20.
111-1, Senat Cl. VII, Lit. Ec Nr. 12 (Lübeckische Zölle), Vol. 1b, Vol. 4.
111-1, Senat Cl. VII, Lit. Ec Nr. 12 (Lübeckische Zölle), Vol. 1b, fol. 34r.
111-1, Senat Cl. VII, Lit. Kc Nr. 5 (Commercium mit Dänemark), Vol. 2, fol. 3v.
111-1, Senat Cl. VII, Lit. Kc Nr. 5 (Commercium mit Dänemark), Vol. 7, fols. 14r–23v.
111-1. Senats Cl. VII, Lit. Ec Nr. 12 (Lübeckische Zölle), Vol. 1b, fol. 34r.
211-2, Reichskammergericht, S150.
371-2, Admiralitätskollegium F12 (Verzeichnis der zu Wasser und zu Lande angekommenen Waren mit Angabe der Kaufleute [Makler] sowie der Herkunft und der Menge der Ware [Contentbuch]), Bd. 2–15.
371-2, Admiralitätskollegium F3 (Verzeichnis der dem Admiralitätszoll unterliegenden, auf Seeschiffen ein und ausgehenden Waren, geordnet nach Kaufleuten [Maklern] mit Angabe der Schiffer und der Zollabgabe), Bd.1 and 2.
Familienarchiv, 622-1/65 (Lorenz-Meyer), Kopiebücher A1, fol. 48.
Familienarchiv, 622-1/65 (Lorenz-Meyer), Kopiebücher A1, fol. 147.
Firmenarchiv, 621-1/54 (Friedrich Justus), Kopiebücher 12c, fol. 708.
Firmenarchiv, 621-1/54 (Friedrich Justus), Kopiebücher 12b, fol. 27.
supplément Danemark, microfilm 5988.

The National Archives, London UK

CO 158/1 (Memorandum on Malta from Al. Ball, 6 March 1801).

Online Databases and Websites

CrespoDynCoopNet Data Collection, http://hdl.handle.net/10261/23894
http://toflit18.hypotheses.org/
http://www.genefourneau.com/mesures. html http://www.cnrtl.fr/definition/millerolle
Sound Toll Registers Online (STRO), www.soundtoll.nl
www.gahetna.nl/collectie/index/nt00338
www.let.rug.nl/welling/sont/johansen.htm

Literature

A Collection of State Papers relative to the War against France (London, 1794).
Acemoglu, Daron, Jonson; Simon, Robinson, James, “The Rise of Europe: Atlantic trade, institutional Change and economic Growth,” *American Economic Review* 95, 3 (2005) 546–579.

Ahonen, Kalevi, *From Sugar Triangle to Cotton Triangle: Trade and Shipping between America and Baltic Russia, 1783–1860* (Jyväskylä, 2005).

Alcalá-Zamora, José; de Llano, Queipo, *España, Flandes y el Mar del Norte (1618–1639)* (Madrid, 2001).

Allan, Francis, *Het eiland Ameland en zijne bewoners* (Amsterdam, 1857).

Allen, Robert C., *The industrial Revolution in Global Perspective* (Cambridge, 2009).

Andersen, Dan; Voth, Hans-Joachim, "The Grapes of War: Neutrality and Mediterranean Shipping under the Danish flag, 1747–1807," *Scandinavian Economic History Review* 48 (2000) 5–27.

Anton Zottmann, *Die Wirtschaftspolitik Friedrichs des Grossen: mit besonderer Berücksichtigung der Kriegswirtschaft* (Leipzig, 1937).

Aretin, Karl-Otmar von, "Teilung und Länderschacher als Folgen des Gleichgewichtssystems der europäischen Großmächte. Die polnischen Teilungen als europäisches Schicksal," *Polen und die polnische Frage in der Geschichte der Hohenzollernmonarchie 1701–1871*, ed. Klaus Zernack (Berlin, 1982).

Armstedt, Richard, *Geschichte der Königl. Haupt- und Residenzstadt Königsberg in Preussen* (Stuttgart, 1899).

Åström, Sven-Erik, *From Cloth to Iron: the Anglo-Baltic Trade in the late Seventeenth Century Part II, The Customs Accounts as Sources for the Study of the Trade* (Helsinki, 1965).

Åström, Sven-Erik, *From Tar to Timber. Studies in Northeast European Forest Exploitation and Foreign Trade 1660–1860* (Helsinki, 1988).

Baasch, Ernst, "Die »Durchfuhr« in Lübeck. Ein Beitrag zur Geschichte der lübischen Handelspolitik im 17. und 18. Jahrhundert," *Hansische Geschichtsblätter* 13 (1907) 109–152.

Baasch, Ernst, *Beiträge zur Geschichte des deutschen Seeschiffbaues und der Schiffbaupolitik* (Hamburg, 1899).

Baasch, Ernst, *Quellen zur Geschichte von Hamburgs Handel und Schiffahrt im 17., 18. und 19. Jahrhundert* (Hamburg, 1910).

Baczko, Ludwig von, *Versuch einer Geschichte und Beschreibung Königsbergs* (Königsberg, 1787).

Balbi, Adrien, *Essai statistique sur le Royaume de Portugal et d'Algarve, comparé aux autres états de l'Europe, et suivi d'un coup d'oeil sur l'état actuel des sciences, des lettres et des beaux-arts parmi les portugais des deux hemispheres* (Paris, 1822).

Barnewitz, Friedrich, *Geschichte des Hafenortes Warnemünde* (Rostock, 1925).

Baumann, Wolf-Rüdiger, *The Merchants Adventurers and the Continental Cloth-Trade (1560s–1620s)* (Berlin, 1990).

Baxa, Jakob; Bruns, Guntwin, *Zucker im Leben der Völker. Eine Kultur- und Wirtschaftsgeschichte* (Berlin, 1967).

Berner, Ernst, *Geschichte des Preußischen Staates* (Bonn, 1896).

Beutin, Ludwig, "Die Wirkung des Siebenjährigen Krieges auf die Volkswirtschaft in Preußen," *Vierteljahresschrift für Sozial- und Wirtschaftsgeschichte* 26 (1933) 219.

Beutin, Ludwig, *Bremen und Nordeuropa* (Weimar, 1937).

Biernat, Czesław, *Statystika obrotu towarowego Gdańska w latach 1651–1815* (Warsaw, 1962).

Black, Jeremy, *British foreign policy in an age of revolutions 1783–1793* (Cambridge, 1994).

Blanc, Olivier, *Les hommes de Londres, Histoire secrète de la Terreur* (Paris, 1989).

Bloothooft, Gerrit, "Assessment of Systems for Nominal Retrieval and Historical Record Linkage," *Computers and the Humanities* 32 (1998) 39–56.

Bochove, C.J. van, *The economic consequences of the Dutch. Economic integration around the North Sea, 1500–1800* (Utrecht, 2008).

Bogucka, M., "The role of Baltic trade in European development from the XVIth to the XVIIIth centuries," *The Journal of European Economic History* IX, 1 (1980) 5–20. Reprint in Maria Bogucka, *Baltic commerce and urban society, 1500–1700. Gdansk/ Danzig and its Polish context* (Aldershot and Burlington, 2003).

Bogucka, Maria, "Danzig als Metropole in der Frühen Neuzeit," *Kulturgeschichte Preußens königlich polnischen Anteils in der Frühen Neuzeit*, ed. Sabine Beckmann (Tübingen, 2005) 89–98.

Bömelburg, Hans-Jürgen, *Zwischen polnischer Ständegesellschaft und preussischem Obrigkeitsstaat. Vom königlichen Preußen zu Westpreussen (1756–1806)* (Munich, 1995).

Boon, P., 'West Friesland and the Sound (1681–1720)' in: W.G. Heeres e.a. ed., *From Dunkirk to Danzig. Shipping and trade in the North Sea and the Baltic, 1350–1850* (Hilversum, 1988) 171–189.

Bottari, Salvatore, "Relations between Sicily and Great Britain, 1750–1800: the Interplay of Culture and Economy," in *Anglo-Saxons in the Mediterranean*, eds. Carmel Vassallo and Michela D'Angelo (Malta, 2007) 81–95.

Braun, Wilhelm, "Zur Stettiner Seehandelsgeschichte 1572–1813, Teil II," *Baltische Studien* N.F. 52 (1966) 65–98.

Briels, Johannes G.C.A, *Zuid-Nederlandse immigratie 1572–1630* (Haarlem, 1978).

Bruijn, J.R., 'De vaart in Europa' in: *Maritieme geschiedenis der Nederlanden* II (Bussum, 1977) 200–241.

Bruijn, J.R., 'Scheepvaart in de Noordelijke Nederlanden 1580–1650' in: *Algemene Geschiedenis der Nederlanden* VII (Haarlem, 1980) 137–155.

Bruijn, J.R., 'Scheepvaart in de Noordelijke Nederlanden 1650–1800' in: *Algemene Geschiedenis der Nederlanden* VIII (Haarlem, 1979) 209–238.

Bruijn, Jaap, "Productivity, profitability, and costs of private and corporate Dutch ship owning in the seventeenth and eighteenth centuries," in *The rise of merchant empires: Long distance trade in the early modern world, 1350–1750*, Ed. James Tracy (Cambridge 1990) 174–194.

Bruijn, Jaap, "Scheepvaart in de Noordelijke Nederlanden, 1580–1650," *Algemene Geschiedenis der Nederlanden*, 7 (Haarlem, 1977) 137–155.

Buck, P. De; Lindblad, J.Th. "De scheepvaart en handel uit de Oostzee op Amsterdam en de Republiek, 1722–1780," *Tijdschrift voor Geschiedenis* 96 (1983) 536–562.

Büsch, Johann Georg, *Versuch einer Geschichte der Hamburgischen Handlung* (Hamburg, 1797).

By-Laws of the Levant Company, 1812 (London, 1813).

Byron, Lew; Cater, Bruce, "The telegraph, co-ordination of tramp shipping, and growth in world trade, 1870–1910," *European Review of Economic History* 10 (2006) 147–173.

Cameron, Alan; Farndon, Roy, *Scenes from Sea and City: Lloyd's List 1734–1984* (London, 1984).

Carlén, Stefan, *Staten som marknadens salt: en studie i institutionsbildning, kollektivt handlande och tidig välfärdspolitik på en strategisk varumarknad i övergången mellan merkantilism och liberalism 1720–1862* (Stockholm, 1997).

Carlson, Bengt, "Sveriges handel och sjöfart på Medelhavet 1797–1803," in *Handel och Sjöfart under Gustaviansk Tid*, ed. Åke Holmberg (Gothenburg, 1971) 1–25.

Carrière, Charles, *Le problème des grains et farines à Marseille pendant la période du maximum 4 mai 1793–4 nivôse an II* (Paris, 1958).

Carrière, Charles, *Negoçiants Marsellais au XVIII*^me^ *siècle* (Marseilles, 1973).

Charles, Loïc; Coenen, Ann; Daudin, Guillaume, "Comparing Early Trade Statistics: The Case of Austrian Netherlands and France from 1759 to 1791" (presented at the ESSHC Conference, Glasgow (United Kingdom), April 2012).

Charles, Loïc; Daudin, Guillaume, "La Collecte Du Chiffre Au XVIIIe Siècle: Le Bureau de La Balance Du Commerce et La Production Des Données Sur Le Commerce Extérieur de La France," *Revue d'Histoire Moderne et Contemporaine*, 1 (2011) 128–55.

Charles, Loïc; Daudin, Guillaume, eds., *18th Century International Trade Statistics: Sources and Methods, spécial issue of the Revue de l'O.F.C.E.*, 140 (Paris, 2015).

Christensen, A.E., "Der handelsgeschichtliche Wert der Sundzollregister. Ein Beitrag zu seiner Beurteilung," *Hansische Geschichtsblätter* 59 (1934) 28–142.

Christensen, A.E., *Dutch trade to the Baltic around 1600* (Kopenhagen en Den Haag, 1941).

Christensen, Aksel E., *Dutch trade to the Baltic about 1600: Studies in the Sound Toll Register and Dutch Shipping Records* (Copenhagen, 1941).

Cieślak, Edmund, "Aspects of Baltic Sea-borne Trade in the XVIIIth Century: the Trade Relations between Sweden, Poland, Russia and Prussia," *The Journal of European Economic History* 12–2 (1983) 239–270.

Cieślak, Edmund, "Bilan et structure du commerce de Gdańsk dans la seconde moitié du XVIIIe siècle," *Acta Poloniae Historica* 23 (1971) 105–118.

Cieślak, Edmund, "Sea-borne Trade between France and Poland in the XVIIIth Century," *The Journal of European Economic History* 6–1 (1977) 54–55.

Cieślak, Edmund; Biernat, Czesław, *History of Gdańsk* (Gdansk, 1995).

Clive, Emsley, "The Home office and Its Sources of Information and Investigation 1792–1801," *The English Historical Review*, 94, 372 (1979) 532–561.

Cooper, Julia Promisel, *The Decline of Spain and the Thirty Years War, 1609–59* (Cambridge, 1970).

Cowan, Brian, *The Social Life of Coffee: The Emergence of the British Coffeehouse* (Yale, 2005).

Crespo Solana, Ana, "A Network-based Empire: Dutch Trade in the Hispanic Atlantic (1680–1740)," in *Dutch Atlantic Connections, 1680–1800. Linking Empires, bridging borders*, eds. Gert Oostindie and Jessica Vance Roitman (Leiden, 2014) 139–159.

Crespo Solana, Ana, "El comercio holandés y la integración de espacios económicos entre Cádiz y el Báltico en tiempos de guerra (1699–1723)," *Investigaciones de Historia Económica* 8 (2007) 45–77.

Crespo Solana, Ana, "Legal Strategies and Smuggling Mechanisms in the Trade with the Hispanic Caribbean," *Jahrbuch für Geschichte Lateinamerikas/Anuario de Historia de América Latina*, 47 (2010) 181–213.

Crespo Solana, Ana, *El comercio marítimo entre Amsterdam y Cádiz (1713–1778)* (Madrid, 2000).

Crespo Solana, Ana, *La Casa de la Contratación y la Intendencia General de Marina en Cádiz, 1717–1730* (Cadiz, 1996).

Crespo Solana, Ana, *Mercaderes atlánticos: Redes del comercio flamenco y holandés entre Europa y el Caribe* (Córdoba, 2009).

Crouzet, François, *L'Économie Britannique et le Blocus Continental* (Paris, 1958).

D' Angelo, Michela, *Mercanti Inglesi a Livorno, 1573–1737* (Messina, 2004).

D'Angelo, Michela, *Mercanti inglesi a Malta, 1800–1825* (Milan, 1990).

D'Angelo, Michela; Vassallo, Carmel, eds., *Anglo-Saxons in the Mediterranean: Commerce, Politics and Ideas (XVII–XX centuries)* (Malta, 2007).

Damus, Rudolf, "Die Stadt Danzig gegenüber der Politik Friedrichs des Großen und Friedrich Wilhelms II.," *Zeitschrift des Westpreußischen Geschichtsvereins* 20 (1887) 102–136.

Darcy-Bertuletti, Yvette, "Tableau Des Mesures Les plus Courantes En Usage Dans Le Pays Beaunois," 2005, http://www.beaune.fr/IMG/pdf/Metrologie.pdf.

Dardel, Pierre, *Navires et marchandises dans les ports de Rouen et du Havre au XVIII*[e] (Paris, 1963).

Daudin, Guillaume; Pourchasse, Pierrick, "Cross-Checking the Sound Database with the French Balance Du Commerce" (presented at the Sound Toll Registers online – to the test STR online as an instrument for historical research, Leeuwarden (Netherlands), October 2010).

Davey, James, "Securing the Sinews of Sea Power: British Intervention in the Baltic, 1780–1815," *The International History Review* 33/2 (2011) 161–184.

Davey, James, *War, Naval Logistics and the British State: Supplying the Baltic Fleet, 1808–1812*, Ph.D thesis, University of Greenwich 2009.

Davis, Ralf, *The Rise of the English Shipping Industry* (Newton Abbot, 1972).

Dekker, Peter, "De Amelander walvisvaart," *It Baeken* 36 (1974) 206–223.

Dekker, Peter, "Friese schippers op de Amsterdamse Oostzeevaart in 1731," *It Beaken* 39 (1977) 233–240.

Denzel, Markus A., *Handbook of World Exchange Rates, 1590–1914* (Farnham, 2010).

Desfeuilles, P., "La Navigation à travers le Sund en 1784: d'après les registres de la Douane danoise," *Annales. Économies, Sociétés, Civilisations* 14, 3 (1959) 492–520.

Desfeuilles, P., "La Navigation à travers le Sund et la guerre russo-suédoise de Finlande (1788–1790)," *Vierteljahrschrift für Sozial- und Wirtschaftsgeschichte* 48 (1961) 56–74.

Devine, Thomas Martin, *Exploring the Scottish Past: Themes in the History of Scottish Society* (East Linton, 1995).

Devine, Thomas Martin; Lythe, Samuel George Edgar, "The economy of Scotland under James VI," *Scottish Historical Review* 50 (1971) 91–106.

Dillen, Johannes Gerard van, *Van rijkdom en regenten. Handboek tot de economische en sociale geschiedenis van Nederland tijdens de Republiek* (Gravenhage, 1970).

Doursther, Horace, *Dictionnaire universel des poids et mesures anciens et modernes: contenant des tables de monnaies de tous les pays* (1840).

Dow, James, "A Comparative Note on the Sound Toll Registers, Stockholm Customs Accounts, and Dundee Shipping Lists, 1589, 1613–1622," *Scandinavian Economic History Review* 12 (1964) 79–85.

Duffy, Michael, "World-wide War and British Expansion, 1793–1815," in *The Oxford History of the British Empire. The Eighteenth Century*, eds. P.J. Marshall, Alaine Low and William Roger Louis (Oxford, 2011) 184–207.

Dziembowski, Edmond, *Les Pitt. L'Angleterre face à la France, 1708–1806* (Paris, 2006).

Ebben, Maurits; Fagel, Raymond; Vermeir, René (eds.), *Agentes e identidades en movimiento. España y los Países Bajos, siglos XVI–XVIII* (Madrid, 2011).

Eckard, Julius, *Livland im achtzehnten Jahrhundert: Umrisse zu einer livländischen Geschichte* (Leipzig, 1876).

Ekegård, Einar, *Studier i svensk handelspolitik under den tidigare frihetstiden* (Uppsala, 1924).

Ellinger Bang, N., and Knud Korst, *Tabeller over skibsfart og vaeretransport gennem Oeresund 1497–1783*, 7 volumes (Copenhagen and Leipzig, 1906–1953).

Ellinger Bang, Nina ed., *Tabeller over Skibsfart og Varetransport gennem Øresund 1497–1660*, 1, *Skibsfarten* (Copenhagen and Leipzig, 1906).

Ellinger Bang, Nina, ed., *Tabeller over Skibsfart og Varetransport gennem Øresund 1497–1660*, 2 A-B, *Varetransporten* (Copenhagen and Leipzig, 1922–33).

Eltis, David, *The rise of African slavery in the Americas* (Cambridge 2000).

Eltis, David; Richardson, David, "Productivity in the Transatlantic slave trade," *Explorations in Economic History* 32 (1995) 465–484.

Emmer, Pieter, "The Dutch Atlantic, 1600–1800: Expansion without Empire," *Jahrbuch für Geschichte Lateinamerikas* 38 (2001) 31–49.

Engels, Marie-Christine, *Merchants, Interlopers, Seamen and Corsairs: the Flemish Community in Livorno and Genoa (1615–1635)* (Hilversum, 1997).

Epstein, Mortimer, *The Early History of the Levant Company* (London, 1908).

Evans, Chris; Rydén, Göran, *Baltic Iron in the Atlantic World in the Eighteenth Century* (Leiden, 2007).

Faber, J.A., "De Sontvaart als spiegel van de structuurveranderingen in de Europese economie gedurende de achttiende eeuw," *Tijdschrift voor Zeegeschiedenis* 1, 2 (1982) 91–101.

Faber, J.A., "Friesland and the Baltic trade," in: W.G. Heeres e.a. ed., *From Dunkirk to Danzig. Shipping and trade in the North Sea and the Baltic, 1350–1850* (Hilversum, 1988) 13–21.

Faber, J.A., "Shipping to the Netherlands during a turbulent period 1784–1810," in: W.G. Heeres e.a. ed., *From Dunkirk to Danzig. Shipping and trade in the North Sea and the Baltic, 1350–1850* (Hilversum, 1988) 95–106.

Faber, J.A., "Structural changes in the European economy during the eighteenth century as reflected in the Baltic trade," in: W.G. Heeres e.a. ed., *From Dunkirk to Danzig. Shipping and trade in the North Sea and the Baltic, 1350–1850* (Hilversum, 1988) 83–94.

Faber, J.A., "The decline of the Baltic grain-trade in the second half of the seventeenth century," in: W.G. Heeres e.a. ed., *From Dunkirk to Danzig. Shipping and trade in the North Sea and the Baltic, 1350–1850* (Hilversum, 1988) 31–51.

Faber, Johannes Alle, "Friesland and the Baltic trade," in *From Dunkirk to Danzig. Shipping and trade in the North Sea and the Baltic, 1350–1850. Essays in honour of J.A. Faber on the occasion of his retirement as professor of economic and social history at the University of Amsterdam*, ed. W.G. Heeres (Hilversum, 1988) 13–21.

Fayle, Ernest, "The Employment of British Shipping," in *The Trade Winds: a Study of British trade during the French Wars, 1793–1815*, ed. C. Northcote Parkinson (London, 1948) 72–86.

Fechner, Hermann, *Wirtschaftsgeschichte der preussischen Provinz Schlesien in der Zeit ihrer provinziellen Selbständigkeit, 1741–1806* (Wrocław, 1907).

Findeisen, Jörg-Peter, "Progressive Kameralisten in Schwedisch-Pommern nach 1750. Die schwedisch-pommersche Reformpublizistik während des Übergangs vom Feudalismus zum Kapitalismus," *Jahrbuch für Wirtschaftsgeschichte* 27–1/2 (1986) 105–129.

Fisher, Frederick J., *Letters relating to Lionel Cranfield's business overseas, 1597–1612* (London, 1966).

Francœur, Louis-Benjamin, et al., *Dictionnaire technologique, ou Nouveau dictionnaire universel des arts et métiers, et de l'économie industrielle et commerciale* (Paris, 1828).

French, Christopher, "Productivity in the Atlantic shipping industry: a quantitative study," *Journal of Interdisciplinary History* 17–3 (1987) 613–638.

Friberg, Nils, *Stockholm i bottniska farvatten. Stockholms bottniska handelsfält under senmedeltiden och Gustav Vasa. En historisk-geografisk studie i samarbete med Inga Friberg* (Stockholmsmonografier 53) (Uppsala, 1983).

Fritz, Sven, *Historisk statistik för Sverige. Utrikeshandel 1732–1970* (vol. 3) (Stockholm, 1972).

Gadebusch, Thomas Heinrich, *Schwedisch-Pommersche Staatskunde, Vol. II* (Greifswald, 1788).

Galani, Katerina, "Caught between Empires: Alliances, Neutrality and Middlemen Minority," in *Greek Maritime History: From the Periphery to the Centre*, eds. Katerina Galani, Panos Kapetanakis, Alexandra Papadopoulou, Research in Maritime History, forthcoming.

Galani, Katerina, "Foreigners in an unfamiliar Market: British Business Strategies in the Eastern Mediterranean (18th century)," in *Making Waves in the Mediterranean*, eds. Michela D'Angelo, Gelina Harlaftis and Carmel Vassallo (Messina, 2010) 359–371.

Galani, Katerina, "The Napoleonic Wars and the Disruption of Mediterranean Shipping and Trade: British, Greek and American merchants in Livorno," *The Historical Review/La Revue Historique* VII (2010) 179–198.

Galani, Katerina, *British Shipping and Trade in the Mediterranean in the Age of War, 1770–1815*, Ph.D thesis University of Oxford, 2011.

Gallant, Thomas, *Experiencing Dominion: Culture, Identity and Power in the British Mediterranean* (Notre Dame, 2002).

García-Baquero González, Antonio, *El Libre comercio a examen gaditano. Crítica y opinión en el Cádiz mercantil de fines del siglo XVIII* (Cádiz, 1998).

Gaziński, Radosław, *Handel morski Szczecina w latach 1720–1805* (Stettin, 2000).

Gestrich, Andreas, et al., "Die Teilungen Polen-Litauens als Zäsur einer europäischen Strukturgeschichte. Komparative Überlegungen jenseits der Nationalgeschichtsschreibung," in *Die Teilungen Polen-Litauens: Inklusions- und Exklusionsmechanismen – Traditionsbildung – Vergleichsebenen*, eds. Hans-Jürgen Bömelburg et al. (Osnabrück, 2013) 9–35.

Gøbel, E., "The Sound Toll Registers Online Project, 1497–1857," in: *International Journal of Maritime History* XXII, 2 (2010) 305–324.

Gøbel, Erik, "The Sound Toll Registers Online Project, 1497–1857," *International Journal of Maritime History* 22 (2010) 305–324.

Gøbel, Erik; Hansen, Ulrich Flaskager, "Denmark," in *Baltic connections: archival guide to the maritime relations of the countries around the Baltic Sea (including the*

Netherlands) 1450–1800, 1, eds. Lennart Bes, Edda Frankot and Hanno Brand (Leiden, 2007) 25–86.

Goldbeck, Johann Friedrich, *Vollständige Topographie des Königreichs Preussen. Erster Theil* (Leipzig, 1785).

Gregory, Desmond, *Malta, Britain and the European Powers, 1793–1815* (Cranbury, 2006).

Grochulska, Barbara, *Handel zagraniczny Księstwa Warszawskiego* (Warsaw, 1967).

Großhaupt, Walter, "Waren, Geldhandel und Nachrichtenübermittlung in der Neuzeit," in *Brücke zwischen den Völkern. Zur Geschichte der Frankfurter Messe*, ed. Rainer Koch, 1 (Frankfurt, 1991) 219–247.

Hamilton, Alastair; Groot, Alexander de; Boogert, Maurits van den, eds., *Friends and Rivals in the East: Studies in Anglo-Dutch Relations in the Levant from the 17th to the early 19th century* (Leiden, 2000).

Hammel-Kiesow, Rolf, "Schoßeinnahmen in Lübeck (1424–1811) und Hamburg (1461–1650). Überlegungen zur Interpretation vorindustrieller Zeitreihen," *Das Gedächtnis der Hansestadt Lübeck. Festschrift für Antjekathrin Grassmann zum 65. Geburtstag*, eds. Michael Hundt and Rolf Hammel-Kiesow (Lübeck, 2005) 301–312.

Handrack, Udo, *Der Handel der Stadt Riga im 18. Jahrhundert* (Jena, 1932).

Harder-Gersdorff, Elisabeth, "Avoiding Sound Traffic and Sound Toll. Russian Leather and Tallow going West via Archangel and Narva-Lübeck (1650–1710)," in *From Dunkirk to Danzig. Shipping and Trade in the North Sea and the Baltic 1350–1850*, eds. Wim G. Heeres et al. (Den Haag, 1988) 237–261.

Harder-Gersdorff, Elisabeth, "Lübeck, Danzig und Riga. Ein Beitrag zur Frage der Handelskonjunktur im Ostseeraum am Ende des 17. Jahrhunderts," *Hansische Geschichtsblätter* 96 (1978) 106–138.

Harder-Gersdorff, Elisabeth, "Riga als Handelsmetropole des Ostseeraums in der Frühen Neuzeit, 16.–18. Jahrhundert," *Riga und der Ostseeraum. Von der Gründung 1201 bis in die Frühe Neuzeit*, ed. Horst Wernicke (Marburg, 2005) 261–294.

Harder-Gersdorff, Elisabeth, "Seehandel zwischen Lübeck und Rußland im 17./18. Jahrhundert nach Zollbüchern der Novgorodfahrer, Part 1," *Zeitschrift des Vereins für lübeckische Geschichte und Altertumskunde* 41 (1961) 5–53.

Hasse, Ernst, *Geschichte der Leipziger Messen* (Leipzig, 1885).

Hausman, William, "The English Coastal Coal Trade, 1691–1910: How rapid was productivity growth?" *Economic History Review* 40–4 (1987) 588–596.

Heckscher, Eli F., "Öresundstullräkenskaperna och deras behandling," *Historisk tidskrift* (1942) 170–186.

Heckscher, Eli F., *Svenskt arbete och liv. Från medeltiden till nutiden*, 6th ed. (Stockholm, 1969).

Heckscher, Eli F., *Sveriges ekonomiska historia från Gustav Vasa*, 2, *Det moderna Sveriges grundläggning 1720–1815*, 1–2 (Stockholm, 1949).

Heeres, W.G., e.a., eds., *From Dunkirk to Danzig: Shipping and trade in the North Sea and the Baltic, 1350–1850. Essays in Honour of J.A. Faber on the Occasion of His Retirement as Professor of Economic and Social History at the University of Amsterdam* (Hilversum, 1988).

Heeringa, Klaas, *Bronnen tot de Geschiedenis van de Levantse Handel*, (Rijks Geschiedkundige Publicatiën 9, 10, 34, 95, 115, 120) ('s-Gravenhage, 1910–1966).

Henderson, William, *Studies in the Economic Policy of Frederick the Great* (London, 1963).

Herrero Sánchez, Manuel, "La Monarquía Hispánica y el Tratado de La Haya de 1673," in *V Coloquio Hispano-holandés de historiadores, Diálogos Hispánicos* 16, eds. J. Lechner and H. de Boer (1995) 105–110.

Hildebrandt, Reinhard, ed., *Quellen und Regesten zu den Augsburger Handelshäusern Paler und Rehlinger 1539–1642. Wirtschaft und Politik im 16. und 17. Jahrhundert*, 2 vols (Stuttgart, 1996 and 2004).

Hill, C.E., *The Danish Sound Dues and the command of the Baltic. A study of international relations* (Durham, N.C. 1926).

Hill, Richard, *The Prizes of War, The naval prize system in the Napoleonic wars* (Stroud, 1998).

Hobsbawm, Eric, *Industry and Empire* (London, 1999).

Hodgson, Godfrey, *Lloyd's of London: A Reputation at Risk* (London, 1986).

Högberg, Staffan, *Utrikeshandel och sjöfart på 1700-talet. Stapelvaror i svensk export och import 1738–1808* (Lund, 1969).

Hughes, Lindsey, *Peter the Great and the West: New Perspectives* (New York, 2000).

Huhnhäuser, Alfred, *Rostocks Seehandel von 1635–1648* (Rostock, 1914).

Hutchinson, Ragnhild, "The Norwegian and Baltic Timber Trade to Britain 1780–1835 and its interconnections," *Scandinavian Journal of History*, 37, 5 (2012) 578–599.

Israel, J.I., *Dutch primacy in world trade, 1585–1740* (Oxford, 1989).

Israel, Jonathan I., "The Phases of the Dutch Straatvaart (1590–1713): A Chapter in the Economic History of the Mediterranean, *Tijdschrift voor Geschiedenis* 99 (1986) 1–30.

Israel, Jonathan I., *The Dutch Republic: Its Rise, Greatness and Fall, 1477–1806* (Oxford, 1995).

Jacks, David, "What drove 19th century commodity market integration?" *Explorations in Economic History* 43 (2006) 383–412.

Jacks, David; Novy, Dennis, "Trade costs in the first wave of globalization," *Explorations in Economic History* 47 (2010) 127–141.

Jeannin, P., "Les comptes du Sund comme source pour la construction d'indices généraux de l'activité économique en Europe (XVIe–XVIIe siècle)," in: P. Jeannin, *Marchands du Nord. Espaces et trafics à l'époque modern* (Paris, 1996) 1–62.

Jeannin, Pierre, "Die Rolle Lübecks in der hansischen Spanien- und Portugalfahrt des 16. Jahrhunderts," *Zeitschrift des Vereins für Lübeckische Geschichte und Altertumskunde* 55 (1975) 5–40.

Jeannin, Pierre, "Les Marchés Du Nord Dans Le Commerce Français Au XVIIIe," in *Aires et Structures Du Commerce Français Au XVIIIe Siècle* (Lyon, 1975) 47–74.

Jeannin, Pierre, *Marchands d'Europe: pratiques et savoires à l'époque moderne* (Paris, 2002).

Jespersen, Knud J.V., e.a., *Revanche og Neutralitet 1648–1814* (Copenhagen, 2002).

Jevrejeva, Svetlana, "Severity of winter seasons in the northern Baltic Sea between 1529 and 1990: reconstruction and analysis," *Climate Research* 17 (2001) 55–62.

Johansen, H.C., "Demand and supply factors in late eighteenth century grain trade," in: W.G. Heeres e.a. ed., *From Dunkirk to Danzig. Shipping and trade in the North Sea and the Baltic, 1350–1850* (Hilversum, 1988) 281–298.

Johansen, H.C., *Shipping and trade between the Baltic and Western Europe, 1784–95* (Odense, 1983).

Johansen, H.C., "Ships and cargoes in the traffic between the Baltic and Amsterdam in the late eighteenth century," in: *Interactions of Amsterdam and Antwerp with the Baltic region 1400–1800* (Leiden, 1983) 161–170.

Johansen, Hans C., "Danish Shipping Service as a Link between the Mediterranean and the Baltic, 1750–1850," in *Shipping and Trade (1750–1959)*, eds. Lewis Fisher and Helge Nordvik, Proceedings of the Tenth International Economic History Congress (Leuven, 1990) 470–493.

Johansen, Hans Christian, "Østersjøhandelen og den svensk-russiske krig 1788–90," *Erhvervshistorisk årbog. Meddelelser fra Ehrvervsarkivet* 27 (1976–77) 35–54.

Johansen, Hans Christian, *Shipping and Trade between the Baltic Area and Western Europe 1784–95* (Odense, 1983).

Jørgensen, Johan, "Denmark's Relations with Lübeck and Hamburg in the Seventeenth Century," *Scandinavian Economic History Review* 11–2 (1963) 73–116.

Jörn, Nils, "Dietrich von Brömbsen – die gescheiterte Karriere eines Lübeckers am Reichshofrat," *Die Integration des südlichen Ostseeraumes in das Alte Reich*, eds. Michael North and Nils Jörn (Cologne, 2000) 205–213.

Kaplan, Herbert, *Russian Overseas Commerce with Great Britain during the Reign of Catherine II*, (Philadelphia, 1995).

Kargol, Tomasz, "Wirtschaftliche Beziehungen zwischen Galizien und den Ländern der österreichisch-ungarischen Monarchie in der ersten Hälfte des 19. Jahrhunderts," *Die galizische Grenze 1772–1867: Kommunikation oder Isolation*, eds. Christoph Augustynowicz and Andreas Kappeler (Münster, 2007) 33–50.

Karonen, Petri, *Pohjoinen suurvalta. Ruotsi ja Suomi 1521–1809* (3th ed., Helsinki, 2008).

Karttunen, Marie-Louise, *Making a Communal World. English Merchants in Imperial St. Petersburg* (Helsinki, 2005).

Katsiardi-Hering, Olga, *Η ελληνική παροικία της Τεργέστης (1751–1830)*, 2 vols. (Athens, 1986).

Kaukiainen, Yrjö, "Shrinking the world: Improvements in the speed of information transmission, c. 1820–1870," *European Review of Economic History* 5 (2001) 1–28.

Kazusek, Szymon, *Handel zagraniczny Korony w końcu XVIII wieku. Tabele statystyczne 1786–1790, Vols. I & II* (Kielce, 2012).

Kellenbenz, Hermann, "Landverkehr, Fluß- und Seeschiffahrt im europäischen Handel (Spätmittelalter – Anfang des 19. Jahrhunderts)," in *Les grandes voies maritimes dans le monde XVe–XIXe siècles*, ed. Jacque Heers (Paris, 1965) 65–174.

Kellenbenz, Hermann, *Unternehmerkräfte im Hamburger Portugal-und Spanienhandel 1590–1625* (Hamburg, 1954).

Kellenbenz, Hermann, "Das Verkehrswesen zwischen den deutschen Nord- und Ostseehäfen und dem Mittelmeer im 16. und in der ersten Hälfte des 17. Jahrhunderts," in *Trasporti e sviluppo economico, secoli XIII–XVIII*, ed. Anna Vannini Marx (Florence, 1986) 99–121.

Kent, Heinz, *War and Trade in Northern Seas: Anglo-Scandinavian Economic Relations in the Mid-Eighteenth Century* (Cambridge, 1973).

Keyser, Erich, *Danzigs Geschichte* (Gdansk, 1921).

Kikuchi, Yuta, "Hamburg's overland trade 1630–1806: commodity distribution to the inland and the Baltic Sea region," *Socio-Economic History* 78–2 (2012) 27–51.

Kikuchi, Yuta, "Hamburg's seaborne trade in the Baltic Sea area during the early modern period: a study of the distribution structure of an intermediate port," *Socio-Economic History* 79–2 (2013) 109–126.

Kikuchi, Yuta, "Sound Toll Registers online for study of Hamburg's Baltic trade in the 17th century," http:www.soundtoll.nl (accessed Nov. 1, 2013).

Kikuchi, Yuta, *Hamburgs Handel mit dem Ostseeraum und dem mitteleuropäischen Binnenland vom 17. bis zum Beginn des 19. Jahrhunderts. Warendistribution und Hinterlandnetzwerke auf See-, Fluss- und Landwegen* (Greifswald, 2013).

Klein, Herbert, *The Middle Passage. Comparative studies in the Atlantic slave trade* (Princeton 1978).

Knick Harley, C. "Ocean freight rates and productivity, 1740–1913: The Primacy of Mechanical Invention reaffirmed," *Journal of Economic History* 48, 4 (1988) 851–876.

Knick Harley, C., "Coal exports and British shipping, 1850–1913," *Explorations in Economic History* 26 (1989) 311–338.

Knick Harley, C., "Steers afloat: The North Atlantic meat trade, liner predominance, and freight rates, 1870–1913," *Journal of Economic History* 68–4 (2008) 1028–1058.

Knight, Roger, *Britain against Napoleon. The Organization of Victory, 1793–1815* (London, 2013).

Knight, Roger; Wilcox, Martin, *Sustaining the Fleet, 1793–1815. War, the British Navy and the Contractor State* (Woodbridge, 2010).

Knitter, Michał, "Verifizierung von Schifffahrtsstatistiken des Stettiner Hafens in der zweiten Hälfte des 18. und Anfang des 19. Jahrhunderts," *Studia Maritima* 25 (2012) 23–51.

Knoppers, J.V.Th., "De vaart in Europa," in: *Maritieme Geschiedenis de Nederlanden* 3 (Bussum, 1977) 226–261.

Koningsbrugge, Hans S.A.M. van, "Tussen Mars en Mercurius: De Republiek der Verenigde Nederlanden, Spanje en de Quadruple Alliantie (1716–1720)," in *Tussen twee culturen: de Nederlanden en de Iberische wereld, 1550–1800*, eds. P.J.A.N. Rietbergen, F.M.A. Robben and Hugo de Schepper (Amsterdam, 1991) 51–86.

Kozłowski, Paweł, *Rekonstruktion der preussischen Handelsflotte sowie Probleme der Schiffahrt und Häfen der südlichen Ostseeküste 1793–1830* (Marburg, 1999).

Kraus, Hans-Christof, "Der „nervus rerum" in Publizistik und Wissenschaft – Staatsfinanzen im kameralistischen und staatswissenschaftlichen Diskurs in Preußen um 1800," in *Krise, Reformen – und Finanzen. Preußen vor und nach der Katastrophe von 1806*, eds. Jürgen Kloosterhuis and Wolfgang Neugebauer (Berlin, 2008) 25–58.

Krawehl, Otto-Ernst, et al., eds., *Statistik des seewärtigen Hamburger Einfuhrhandels im 18. Jahrhundert* (St. Katharinen, 2001).

Kresse, Walter, *Materialien zur Entwicklung der Hamburger Handelsflotte 1765–1823* (Hamburg, 1966).

Kriedte, Peter, "Trade," in *Germany. A New Social and Economic History*, ed. Sheilagh Ogilvie, 1 (London, 1996) 100–133.

Kutz, Andreas, *Deutschlands Außenhandel von der Französischen Revolution bis zur Gründung des Zollvereins. Eine statistische Strukturuntersuchung zur vorindustriellen Zeit* (Wiesbaden, 1974).

Kynaston, David, *City of London. The History* (London, 2011).

Lawaty, Andreas, et al., *Deutsch-polnische Beziehungen in Geschichte und Gegenwart: Bibliographie 1900–1998* (Wiesbaden, 2000).

Le Moine de L'Espine and Isaac Le Long, *De koophandel van Amsterdam, en andere Nederlandsche steden, naar alle gewesten der waereld* (Rotterdam, 1763).

Leijonhufvud, Lotta; Wilson, Rob; Moberg, Anders, "Documentary data provide evidence of Stockholm average winter to spring temperatures in the eighteenth and nineteenth centuries," *The Holocene* 13, 2 (2008) 333–343.

Lesger, Clé, *Handel in Amsterdam ten tijde van de Opstand. Kooplieden, commerciële expansie en verandering in de ruimtelijke economie van de Nederlanden, ca. 1550–ca. 1630* (Hilversum, 2003).

Leunen, Pieter van, *Terschelling en de visserij* (Harlingen, 1998).

Lilja, Sven, "Peoples, Towns and States. Structural Power Resources and State Power in the Scando-Baltic Region (1500–1820)," in *The Dynamics of Economic Culture in the*

North Sea and Baltic Region in the late Middle Ages and Early Modern period, eds. Hanno Brand and Leos Müller (Hilversum, 2007) 24–46.

Lindberg, Erik, "An 18th Century Swedish Perspective on the Portuguese Salt Industry. With trade and production figures," in *Actas I Seminário Internacional sobre o sal português* (Porto, 2005) 179–196.

Lindblad, Thomas, *Sweden's trade with the Dutch Republic 1738–1795: a quantitative analysis of the relationship between economic growth and international trade in the eighteenth century* (Assen, 1982).

Loose, Hans-Dieter, *Hamburg und Christian IV. von Dänemark während des Dreißigjährigen Krieges. Ein Beitrag zur Geschichte der hamburgischen Reichsunmittelbarkeit* (Hamburg, 1963).

Lord, Robert, *The second partition of Poland: a study in diplomatic history* (Cambridge (Mass.), 1915).

Lucassen, Jan; Unger, Richard, "Labour Productivity in Ocean Shipping, 1450–1875," *International Journal of Maritime History* 12 (2000) 127–141.

Lucassen, Jan; Unger, Richard, "Shipping, Productivity and Economic Growth," in *Shipping and economic growth 1350–1850*, eds. Jan Lucassen and Richard Unger (Leiden, 2011) 3–46.

Lukowski, Jerzy, *The Partitions of Poland 1772, 1793, 1795* (London, 1999).

Macgregor, John, *Commercial Statistics: A Digest, Vol. I* (London, 1844).

Mackesy, Piers, *The War in the Mediterranean, 1803–1810* (London, 1957).

Marzagalli, Silvia, "American Shipping into the Mediterranean during the French Wars: A first Approach," *Research in Maritime History* 44 (2010) 43–62.

Matschoss, Conrad, *Friedrich der Große als Beförderer des Gewerbfleißes* (Berlin, 1912).

McCloskey, Donald, "The industrial revolution 1780–1860: A survey," in *The economics of the Industrial Revolution*, Ed. Joel Mokyr (Savage 1985) 103–127.

McDonald, Janet, *Feeding Nelson's Fleet: The True Story of Food at Sea in the Georgian* (London, 2006).

Meinig, Donald W., *The Shaping of America: A Geographical Perspective on 500 Years of History*, 1, *Atlantic America, 1492–1800* (New Haven, 1986).

Menard, Russell, "Transports costs and long-range trade, 1300–1800: Was there a European 'transport revolution' in the early modern era?" in *The political economy of merchant empires. State power and world trade 1350–1750*, Ed. James Tracy (Cambridge 1991) 228–275.

Michela, D'Angelo, *Mercanti Inglesi in Sicilia 1806–1815* (Milan, 1988).

Minchinton, W.E., en D. Starkey, "Ships and cargoes in the traffic between the Baltic and Amsterdam in the late eighteenth century," in: *Interactions of Amsterdam and Antwerp with the Baltic region 1400–1800* (Leiden, 1983) 181–191.

Mitchell, Brian R., *British Historical Statistics* (Cambridge, 1988).

Mitchell, Brian R.; Deane, Phyllis, *Abstract of British Historical Statistics* (Cambridge, 1962).

Mola, Marina Alfonso, "El comercio marítimo de Cádiz, 1797–1805," in *Trafalgar y el mundo atlántico*, eds. Agustín Guimerá, Alberto Ramos and Gonzalo Butrón (Madrid, 2004) 255–299.

Montojo, Vicente, "Guerra y paz bajo Felipe III: el comercio del Levante español y sus relaciones clientelares, familiares y profesionales," *Chronica Nova* 31 (2005) 349–378.

Moreira, Cristina, et al., "Comparing Trade Flows between Portugal and Scandinavia: Methodological Lessons Arising from the Use of Multiple Sources" (presented at the Early trade statistics: What are they and why do we care, Paris (France), May 2014).

Morell, Mats, *Om mått- och viktsystemens utveckling i Sverige sedan 1500-talet: vikt- och rymdmått fram till metersystemets införande* (Uppsala, 1988).

Morgan, Kenneth, *Bristol and the Atlantic trade in the eighteenth century* (Cambridge 1993).

Morineau, Michel, "La Balance du commerce franco-néerlandais et le resserrement économique des Provinces-Unis au XVIIIe siècle," *Economisch-Historisch Jaarboek*, 30 (1965) 170–233.

Müller, Leos, "Swedish-Portuguese trade and Swedish consular service, 1700–1800," in *A articulação do sal Português aos circuitos mundiais antigos e novos consumes*, ed. Inês Amorim (Porto, 2008).

Müller, Leos, "The Forgotten Age of Swedish Shipping. The Eighteenth Century," *International Journal of Maritime History* 24 (2012) 1–18.

Müller, Leos, *Consuls, Corsairs and Commerce: The Swedish Consular Service and Long-Distance Shipping, 1720–1815* (Uppsala, 2004).

Müller, Lotte, *Die Entwicklung des Stralsunder Seehandels in der Zeit der schwedischen Herrschaft (1648–1814)* (Königsberg, 1926).

Müller, Michael, *Die Teilungen Polens 1772, 1793, 1795* (Munich, 1984).

Müller, Walther, *Rostocks Seeschiffahrt und Seehandel im Wandel der Zeiten* (Rostock, 1930).

Naudé, Wilhelm, *Deutsche städtische Getreidehandelspolitik vom 15.–17. Jahrhundert* (Leipzig, 1889).

Naudé, Wilhelm, et al., *Die Getreidehandelspolitik und Kriegsmagazinverwaltung Preußens (1740–1756)* (Berlin, 1910).

Neugebauer, Wolfgang, "Marktbeziehung und Desintegration. Vergleichende Studien zum Regionalismus in Brandenburg und Preußen vom 16. bis zum frühen 19. Jahrhundert," *Jahrbuch für die Geschichte Mittel- und Ostdeutschlands* 45 (1999) 157–207.

Newman, Karin, "Hamburg in the European Economy, 1660–1750," *Journal of European Economic History* 14–1 (1985) 57–93.

Nissen, Nis R., "Neue Forschungsergebnisse zur Geschichte der Schifffahrt auf der Elbe und dem Stecknitzkanal," *Zeitschrift des Vereins für lübeckische Geschichte und Altertumskunde* 46 (1966) 5–14.

North, Douglass, "Ocean freight rates and economic development 1750–1913," *Journal of Economic History* 18–4 (1958) 537–555.

North, Douglass, "Sources of Productivity Change in Ocean Shipping, 1600–1850," *Journal of Political Economy* 76–5 (1968) 953–970.

North, Michael, "The Export of Timber and Timber By-products from the Baltic Region to Western Europe, 1575–1775," in *From the North Sea to the Baltic. Essays in Commercial, Monetary and Agrarian History 1500–1800*, ed. Michael North (Aldershot, 1998) 1–14.

North, Michael, *Geschichte der Ostsee: Handel und Kulturen* (Munich, 2011).

Nyberg, Klas, *Köpes: ull, säljes: kläde. Yllemanufakturernas företagsformer i 1780-talets Stockholm* (Uppsala, 1992).

Nye, John V.C., *War, Wine, and Taxes: The Political Economy of Anglo-French Trade 1689–1900* (Princeton, 2007).

O'Brien, Patrick K., "European Economic Development: The Contribution of the Periphery," *Economic History Review* 35/1 (1982) 1–18.

O'Brien, Patrick K.; Escosura, Leandro P., eds., "The Costs and Benefits for Europeans from Their Empires Overseas," *Revista de Historia Económica (Second Series)*, 16–01 (1998) 29–89.

O'Rourke, Kevin; Williamson, Jeffrey, *Globalization and history. The evolution of a nineteenth century Atlantic economy* (Cambridge 1999).

Oddy, Joshua, *European Commerce, Shewing New and Secure Channels of Trade with the Continent of Europe* (Philadelphia, 1807).

Ojala, Jari, *Tehokasta liiketoimintaa Pohjanmaan pikkukaupungeissa. Purjemerenkulun kannattavuus ja tuottavuus 1700–1800-luvulla* (Helsinki, 1999).

Ojala, Jari; Karvonen, Lauri, "Assessing the Reliability of the Sound Toll Accounts: Comparing the Data to the Swedish and Portuguese Sources" (presented at the STRO conference, Groningen (Netherlands), October 2012).

Olechnowitz, Karl-Friedrich, *Handel und Seeschiffahrt der späten Hanse* (Weimar, 1965).

Olesen, J.E., '"Den rette, sædvanlige Strøm." Øresundstolden i 1400–tallet' in: O. Degn ed., *Tolden i Sundet. Toldopkraevning, politik og skibsfart i Oeresund 1429–1857* (Copenhagen, 2010) 27–40.

Ormrod, David, *The Rise of Commercial Empires. England and the Netherlands in the Age of Mercantilism, 1650–1770* (Cambridge, 2003).

O'Rourke, Kevin; Williamson, Jeffrey, "When did globalisation begin?" *European Review of Economic History* 6 (2002) 23–50.

Őzveren, Eyüp, "The Black Sea World as a Unit of Analysis," in *Politics of the Black Sea: The Dynamics of Cooperation and Conflict*, ed. Tunç Aybak (London, 2001) 61–84.

Palmer, Sarah, *Politics, Shipping and the repeal of the Navigation Laws* (Manchester, 1990).

Pantel, Isabelle, *Die hamburgische Neutralität im Siebenjährigen Krieg* (Münster, 2011).

Pelus-Kaplan, Marie-Louise, "Eine Hansestadt im Planetensystem des Sonnenkönigs. Der Handel mit Frankreich und seine Bedeutung für die Lübeckische Wirtschaft in der Epoche Ludwigs XIV.," *Zeitschrift des Vereins für Lübeckische Geschichte und Altertumskunde* 65 (1985) 119–142.

Persson, Karl Gunnar, "Mind the gap! Transport costs and price convergence in the nineteenth century Atlantic economy," *European Review of Economic History* 8 (2004) 125–147.

Petersson, Astrid, "Zuckersiedergewerbe und Zuckerhandel in Hamburg. Von den Anfängen bis zum Ende der Kontinentalsperre," *Hamburger Wirtschafts-Chronik* Neue Folge 1 (2000) 53–81.

Pitz, Ernst, *Die Zolltarife der Stadt Hamburg* (Wiesbaden, 1961).

Pomeranz, Kenneth, *The Great Divergence: China, Europe, and the Making of the Modern World Economy*, (Princeton University Press, 2000).

Posthumus, Nicolaas W., *Nederlandse prijsgeschiedenis*, 3 vols. (Leiden, 1943).

Pourchasse, Pierrick, *Le Commerce Du Nord: Les Échanges Commerciaux Entre La France et l'Europe Septentrionale Au XVIIIe Siècle* (Rennes, 2006).

Rachel, Hugo, "Der Merkantilismus in Brandenburg-Preußen," *Moderne Preußische Geschichte. 1648–1947: Vol. III*, eds. Otto Büsch and Wolfgang Neugebauer (Berlin, 1981).

Rachel, Hugo, *Die Handels, Zoll- und Akzisepolitik Preußens 1740–1786, Vol. III* (Berlin, 1928).

Rasch, Aage, "Die Beziehungen Dänemark – Norddeutschland im 18. Jahrhundert. Ein Beitrag zur Geschichte des Ostseehandels," *Zeitschrift des Vereins für lübeckische Geschichte und Altertumskunde* 46 (1966) 15–24.

Rasch, Aage, "Kopenhagen und die deutschen Ostseestädte 1750–1807," *Hansische Geschichtsblätter* 82 (1964) 55–68.

Reichenbach, Johann David von, *Patriotische Beyträge zur Kenntniß und Aufnahme des Schwedischen Pommern*, Vol. IV (Greifswald, 1785).

Ressel, Magnus, "Swedish Pomeranian Shipping in the Revolutionary Age (1776–1815)," Forum Navale 68 (2012) 76–77.

Rice, Howard C., "Documents sur le commerce avec les neutres en l'an II et III (1794-1795)," *Annales historiques de la révolution française*, XVII (1940) 166–183.

Rich, Edwin E.; Wilson, Charles H. (eds.), *The Cambridge Economic History of Europe. Vol. 5. The Economic Organization of Early Modern Europe.* (Cambridge, 1977).

Rodger, Nicholas A.M., *The Command of the Ocean* (London, 2004).

Roitman, Jessica V.; Pétré-Grenouilleau, Olivier; Emmer, Pieter C., eds., *A Deus Ex Machina Revisited: Atlantic Colonial Trade and European Economic Development* (Leiden, 2006).

Romano, Ruggero, "Per una valutazione della flotta mercantile Europea alla fine del secolo XVIII", *Studi in onore di Amintore Fanfani* 5 (Milan, 1962) 573–591.

Rönnbäck, Klas, "New and Old Peripheries: Britain, the Baltic and the Americas in the Great Divergence," *Journal of Global History*, 5/3 (2010) 373–394.

Rönnbäck, Klas, "The Speed of Ships and Shipping Productivity in the Age of Sail," *European Review of Economic History*, 16–4 (2012) 469–489.

Rössner, Philipp Robinson, *Scottish Trade in the Wake of Union (1700–1760): The Rise of a Warehouse Economy* (Stuttgart, 2008).

Rössner, Philipp Robinson, *Scottish Trade with German Ports, 1700–1770* (Stuttgart, 2008).

Royen, Paul C. van, "The First Phase of Dutch Straatvaart (1591–1605): Facts and Fiction," *International Journal of Maritime History* 2 (1990) 69–102.

Ryan, Anthony N., "The Defence of British Trade with the Baltic, 1808–1813," *English Historical Review* 74/292 (1959) 443–466.

Ryan, Anthony N., "Trade with the Enemy in the Scandinavian and Baltic Ports during the Napoleonic Wars; for and against," *Transactions of the Royal Historical Society* 12 (1962) 123–140.

Sakuma, Hironobu, *Die Nürnberger Tuchmacher, Weber, Färber und Bereiter vom 14. bis 17. Jahrhundert* (Nürnberg, 1993).

Sandström, Åke, *Mellan Torneå och Amsterdam. En undersökning av Stockholms roll som förmedlare av varor i regional- och utrikeshandel 1600–1650* (Stockholm, 1990).

Savary, Jacques Des Brulons, *Dictionnaire universel de commerce* (Paris, 1723).

Scheltjens, W., *Dutch Deltas: emergence, structure and functions of the first modern transport system*, Brill's Studies in Maritime History, 1 (Leiden and Boston, 2015).

Scheltjens, W., "Die krisenhaften Auswirkungen der polnischen Teilungen auf die Struktur der Ostseehandel, 1772–1846," in: D. Adamczyk and S. Lehnstädt (eds.), *Wirtschaftskrisen als Wendepunkte. Ursachen, Folgen und historische Einordnungen vom Mittelalter bus zur Gegenwart (Warschau, 2015) 215–232.*

Scheltjens, W., "Het ontstaan van een geïntegreerde maritieme transportruimte in de Lage Landen, ca. 1300–1800," *Revue belge de la Philologie et d'Histoire* 92 (2014) 293–365.

Scheltjens, W., "Maße und Gewichte: Konvertierungsmöglichkeiten am Beispiel der Sundzollregister," in: P. Rauscher and A. Serles (eds.), *Wiegen – Zählen – Registrieren:*

Handelsgeschichtliche Massenquellen und die Erforschung mitteleuropäischer Märkte (13.– 18. Jahrhundert) (*Innsbruck, Wien and Bozen, 2015*) *455–479*.

Scheltjens, W., "The influence of spatial change on operational strategies in early-modern Dutch maritime shipping: a case-study on Dutch maritime shipping in the Gulf of Finland and on Archangel, 1703–1740," *International Journal of Maritime History, XXIII*, 1 (2011) 115–147.

Scheltjens, W.; Veluwenkamp, J.W. "Sound Toll Registers online. Introduction and first research examples," *International Journal of Maritime History* XXIV, 1 (2012) 301–330.

Scheltjens, Werner, "French Imports to the Baltic, 1670–1850," in *Eighteenth-Century International Trade Statistics: Sources and Methods*, eds. Loïc Charles and Guillaume Daudin, Special Issue of the Revue de l'OFCE 140 (2015) 137–173.

Scheltjens, Werner, "The changing geography of demand for Dutch maritime transport in the 18th century," *Histoire & mesure* 27–2 (2012) 5–47.

Scheltjens, Werner, "The Volume of Dutch Baltic Shipping at the End of the Eighteenth Century: A New Estimation Based on the Danish Sound Toll Registers," in *Scripta Mercaturae – Zeitschrift Für Wirtschafts- und Sozialgeschichte* 43–1/2 (2009) 83–110.

Scheltjens, Werner, *De invloed van ruimtelijke verandering op operationele strategieën in de vroeg-moderne Nederlandse scheepvaart: een case-study over de Nederlandse scheepvaart in de Finse Golf en op Archangel, 1703–1740* (Groningen, 2009).

Scheltjens, Werner; Dopfer, Kurt, "Unified Rule Approach and the Semantic Enrichment of Economic Movement Data," in *Universal ontology of geographic space: semantic enrichment for spatial data*, eds. Tomaz Podobnikar and Marjan Ceh (Hershey, 2012) 222–239.

Schmidt, Theodor, "Geschichte des Handels und der Schifffahrt Stettins I," *Baltische Studien* 19–1 (1863) 46–58.

Schmidt, Theodor, "Geschichte des Handels und der Schiffahrt Stettins III," *Baltische Studien* 25–2 (1875) 1–4.

Schmidt-Händel, Astrid, "Landtransport im Spätmittelalter und in der Frühen Neuzeit am Beispiel des Erfurter Waidhandels," in *Von Nowgorod bis London. Studien zu Handel, Wirtschaft und Gesellschaft im mittelalterlichen Europa*, ed. Marie-Luise Heckmann and Jens Röhrkasten (Göttingen, 2008) 197–212.

Schneid, Frederick, *Napoleon's Conquest of Europe: The War of the Third Coalition* (Westport CN, 2005).

Schoorl, Henk, *De convexe kustboog Texel-Vlieland-Terschelling. Bijdragen tot de kennis van het westelijk Waddengebied en de eilanden Texel, Vlieland en Terschelling*, 1 (Schoorl, 2000).

Schrader, Paul, *Geschichte der Königlichen Seehandlung* (*Preußische Staatsbank*) (Berlin, 1911).

Schreiner, Johan, *Nederland og Norge 1625–1650: Trelastutførsel og handelspolitik* (Oslo, 1933).

Sembritzki, Johannes, *Geschichte der königlich preussischen See- und Handelsstadt Memel* (Memel, 1926).

Shah, Mohammed Saif; Williamson, Jeffrey, "Freight rates and productivity gains in British tramp shipping 1869–1950," *Explorations in Economic History* 41 (2004) 172–203.

Shepherd, James; Walton, Gary, *Shipping, maritime trade, and the economic development of Colonial North America* (Cambridge 1972).

Simsch, Adelheid, *Die Wirtschaftspolitik des preußischen Staates in der Provinz Südpreußen 1793–1806/07* (Berlin, 1983).

Sjöberg, Åke G., "Gotlands Handel im frühen 17. Jahrhundert," in *Gotland. Tausend Jahre Kultur- und Wirtschaftsgeschichte im Ostseeraum*, ed. Robert Bohm (Sigmaringen, 1988) 105.

Snapper, F., "Commerce, ships and war in the Baltic from the rise of the Hanseatic League till the French Revolution," in: W.G. Heeres e.a. ed., *From Dunkirk to Danzig. Shipping and trade in the North Sea and the Baltic, 1350–1850* (Hilversum, 1988) 405–428.

Sogner, Sølvi, "Norwegian-Dutch Migrant Relations in the Seventeenth Century," in *Dutch Light in the 'Norwegian Night'. Maritime Relations and Migration across the North Sea in Early Modern Times*, eds. Louis Sicking, Harry de Bles and Erlend des Bouvrie (Hilversum, 2004) 43–56.

Solar, Peter M., "Opening to the East: Shipping Between Europe and Asia, 1770–1830," *Journal of Economic History* 73–3 (2013) 625–661.

Spanjer, T.J., "Groot-Schippersbuidel of Zeemans-Assurantiebeurs der vijf oostersche dorpen, sedert 1587," in *De Buul: 400 jaar zeeverzekering op Terschelling*, ed. W.Smit (Urk, 1987) 3–8.

Sparrow, Elisabeth, *Secret Service, British Agents in France 1792–1815* (Woodbridge, 1999).

Steensgaard, Niels, "The Growth and Composition of the Long-Distance Trade of England and the Dutch Republic before 1750," in *The Rise of Merchant Empires*, ed. James D. Tracy (Cambridge, England, 1991) 102–152.

Stopford, Martin, *Maritime Economics* (Abington, 2008).

Straube, Manfred, "Leipzig und Sachsen im ost- und südeuropäischen Handel des 18. Jahrhunderts," *Jahrbuch für Wirtschaftsgeschichte* 1 (1978) 239–244.

Straube, Manfred, "Zum Warenaustausch im Ost-West-Handel auf dem Landwege in der ersten Hälfte des 16. Jahrhunderts," *Wissenschaftliche Zeitschrift der Pädagogischen Hochschule Leipzig* 3 (1977) 22–36.

Straubel, Rolf, *Die Handelsstädte Königsberg und Memel in friderizianischer Zeit. Ein Beitrag zur Geschichte des ost- und gesamtpreußischen « Commerciums » sowie seiner sozialen Träger (1763–1806/15)* (Berlin, 2003).

Straubel, Rolf, *Zwischen monarchischer Autokratie und bürgerlichem Emanzipationsstreben. Beamte und Kaufleute als Träger handels- und gewerbepolitischer Veränderungen im friderizianischen Preußen* (Berlin, 2012).

Tarrade, Jean Le, *Commerce colonial de la France à la fin de l'Ancien Régime: l'évolution du régime de l'exclusif de 1763 à 1782* (Paris, 1972).

Techen, Friedrich, *Geschichte der Seestadt Wismar* (Wismar, 1929).

Tielhof, M. van, "Ostseehandel," in: *Enzyklopädie der Neuzeit*. Vol. 9 (Stuttgart, 2009) 728–731.

Tielhof, M. van, *The 'Mother of all Trades'. The Baltic Grain Trade in Amsterdam from the Late 16th to the Early 19th Century* (Leiden, Boston and Köln, 2002).

Tielhof, Milja van, *The "mother of all trades". The Baltic grain trade in Amsterdam from the late 16th to the early 19th century* (Leiden, 2002).

Töpffer, J.C., "Unvorgreifliches Bedenken betreffend den im Jahr 1771 eingeführten Tariff aller zur See aus der ersten Hand in den Pommerschen Stapel- Städten einkommenden Waaren," in *Pommersche Sammlungen. Vol. II*, ed. Johann H. Gadebusch (Greifswald, 1786) 203–226.

Torres Sanchez, Rafael, "The Triumph of the Fiscal-Military State in the Eighteenth Century: War and Mercantilism," Rafael Torres Sanchez ed., *War, State and Development: States in the Eighteenth Century* (Navarra, 2007) 20–34.

Treue, Wilhelm, *Wirtschafts- und Technikgeschichte Preussens* (Berlin, 1984).

Unger, Eike E., "Nürnbergs Handel mit Hamburg im 16. und beginnenden 17. Jahrhundert," *Mitteilungen des Vereins für Geschichte der Stadt Nürnberg* 54 (1966) 1–85.

Unger, R.W., "The Dutch trade in rye. Comparative capital requirements in the seventeenth and eighteenth centuries," in: C.A. Davids, W. Fritschy en L.A. van der Valk ed., *Kapitaal, ondernemerschap en beleid. Studies over economie en politiek in Nederland, Europa en Azië van 1500 tot heden. Afscheidsbundel voor prof.dr. P.W. Klein* (Amsterdam, 1996) 121–140.

Unger, Richard W. *Shipping and economic growth 1350–1800* (Leiden, 2011).

Unger, Richard; Allen, Robert, "The Depth and Breadth of the Market for Polish Grain, 1500–1800," in *Baltic Affairs: Relations between the Netherlands and North-Eastern Europe, 1500–1800. Essays*, Baltic Studies 1, eds. J.P.S. Lemmink and J.S.A.M. Van Koningsbrugge (Nijmegen, 1990) 1–18.

Unger, W.S., "De publikatie der Sonttabellen voltooid," *Tijdschrift voor Geschiedenis* 71 (1958) 147–205.

Unger, W.S., "De Sonttabellen," *Tijdschrift voor Geschiedenis* 41 (1926) 137–155.

Unger, Willem, "Trade Through the Sound in the Seventeenth and Eighteenth Centuries," *The Economic History Review. New Series* 12–2 (1959) 206–221.

Vallerö, Rolf, *Svensk handels- och sjöfartsstatistik 1637–1813* (Stockholm, 1969).

Veluwenkamp, J.W., "'Die Sound Toll Registers Online' als Instrument für die Erforschung des frühneuzeitlichen Ostseehandels," in: Peter Rauscher en Andrea

Serles, eds., *Wiegen – Zählen – Registrieren. Handelsgeschichtliche Massenquellen und die Erforschung mitteleuropäischer Märkte (13.-18. Jahrhundert)* (Innsbruck, Wien and Bozen, 2015) 365–384.

Veluwenkamp, J.W., "Lading voor de Oostzee," in: R. Daalder e.a. (ed.), *Goud uit graan. Nederland en het Oostzeegebied 1600–1850* (Zwolle, 1998) 42–55.

Veluwenkamp, J.W., Sound Toll Registers. Concise source criticism (2011), www.soundtoll.nl > about the project > Sound Toll Registers.

Veluwenkamp, Jan Willem, "Het Nederlandse handelsstelsel in de vroegmoderne tijd. Oude en nieuwe visies," *Leidschrift* 23–2 (2008) 73–76.

Veluwenkamp, Jan Willem, "International Business Communication Patterns in the Dutch Commercial System, 1500–1800," in *Your Humble Servant. Agents in Early Modern Europe*, eds. Cools, H., M. Keblusek & B. Noldus (Hilversum, 2006) 121–134.

Vergleich, welcher zwischen dem Hochfürstlichen Gesamt-Hause Holstein und der Kayserlichen Freyen Reichs-Stadt Hamburg zu Gottorff am 27ten May 1768 geschlossen [...] worden, printed by Jeremias C. Piscator, Hamburg 1768.

Vermeulen, D., *Op zoek naar Vlielands verleden* (Baarn, 1979).

Ville, Simon, "Defending productivity growth in the English Coal Trade during the Eighteenth and Nineteenth Centuries," *Economic History Review* 40–4 (1987) 597–602.

Ville, Simon, "Total factor productivity in the English shipping industry: The North-East Trade, Coal 1700–1850," *Economic History Review* 39–3 (1986) 355–370.

Vlachovič, Jozef, "Die Kupfererzeugung und der Kupferhandel in der Slowakei vom Ende des 15. Bis zur Mitte des 17. Jahrhunderts," in *Schwerpunkte der Kupferproduktion und des Kupferhandels in Europa 1500–1650*, ed. Hermann Kellenbenz (Köln, 1977) 148–171.

Vlachovič, Jozef, "Produktion und Handel mit Ungarischem Kupfer im 16. und im ersten Viertel des 17. Jahrhunderts," in *Der Außenhandel Ostmitteleuropas 1450–1650. Die ostmitteleuropäischen Volkswirtschaften in ihren Beziehungen zu Mitteleuropa*, ed. Ingomar Bog (Köln, 1971) 624–627.

Voelcker, Tim, *Admiral Saumarez versus Napoleon: The Baltic, 1807–1812* (Woodbridge, 2008).

Vogel, Walther, "Beiträge zur Statistik der deutschen Seeschiffahrt im 17. und 18. Jahrhundert I," *Hansische Geschichtsblätter* 53 (1928) 137–138.

Vogel, Walther, "Beiträge zur Statistik der deutschen Seeschiffahrt im 17. und 18. Jahrhundert II," *Hansische Geschichtsblätter* 54 (1932) 114–115.

Vries, J. de, and A. van der Woude, *Nederland 1500–1815. De eerste ronde van moderne economische groei* (Amsterdam, 1995).**

Vries, Jan de; Woude, Ad van der, *Nederland 1500–1815. De eerste ronde van moderne economische groei* (Amsterdam, 1995).

Vries, Jan de; Woude, Ad van der, *The First Modern Economy: Success, Failure, and Perseverance of the Dutch Economy, 1500–1815* (Cambridge, 1997).

Vries, Johannes De, *De Economische achteruitgang der Republiek in de achttiende eeuw* (Amsterdam, 1959).

Wachowiak, Bogodan, "Stettin in der Neuzeit (1478–1805)," in *Stettin. Kurze Stadtgeschichte*, ed. Jan Piskorski (Poznań, 1994) 83–96.

Wal, Johan van der, *We vieren het pas als iedereen terug is* (Franeker, 2007).

Wallerstein, Immanuel, *The Modern World-System, 2, Mercantilism and the Consolidation of the European World-Economy, 1600–1750* (New York etc. 1980).

Wallerstein, Immanuel, *The Modern World-System. Capitalist Agriculture and the Origins of the European World-Economy in the Sixteenth Century* (New York etc., 1974).

Wallerstein, Immanuel, *World-Systems Analysis – An Introduction* (Durham, NC, 2004).

Walton, Gary, "A measure of productivity change in American colonial shipping," *Economic History Review* 21–2 (1968) 268–282.

Walton, Gary, "A quantitative study of American colonial shipping: A summary," *Journal of Economic History* 26–4 (1966) 595–598.

Walton, Gary, "Obstacles to technical diffusion in ocean shipping, 1675–1775," *Explorations in Economic History* 8–2 (1970) 123–140.

Walton, Gary, "Sources of productivity change in American colonial shipping, 1675–1775," *Economic History Review* 20–1 (1967) 67–78.

Weber, Klaus, *Deutsche Kaufleute im Atlantikhandel 1680–1830. Unternehmen und Familien in Hamburg, Cadiz und Bordeaux* (Munich, 2004).

Welling, George M., *The Prize of Neutrality. Trade Relations between Amsterdam and North America, 1771–1817: A Study in Computational History* (Hilversum, 1998).

Wendt, Heinrich, *Schlesien und der Orient. Ein geschichtlicher Rückblick* (Wrocław, 1916).

Werner, Johannes, *En Dansk Storkøbmand fra den Glimrende Handelsperiode* (Copenhagen, 1927).

Wiskemann, Erwin, *Hamburg und die Welthandelspolitik von den Anfängen bis zur Gegenwart* (Hamburg, 1929).

Witthöft, Harald; Göbel, Gerhard W., *Deutsche Masse und Gewichte des 19. Jahrhunderts: Die Mass- und Gewichtseinheiten* (St. Katharinen, 1993).

Wohlwill, Adolph, *Aus drei Jahrhunderten der hamburgischen Geschichte (1648–1888)* (Hamburg, 1897).

Wood, Alfred C., *A History of the Levant Company* (London, 1964).

Zanden, Jan Luiten van; Tielhof, Milja van, "Roots of growth and productivity change in Dutch shipping industry, 1500–1800," *Explorations in Economic History* 46 (2009) 389–403.

Zimmermann, Alfred, *Geschichte der preussisch-deutschen Handelspolitik* (Leipzig, 1892).
Zins, Henryk, *England and the Baltic in the Elizabethan Era* (Manchester, 1972).
Zwaal, A.J., *Terschellinger historie*, 2nd ed. (Terschelling, 2000).

Index

www.ingramcontent.com/pod-product-compliance
Lightning Source LLC
Chambersburg PA
CBHW071323230926
51849CB00002B/300